THE LAST NAVIGATOR

Paul Goodwin is retired and living in Sydney, having had a long and very successful career in marketing and executive positions. Gordon Goodwin died aged 94 in 2012. The memoir he wrote in later life forms the basis of this book.

THE LAST NAVIGATOR

PAUL GOODWIN
WITH GORDON GOODWIN

ALLEN&UNWIN
SYDNEY • MELBOURNE • AUCKLAND • LONDON

Allen & Unwin
83 Alexander Street
Crows Nest NSW 2065
Australia
Phone: (61 2) 8425 0100
Email: info@allenandunwin.com
Web: www.allenandunwin.com

A catalogue record for this book is available from the National Library of Australia

ISBN 978 1 76087 743 9

Map and 'corkscrew' manoeuvre diagram by Mika Tabata
Set in 12/17 pt Minion LT by Midland Typesetters, Australia
Printed and bound in Australia by Griffin Press, part of Ovato

10 9 8 7 6 5 4 3 2 1

The paper in this book is FSC® certified. FSC® promotes environmentally responsible, socially beneficial and economically viable management of the world's forests.

For my father, mother and brother.

CONTENTS

'For once you have tasted flight you will walk the earth with your eyes turned skywards, for there you have been and there you will long to return.'

Leonardo da Vinci

FOREWORD

'With memories of exciting times, I was fortunate to have one of
the best navigators in Bomber Command'.

Wing Commander Philip Patrick MBE, DFC

I am privileged to write the foreword to *The Last Navigator*, the
story of Gordon Goodwin, an exceptional Australian navigator who
joined me on my second tour of duty in Lancaster III 'G for George'
with 7 Squadron, 8 Group Pathfinder Force, Bomber Command
at Oakington, England, in November 1943. We flew together over
enemy territory on no fewer than twenty occasions and this volatile
experience alone forged a lifetime bond between us.

After the war Gordon went on to establish from his service with the
RAAF a distinguished civilian flying career in navigation, at a time
when finding your way in the skies still required great skill, courage
and leadership. He spent 26 years with Qantas Empire Airways
guiding Lancasters, Hythe Flying Boats, Constellations and the
L-1049 Super Constellations, DC-4s and the Boeing 707s to the right
and safe destination. He held the position of Qantas Chief Navigator

for thirteen years and, in the end, assisted with the computerisation of his art, making his profession of air navigation obsolete.

Gordon and I served during the war in probably one of the most dangerous wartime occupations of all. The Pathfinders were the aircraft that pinpointed the targets and went in first to mark them with flares, providing illumination for the following bombers to ensure an effective and concentrated hit. Air navigation was the central focus and driving force of the Pathfinders, and also the key to survival, getting to the target and out in minimal time.

Before the formation of Pathfinders, the success rate of bombing against German forces and the industry supporting them was less than satisfactory. The advent of this new saturation bombing technique, with a very large number of bombers in many of the raids dropping their load right on the target, was one of the key turning points of the war in Europe and sapped the German war effort of resources, diverting defending fighters and much anti-aircraft artillery from the Russian front and the Allied invasion of Europe.

Gordon's crew was the first in the formation of RAAF 460 Squadron at Breighton, Yorkshire, operating on Mark IV Wellington bombers. Gordon completed 31 operations on this, his first tour, and his crew was the first to survive this challenge unscathed. He received the Distinguished Flying Medal for this achievement and his outstanding navigation.

In June 1942 he was commissioned pilot officer and took up navigation instructor duties at Lichfield. After completing a three-month Staff Navigator course at Cranage, which included air work and advanced navigational study on the ground, he was posted as officer-in-charge to set up 93 Group Navigation Instructors' schools to improve the quality of Bomber Command's navigational training.

In October 1943, Gordon applied to return to operations and was directed to the Navigation Training Unit, Pathfinder Force, Upwood, Huntingdonshire for re-crewing and crew training. In this time

Gordon's rank had advanced from pilot officer to squadron leader. I approached Gordon to join my crew on the strength of 7 Squadron, Pathfinder Force, at Oakington, Cambridgeshire. It was the second tour of duty for us both and the twenty operations that we flew on together over Germany included nine to Berlin. I was lucky to have one of the best navigators in Bomber Command, which gave us the best chance at making it through our tour intact. Not only was it vital to plot the best route to the target so you arrived at the right time, allowing for any variations in wind and weather, but it was also critical to reach and mark the target without the need for a second run. This minimised exposure to the enemy's coning of searchlights and the barrage of their anti-aircraft fire.

Following our time together, Gordon went on to be posted as navigation leader for the formation of a new Pathfinder Squadron No. 635 at Downham Market, Norfolk, where he completed another twelve operations, remaining until January 1945. He flew with inexperienced crews or crews that had lost a navigator and cut down their chances of 'buying it' in, typically, their first five operations. He used his leadership to intervene, as needed, to ensure their survival. At a time when he was newly married, this feeling of duty to put himself at further high risk is commendable. Gordon completed a total of 65 missions over enemy territory and was awarded the Distinguished Service Order for his brave and relentless service, one of the highest awards for an airman.

We remained close friends for another 68 years. Although separated by great distances we often visited with each other in Australia or England, enjoying good times with our wives, Olive and Joy. Gordon was the second last crew member standing and died on 21 July 2012 at the age of 94 years, his beautiful English bride, his Joy, following him a mere two months later. They were inseparable.

There have been many books written about Bomber Command that have highlighted the lack of recognition for its 'Bomber Boys' and the reasons behind it. It was noteworthy for me that the death notice of my good friend Gordon Goodwin appeared in the same spring edition 2012 of the Pathfinder Force Australia newsletter that included the story of the Bomber Command Memorial in London's Green Park, dedicated by Queen Elizabeth II on 28 June 2012. The headline says it all for me: '67 years after World War II, Britain finally honours the unsung heroes of BOMBER COMMAND'.

I was pleased that Gordon and I were able to share some whimsical words on the resolution of this historic injustice before his passing. His son Paul has applied posthumously for the Bomber Command Clasp to recognise his father's service. It again seems poignant that this award should only have been recently initiated by the British Ministry of Defence, coming into being so long after the end of the war.

This book is about Gordon and is based on his memoirs, telling the story of his early years, his training and wartime experiences, how the war moulded him—giving him the opportunity to escape his early destiny and follow the pathway to a career as an airman and brilliant navigator. In his war and civilian life he completed a total of 13,700 hours guiding aircraft in the air and/or leading and training others in this demanding task.

At 99 years of age, I have had the good fortune to enjoy nearly another 70 years of living since the end of World War II in Europe, 68 of these in the company of my good friend. More than half of our compatriots were not so fortunate. We were young men called upon to do some extraordinary things and this seemingly brief wartime episode shaped our thinking, with survival leaving its defining stamp, and relegating later life challenges to the possible. They were indeed exciting times.

As the last living member of the crew of 7 Squadron, Pathfinder Force, Lancaster III 'G for George', it seems fitting that I pay tribute to my mate Gordon Goodwin. I celebrate our years together. It was extremely appropriate that a navigator as outstanding as Gordon should serve in a force commanded by Air Vice Marshall Don Bennett, who was a fellow Australian and another exceptional navigator, as well as being a very accomplished pilot. Don Bennett's emphasis on navigation was fundamental to the success of the Pathfinder Force. Like his air officer commanding, Gordon maintained extremely high standards in an era when long-range navigation required great skill and dedication. He was truly one of the great Pathfinders.

Philip Patrick
13 June 2014

Author's note: Philip Patrick was the last remaining member of the crew of 'G for George' with 7 Squadron, 8 Group Pathfinder Force, Bomber Command. This foreword was written in June 2014. Philip lived to 101 and died on 10 September 2016.

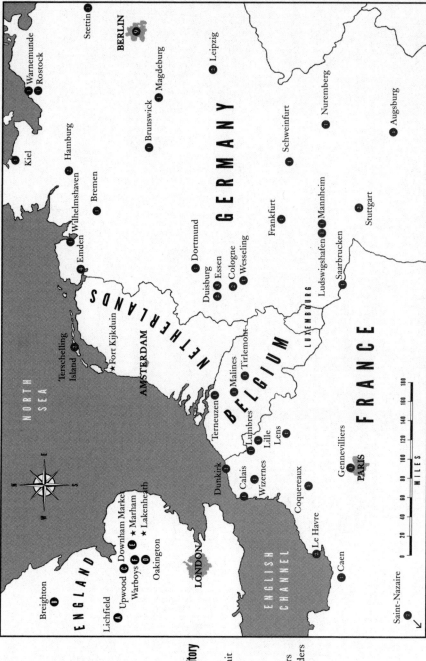

RAF BOMBER COMMAND OPERATIONS OF SQUADRON LEADER GORDON GOODWIN

- 65 operations to 40 targets
- 43 over Germany
- 32 Pathfinder missions
- 9 to Berlin
- 4 sea searches over enemy territory

Ⓐ 27 Operational Training Unit
Ⓑ No. 460 Squadron RAAF, Bomber Command
Ⓒ Pathfinder Navigation Training Unit
Ⓓ No. 7 Squadron, Pathfinders
Ⓔ No. 635 Squadron, Pathfinders
Ⓕ Pathfinder Training Unit

⬤ Target and number of times visited

★ Point of interest

Map labels:

ENGLAND — Breighton Ⓑ, Lichfield Ⓐ Upwood Ⓒ, Downham Market, Warboys Ⓕ ★ Marham Ⓔ, ★ Lakenheath Ⓓ, Oakington, LONDON

NORTH SEA

NETHERLANDS — AMSTERDAM, Terschelling Island, ★ Fort Kijkduin

GERMANY — Stettin ①, Warnemünde ①, Rostock ①, BERLIN ⑨, Kiel, Hamburg, Wilhelmshaven ②, Bremen, Emden, Brunswick ①, Magdeburg ①, Leipzig ①, Dortmund ①, Duisburg ②, Essen ③, Cologne ②, Wesseling ①, Frankfurt ①, Schweinfurt ①, Ludwigshafen ①, Mannheim ①, Saarbrucken ①, Nuremberg ①, Augsburg ①, Stuttgart ②

BELGIUM — Terneuzen ①, Malines ①, Tirlemont ①, Lumbres ①, Lille, Lens ①

LUXEMBURG

NETHERLANDS/BELGIUM border area

FRANCE — Dunkirk ①, Calais ①, Wizernes ①, Coquereaux ①, Le Havre ②, Caen ①, Gennevilliers ①, PARIS, Saint-Nazaire ①

ENGLISH CHANNEL

MILES — 0 20 40 60 80 100 120 140 160 180

AUTHOR'S NOTE

Facing an aircraft on fire at the end of the runway, flames erupting from black mushroom clouds in burnt orange, you prepare to take off on your second attempt at crossing the Atlantic. Two thousand miles in a fuel-laden Lockheed Hudson on your way to war from training in Canada, special tanks filled to the gunnels to make the distance.

Your second operation in a Wellington bomber and first time over enemy territory, suddenly out of the pitch black comes a strange and frightening blue shaft of light picking your aircraft out of the sky. Coned by between 10 and 50 searchlights, locking on and lighting up the cockpit like daylight, you're surrounded by exploding flak, trying to blast you from the heavens with its tumultuous shattering sound. The skipper drops the bomber out of the night sky.

You fear your plane ditching into the ice-cold waters of the English Channel, being the only survivor in a life-raft tossing in the dark, roiling ocean, awaiting possible sea rescue in the dead of night.

The choking, chest-tightening feeling of being trapped in a burning Lancaster, enduring the uncertainty, you count down the requisite 60 seconds for the tanks to blow. Your skip has thrown off the fighters with yet another brilliant corkscrew manoeuvre, but will you get your badly wounded bomber home?

The last, nail-biting trip over Berlin, you briefly ponder how you managed to survive the last eight attempting to bring the 'Big City' to its knees and end the war. You feel your chances for survival have moved to zero.

These are but some of the memories of my father, Gordon Goodwin. A squadron leader with Bomber Command and member of the Pathfinders, the 'corps d'elite' who led the way in virtually every major bomber operation for the last three years of the war in Europe. His ordeals would keep flooding back in his dreams at night, even into his nineties. War was my father's defining moment, releasing him from a mundane life and unpleasant childhood.

My father completed his memoirs in 1997, when he was 80, but they were fairly emotionless, as if he could not really allow himself the perceived indulgence of his good fortune. I wanted to understand what he had been through and so we talked. It was only really towards the end of his life, well into his nineties, that he opened up, letting in the meaning and the emotions behind his wartime experiences. This book is a collaboration between father and son. Wherever possible, I have used my father's words and followed the format of his memoirs. It is written in his voice, as it is his story.

I also drew on his extensive library of books on Bomber Command, interviews recorded with he and his 7 Squadron skip, Philip Patrick, his logs, his other documents and a lifetime of conversations with him. Where my father's story was incomplete, I have drawn on other published sources and internet research to explain and expand on his work. My mother, Joy, also committed pen to paper to reflect her life and war years.

My mother and father were inseparable. My mother died just two months after my father, unable to be persuaded to live on for her great-grandchildren. In their 40-odd years of retirement they enjoyed overseas travel, time up the NSW coast at Nambucca Heads—he fishing for blackfish and she savouring peaceful periods of reading. Children and grandchildren abounded.

In this the year of the Qantas centenary, my dear mother would also have reached her hundredth year. My father would have been pleased with this concurrence at the time when his story is to be told.

Philip Patrick was the last remaining crew member of my father's aircrew in 7 Squadron and died in 2016. There are now not many left to tell this incredible story of Bomber Command and Pathfinders. I am indebted to Philip, with the help of his son Ian, for the writing of the foreword to this book in June 2014.

I have tried to reflect the measure of my father throughout this book—his harsh upbringing, his love of the outdoors and his whimsical humour born out of wartime experiences. I marvelled at my father's tranquillity in times of crisis, a wisp of whimsy would always drift into an intense conversation to relieve the tension. His dices with death in his RAAF years were clearly the architect of his playful humour. Surviving as he did, nothing that followed could be taken too seriously. My father told me that to survive you had to surrender all hope. This was the extraordinary formula followed by the men of Bomber Command to get through—the chances of remaining alive and unhurt were less than 50 per cent for more than 50 operations over enemy territory. You had to blot out all the possibilities of demise and disaster and focus only on the mission at hand. War had also brought him his partner for life, Joy, and an appreciation of civilians at home, under enemy attack.

In his 30-year career and 13,700 hours in the air, my father had covered the full gamut of flight, spanning warfare with Wellingtons and Lancasters to Qantas and Flying Boats, Constellations, the introduction of Doppler navigation, the advent of the jets, and the Boeing 707.

With the arrival of the Boeing 747 jumbo jet, he helped to introduce computerised navigation to Qantas, making his profession obsolete in his own lifetime.

I miss my father and the gripping stories of his adventures. I hope that the telling of his story allows people to see the extraordinary man that he was.

His navigational journey brought him the inspiration of some great role models along the way: Matthew Flinders and his brave circumnavigation of our homeland, learning of John Cabot as the actual European discoverer of America, and lastly the indomitable Donald Bennett, perhaps the finest modern exponent and advocate for his art. Captain Cook also comes to mind in his resolute navigation to our country of birth. They all had exquisitely pursued their craft of making it back to land.

My father's profession, wrought through the instrument of warfare, was to conclude in his lifetime, like the final act of a powerful play. It had brought him an unforgettable panoply of the wonders of weather and nature, as he faced his challenges in the air, seemingly skimming the surface of this spectacular globe, out into the blue, puffed clouds abounding. I was duly proud of him and, on reflection, I have felt my father to have truly been, 'The Last Navigator'.

This is his story.

1

THE MONTVILLE YEARS

It was 1930, in the midst of Australia's Great Depression, I was twelve years of age and my childhood had just been cut short. No longer permitted the stimulation of schooling, I was dispatched with my trusty Winchester Model 60 rifle and charged with providing for the family table. My father's parting words always contained some form of veiled threat: 'I feel like some pigeon tonight, Gordon. Make sure you bag a few but don't waste the ammunition. It's got to last you the month.'

It was my early fate to grow up in Montville, Queensland, on a less than successful orange orchard. My father, Ralph, was a big towering man well over 6 feet packed into a 15-stone frame without any sign of surplus flesh. He had a preponderance for overseeing others, rather than himself taking on the toil needed to glean success from the soil. From an early age he had firmly planted his burdens of life on my unwilling shoulders.

He had named me Ralph Gordon, a life sentence and signature of continuation of the family lineage. Good fortune smiled upon me with early confusion allowing my second name to come to my rescue. I relished 'Gordon' as it set me apart from my father and avoided any suggestion that he could be my role model.

My old man was well educated and had trained and worked as a high school teacher before joining the Colonial Sugar Refining Company as a plantation manager in Fiji. Perhaps I should have been more forgiving of him for using family as a substitute for the 'Indian coolies' he once controlled. He saw his children as mere chattels to give him the lifestyle he deserved. There was no thought as to our lives, future or wellbeing.

'Gordon, I want you up at the crack of dawn, you hear? You need to pick the fruit well before the heat of the day gets hold. No slacking or there'll be hell to pay,' roared my father. Never a kind word, thanks or offers of working together. His job was to rule, mine to manage the menial and comply with his every terse direction.

An authoritarian, he used 'the strap' to record his slightest displeasure. I can recall being beaten for collecting wood for the fuel stove that was not dense enough to give immediate intense heat. I learnt my lessons more from punishment than guidance and devoted more time on the right wood selection. My younger sisters, Rua Jean and Rina, nicknamed Nug for her early stocky build, received the same retribution for the merest of misdemeanours. I never needed to inquire about his treatment of the labour he managed on the estate in Fiji. He was an imperious, oppressive man.

I can still hear my father's words ringing in my ears like an out-of-tune bell tower, 'Gordon, your school results show that you have no real future academically. It's time you earned your keep, helping me on the farm.' Silence and disbelief was my response. My schooling had been my only relief from the tedium and the repressive kingdom my father had created.

I remember sitting in the headmaster's office and hearing his generous words to my parents, 'I would like to offer Gordon a scholarship to continue free of charge as a boarder at Brisbane Boys' College. Only clothing and limited expenses will need to be paid for.'

'Gordon is needed on the farm,' my father had stated singularly and without hesitation. I suspect my father had little money left at that stage but it was never put to me that way. Father was a man with some physical health problems and he needed my labour. He never apologised or recognised the price he made me pay.

The bush became my escape and fruit pigeons, my family's favoured food source, became my best friends. Days spent tramping through the heavy flooded-gum forest into the Blackall Range were my delight and built this unlikely bond.

We had two tracts of land, one for the house, comprising 27 acres perched atop the range and rolling 1300 feet down into the valley below. The second block to the west was about 25 acres of prime red volcanic soil, already planted with 1000 orange and mandarin trees. They coincidentally came into full bearing at the time of my birth in 1917. My bond to them was short-lived as, over my early years, I endured mindless months chipping at their bases to remove any vegetation that would deplete productivity. Despite this, I still retained my affinity for the land.

Around this time I had an interesting encounter with a carpet snake in the woodland twilight. I impart it now just to relieve the tale of torment and tension. My Winchester was a single shot .22 calibre rifle. It was near nightfall and I had taken a short cut for home across the remote Obi Obi ridge, which had led me into some of the thickest undergrowth I had ever seen. I had started to climb over a green, dank mossy log when a massive flat head lurched out, conjuring up thoughts of prehistoric raptor-like monsters. We stared at each other across the rotten trunk until, almost instinctively from the hip, I shot it neatly between those beady, staring eyes. It stayed momentarily erect, before collapsing, writhing in a huge heap of coils. At 15 feet, 8 inches, with the skin stretching to 18 inches at its widest point, it was the largest carpet snake I had ever encountered.

It had looked so immense that it was some minutes before I mustered the courage to check if it was really dead. I reloaded and tentatively eased across the log confirming the fatality. I strung it up for skinning with a cord around its hefty neck and finished as quickly as I could, filling my shooting bag with the snakeskin.

Carpet snakes mate for life. As I struck out for home, the eerie night light magnified the grisly thought that my prey's consort was silently stalking me, intent on avenging its mate's death. I made it home, surviving the journey and my ordeal of imagination. I was proud of that snakeskin—the skin from carpet snakes was particularly prized at the time as it was made into shoes and handbags. It eventually earned us 30 shillings in Brisbane and went a good way to paying for fertiliser and other farm necessities. True to form, my mother chose to take the fruits of my labour with little of this money coming my way.

I only ever hunted for game that had a practical use, either for its food or hide, never for the sake of the kill. My main love was hunting fruit pigeons of seven or eight kinds, scrub turkeys now and then, wallabies for their leather and fur and, very rarely, a dingo. These wild dogs caused carnage for the local livestock so killing them was highly rewarded. A guinea for a dingo scalp was something to dream about, and almost a week's wages then for a farm labourer.

But my true salvation was the lure of the sea only 12 miles away. It filled my soul with a broad band of reflected light. The rising sun would ignite the Sunshine Coast hinterland, blotting out the misery of my childhood. My two younger sisters, Rua and Nug, and I would sit and watch the landscape, mesmerised by the wispy smoke trails of the trains tracking between Landsborough and Woombye stations, the hundred miles of coastline punctuated by the gingered grandeur of Buderim Mountain.

Beatrice, my mother, was perhaps understandably also not one for emotional comfort. She had earned her hard life on the rebound, having been jilted at the altar by her true love. On a visit to Sydney, fleeing the trauma of her broken engagement, she quickly settled for my father, a man she thought could secure her station in life. My father was on holiday from his plantation, with little experience of women or the city. He showered her with gifts and attention and so she was easily persuaded into a marriage that would be filled with regret and hopelessness. She was more a victim of life than a perpetrator.

Mother came from hardy pastoral stock and grew up on a cattle station in northern Queensland where she took her place alongside the sons of the house in mustering, branding and general outside work on the station. Her grandfather, Major North, once resided in Kilduff, Ireland, and held a commission in the 68th Light Infantry. He fought in the Peninsula Wars in the early 1800s under the Duke of Wellington, where large-scale guerilla warfare was first initiated, and was also present with him at the Battle of Waterloo on Sunday, 18 June 1815.

The major had four sons who endured the same cruelty and contempt that he had learnt from the rigours of open warfare. His eldest son, William North, carried on this ruinous tradition, visiting this pitiless legacy upon his three sons and three daughters, including my unfortunate mother. Grandfather North's harsh and unloving nature was further inflamed by the loss of his wife in childbirth in 1904, with the entry into the world of his youngest son, Joe. Funnily enough, Joe escaped the tough love lot of his five siblings and was tenderly raised by his sisters. The lottery of age also saved him from the carnage of World War I.

His brothers, Arthur and Bernard, were not so lucky. They had enlisted at the earliest opportunity to escape the tyranny of their father. Arthur was killed on the Somme in 1916 and Bernard somehow survived the Western Front, giving courageous service as a stretcher-bearer. They were nicknamed the 'Linseed Lancers' as they administered linseed oil to men with stomach and intestinal wounds to help their digestive systems. He was a quietly spoken gent and a gentle soul at that. He has left me with an indelible memory of kindness and caring. The males in my mother's family somehow seemed to cast aside the meanness in their lineage. Perhaps Uncle Bernard's salvation was delivered through his saving of others, providing him with immunity from this tragic trait.

Sugar and books were in my blood. My grandfather on my father's side was registered as a 'sugar planter' on his marriage certificate, with my grandmother shown as a 'gentlewoman'. Grandfather Goodwin died at Branyan, Queensland, four years after my father was born. After a decent interval my grandmother married the local solicitor at Childers and subsequently gave birth to a daughter, my Aunt Isobel. She was my father's half-sister and she then married Stan Moore.

Uncle Stan, as I called him, was a munificent fellow who was to prove to be my salvation from the tawdry sentence of chipping under orange trees in Montville. A large red-headed man, Uncle Stan easily attracted the liking and respect of everyone who knew him. Although even bigger than my father, he used his size like a warm blanket, wrapping everyone up in his cloak of positivity. Never intimidating, he was kind and unpretentious, and went out of his way to help me. He had two sons, Jack and Guy, who were about my age. I envied their good fortune. Uncle Stan was everything I imagined a father should be. He made me realise that you can shape your own life. I remember his simple wisdom, 'Gordon, you can always make a little bit of luck for yourself.'

My parents actually had a good beginning to their married life when they first settled down in Montville as citrus orchardists. They felt they had found their position in this modest society, securing their standing in the social pecking order with the bounty of fruit, easily garnered from the sun's rays. At that time, it delivered a reasonable income. The money obtained by my father from his colonial 'command' in Fiji meant they could afford fruit trees, a modest house and hired help. My father also acquired additional saddle horses, extra work horses and a very handsome buggy for family travel. There was also a two-wheel sulky for the exclusive use of my father and mother. Tennis, cricket, riding and shooting within the sight of the glorious Brisbane coastline betokened a life of opulence and ease. Somehow we were able to afford our own grass tennis court. Several trained gun dogs completed my father's self-image as a country gentleman.

Life was well ordered and serene. We prospered for the first four years of the farm's existence, but I doubt my father had the sense to pay back any of his debts with the proceeds. To fund the purchase of the two plots of land, he had borrowed £900 from his elder brother Hubie, who was a successful pastoralist. He had also further saddled the family fortunes with loans from the bank to undertake his questionable lifestyle improvements. My father was not a man with a head for money or the anticipation of financial fluctuations.

The Depression years began in late 1929 when I was just twelve and they took their toll on my parents, particularly my mother. It brought out the worst in them, bridging back to their tough, almost cruel, childhoods, making them distant and bitter.

They were not alone. At that time most Australians felt the effects of the Great Depression very strongly as the majority had lived well prior to the fall. Many hundreds of thousands suddenly faced the humiliation of poverty and unemployment. There was just no money around and many families broke up, with some parents choosing to give their children to people who could afford to care for them. In retrospect, my experience was not so bad by comparison but I found it hard to accept my treatment, my devaluation as a human being. I became a resource to be milked for all it would bear, with little or nothing in return.

I remember the one bright hope about this time was Uncle Stan's visits. He proved to be a guiding light to me when the lantern had been well blackened. He remained employed at the Bundaberg sugar mill through these dark days and would not only bring food parcels, but regale us with happy tales to brighten the despair.

Joyous stories of a young 21-year-old cricketer from New South Wales named Don Bradman who, in a Sheffield Shield cricket match, had smashed the previous highest batting score in first-class cricket with 452 runs not out in 415 minutes and was chaired off the cricket pitch by his jubilant team. On another occasion Stan captivated us with the tale of the racehorse Phar Lap who had won fourteen races in a row, including the 1930 Melbourne Cup, in spite of an assassination attempt and carrying a whopping 9 stone 12 pounds in handicap weight. Thank god for these legendary yarns of optimism from Uncle Stan.

The orchard was destined for failure. Mother had taken over the whole fruit-packing operation in addition to the cooking and other household chores. We had no funds for fertiliser and my mother and I were reduced to growing cowpea and grass, and spreading it as compost over the thousands of large trees. This was a feckless and futile hope and only produced more oranges of a diminished quality and size. The market price for our produce plummeted.

Towards the end of the ordeal, it was not uncommon for us to receive a debit note for our consignment of 50 to 100 cases to market. Agent's commission, rail freight, cartage to the station and the cost of the orange cases eroded our return to the point where there was none. The Depression ground us down until our fruit became unsaleable. We admitted defeat, broken and despondent.

I remember digging long trenches to bury our whole orchard crop of 5000 bushels, mounding it with dry brush soaked in unaffordable kerosene before setting it alight. My father's bitter words seemed to add to the misfortune. He lined us up like soldiers ready for an unwinnable battle, a general issuing orders from the rear, 'Make sure you lot pack the tinder close to the oranges. We don't want the slightest chance of fruit fly, do we?' This tragic burning was to sterilise the crop and avoid fruit fly contamination, and was followed by the back-breaking and soul-destroying work of filling in the cavity containing our blood, sweat and tears from twelve months of work.

The banks would no longer support my father, a devastating strike to his self-esteem and prestige in our small community. I suspect this paramount social blow stripped him of his last vestiges of resolve, the will to fight.

By the time of that harrowing harvest, I had had three years of indentured labour on 'the farm' with forlorn promises of 'this will be all yours one day, son'.

Those three depressed years of thirteen, fourteen and fifteen bore for me the fruit of initiative, imagination and inventiveness, as they did for many children of the Depression. I became self-sufficient with a yearning to take any opportunity that might come my way. I read the limited number of excellent books my father had retained from his years as a teacher and used them as my instruction. My father never encouraged me in this pursuit but I craved some form of self-improvement. My potential and verve for life were imperilled until Uncle Stan saved me.

Uncle Stan had trained at university as an industrial chemist and was soon to be appointed general manager of the whole Millaquin sugar complex, including the refinery and distillery, in Bundaberg. He became a gentleman of some influence in the local sugar industry and in the town.

Whenever he could get away, he would come to Montville for local shooting expeditions. I became quite close to him as he would often stay a week and draw upon my local hunting knowledge. On one of these visits, I overheard Uncle Stan saying to my father, 'Ralph, you must know that you haven't a hope in hell of making a go of it here on the farm. Give the boy a chance in life . . .'

I didn't hold out much hope as my father was like a charging rhinoceros, never to be swayed from his course. Any earlier suggestions I'd made about doing something to get more money had resulted in a smack on the side of the head that left me dizzy.

That night at dinner, in the muted presence of my diffident parents, Uncle Stan asked me direct, 'Gordon, how would you like to have a job in the sugar mill at Bundaberg? You'll serve as an apprentice for the first three years and, although the pay won't be much, you'll have enough to live on, and send a bit back home.'

'I would really like that,' I heard my distant voice answering hesitantly, my tone belying my building excitement, like a spark from a small brushfire lingering on the outskirts of a tinderbox. I glanced at my parents but could glean no sign of their disapproval.

Uncle Stan continued, 'You'll need to start as a "pan-boy" and offsider to the sugar-boiler, the best-paid process worker in the mill. If you hold the job for three years you'll become a qualified sugar-boiler yourself, with a chance at a permanent position, if one is available.'

It was a dream come true, and I pictured myself leaving home and travelling north to live in a big town, forsaking my parents and their solitary servitude. They had been clearly appeased by the thought of the added income that Uncle Stan had cleverly weaved into my escape plans. There was to be another life for me, away from the folly of the farm. My heart soared as I contemplated my release and dared to imagine this other life.

2

ESCAPE TO BUNDABERG

Two months later, in 1935, I found myself on the train heading north for Bundaberg, ten days before the crushing season at the Millaquin mill. I was to stay at my uncle's house on the Burnett River for a month or so until I could find a room down in the town. I was treated as one of the family by Aunt Isobel and the days were idyllic.

I found the work at the mill very interesting and a welcome relief from the drudgery of the farm. I quickly learnt the processes for the raw sugar mixes and was soon let loose on my own pan of 'Straight A', the easiest grade of sugar.

My meticulous brew got the nod of approval from the sugar dryers and baggers, critically receiving the batch below. 'Not a bad drop, mate. Keep up the good work.' My belief in myself was building and I realised my future lay beyond menial tasks, despite the way my father had treated me. I progressed to boiling the lower grades of sugar, a more exacting procedure requiring real courage and judgement.

At this stage Uncle Stan took me aside for a talk. 'Gordon, you know you've handled things very well at the mill so far. For the life of me I can't see why you shouldn't lift your sights beyond that of sugar-boiler. I suggest you immediately take up the study of sugar chemistry with the aim of becoming an industrial chemist. You've certainly got the ability.' I took his advice, studying at night at the Bundaberg Technical College and revelling in the chance to put some theory into my practical experience. My early love of learning, at school and from my father's books, had prepared me for this pursuit.

The cane-crushing season only lasted three months and I suspect it was again the generous intervention of my uncle that ensured I was not laid off at the end of this spell, being instead kept on in the 'slack' with the other sugar-boilers. My work included odd jobs in the mill yard, climbing into the higher parts of the mill to fix slings, tackles and chain blocks to lift things out for repair. I was fortunate that my years of foraging alone in the bush had forged in me the gift of resilience, making me feel impervious to any physical threat of harm. This was sorely tested one day when the second engineer took me to the boiler house and up two flights of ladders to the very top. Here there was a line of brutishly blackened Babcock boilers that produced the steam to power all of the mill functions.

'Lad,' he said, 'you need to get inside to chip away the rust from the cast iron so that next season it won't flake off and contaminate the syrup or sugar. You've got broad shoulders so we need to make sure you can get through the manhole at the end.'

'Righto, Mr Green,' I replied with a bravado that belied my mounting apprehension. He took me up to the darkened opening of one of the twin oval steel-boiler drums. It was 20 feet long and less than inviting. I managed to get in, but it was a fairly tight squeeze.

'There's your chipping hammer, light and air-hose. Make sure you keep the light intact. If it breaks and touches the side of the boiler you'll be electrocuted. Keep the air-hose close to you so you can get enough air to breathe.'

With that he just left me. I started chipping away, determined to finish the task as soon as possible. The steel of the drum was about three-quarters of an inch thick and rang like church bells chained up close to your ears. My ears ached and it was hot. I would work inside the drum for a desperate hour and then push out through the manhole for fresh air to cool my sweat-streaming body, plastered all over with red-grey rust flakes.

It was on one of these moments of glorious release that I met two men at the mouth of the manhole. They were big burly brutes, but they both held a wry smile that softened their features.

'How are ya getting on, mate?' one of them asked with no real sign of sympathy.

'It's hot work,' I offered, seemingly stating the obvious.

'Did you hear about the jealous husband, a few years back?' he inquired.

I bristled, knowing it would not be a story I wanted to hear. 'The wife's lover was working in the very drum you're in now.'

'What happened?' I felt compelled to ask.

'The husband jerked the air-hose and electric lead out and slammed and bolted the steel door shut. The man suffocated, of course. Made as much noise inside as you were making just now. No one took much notice when it stopped. Just thought it was time he took a rest.' Then, as he turned to leave, he threw a hand grenade into my already tentative, youthful love-life, 'You haven't been playin' around lately have you, young feller?'

This motley pair reappeared regularly like reoccurring bad dreams, with further devastating 'claustro' yarns. I slowed my pace of work, knowing the chiming of my chipping was now a signal, an invitation for the telling of their terrible tales. I served my time with Mr Babcock the best part of one long week.

I was also asked to turn my hand as a blacksmith's striker and, if I succeeded in this, Alec Dick, the blacksmith, would give me regular work in 'the slack'. Farm-work had trained me with axe and adze to hit any spot I wanted to hit so I had no trouble wielding the 28-pound long-handled hammers. I also managed to master control of the

2-ton steam hammer which was actually powered by compressed air. 'Careful with the steam hammer,' Alec chortled calmly. 'It's a devil and can nearly rip a man's shoulder off at the joint. Make sure you keep clear.' I proudly proved my ability to tame the beast by cracking the shell of a walnut on the anvil below without bruising the meat. It was like my graduation prize.

My time with Alec forged a strong friendship with marvellous opportunities for metalwork to build my skills, including occasional 'foreign orders' like fishing knives from old files or ring spanners from bar steel, with jaws cyanide-hardened to resist wear. Alec's encouragement replaced my father's corporal punishment.

Now that I had some money, I wanted to live independently. Uncle Stan put me in touch with Kasmaroski, a Pole who I already slightly knew as he worked on the sugar floor bagging sugar. He and his wife owned a house near the river halfway between the mill and the town. They agreed to let me have a room with use of the kitchen and the bathroom for only a pound a week.

I remember Kasmaroski's wise words about mateship: 'Gordon, I've found the best way to be accepted is to be prepared to just relax and have a good yarn over a beer or two.' With a cool bottle as the heat was going out of the day, he would captivate me on the back verandah with stories of his life in Poland and his days as a deckhand on sailing ships, including a voyage with one of the Antarctic explorers. I came to value our time together as the sultry sun set over the upper reaches of the river. I learnt the joys of socialising and would often buy a bottle to reciprocate his splendid hospitality. I put behind me my mother's letters of demand for weekly payments beyond what I could afford and her snide histrionics about 'letting others starve'. Though I still sent reasonable funds to my parents, I no longer denied myself totally. Money for beer was important. My parents would have to make their own lives, without depending on me. Kasmaroski was a true Aussie, teaching me how to make friends and treating me better than perhaps he had been treated when he first arrived in Australia. I remember telling him once, perhaps after the subtle effects of a chilled ale or two, 'Ivan, you're a bloody good mate.'

Work was not the only thing in my life now. I became firm friends with my cousins, Jack and Guy, and we enjoyed countless expeditions around the bends of the Burnett River, fishing and shooting. Cartridges were a half-penny each for our .22 rifles and well worth the investment. In the mangroves of Paddy Island was a camp of flying foxes, regarded as a pest by the government, who paid sixpence for each pair of claws.

The best fishing was down at the river mouth at Skyringville, 11 miles away. Uncle Stan had bought Jack and Guy a 14-foot 'flattie', a boat with no keel, to get in over the mudflats. We initially got a tow from old John Wilmott, the car painter, but ended up rowing the distance more often than not, taking four hours to get to our fishing nirvana. It was well worth it. The first haul of the prawn net brought in plenty of bait with enough larger prawns to make a decent feed. Using the fresh prawn bait, the bream and trumpeter were definitely 'on', generating meals for two families for a week.

Uncle Stan soon recognised our plight. 'I can see that it's a long row for you guys. How about I put a one-and-a-half horsepower inboard Wilson engine into the flattie? That should give you more fishing time.' It was a godsend. We could now exploit new fishing grounds in the main channel towards Burnett Heads, where the best trumpeter could be found. Making crab pots out of number eight fencing wire and netting, we were rewarded with some very good hauls of 'muddie monsters' around Barraba Island, and also doubled our prawn catches with a better quarter-inch mesh net. We now set our own 50-yard flax cord nets in the main river channels overnight for the big kingfish and the old barramundi. There was also excellent shooting with black duck and wood duck quite plentiful. The best duck shooting was over in the Fairymead cattle run. It was almost accidentally that we made what was to be both our first and last visit there.

The Youngs, the owners of the adjacent property to the river in Fairymead, had recently declared their cattle run a 'bird and game sanctuary', with their stockmen very active in patrolling it. This seemed to us tainted with hypocrisy as rumour had it that their forebears had encouraged the practice of 'blackbirding' starting in the 1860s. This was the cruel capture of native labour, called 'kanakas', from the Pacific Islands for work on the sugar plantations. These people were wrenched from their idyllic atolls and kidnapped to become indentured labour to build the cane wealth of the squattocracy. People, such as the Youngs, showed little regard for the wellbeing of their slaves. There was scuttlebutt of a death rate of one in ten through poor feeding, bad water or overwork. I identified strongly with this sorry servitude. I thought of my father and his Fijian plantation, though this practice of human exploitation had started twenty years before he was born.

We were motoring to Skyringville but decided to camp for the night at a likely looking creek for our crab pots on the Fairymead side of the river. We landed on one of the sandy islands in the Barraba maze of islets and mangrove creeks. It was like an oasis, with shaded she-oaks and a good covering of saltwater couch for comfort. The lure of the ducks was too close to be resisted and we decided to go hunting for them the next morning. Guy said what we were all thinking, 'We'll have to choose the right timing as the stockmen's quarters are not far away. The sound of our shots will certainly stir a hasty response. As duck shooters on foot, we will be no match in speed for expert horsemen.'

At first light, with the boat moored nearby for a quick getaway, we opened up with a barrage from Guy's beloved double-barrelled Greener 12-gauge shotgun and my and Jack's .22s. We secured a bounty of black duck but it took time to collect our treasure as many fell into deeper swampy water. On the way back to the boat, we kept cautiously to the edge of the mangroves, quite impassable to horsemen, but we saw no one. Everything was going according to plan. We arrived on the bank to board the boat, when there was a shout, 'Got you, you bastards!'

A large man on a roan horse lunged forward from the top of the sloping bank. He jabbed his spurs into the half-rearing beast with his stockwhip swinging. That moment conjured up a clear image of my father in a mad rage, whipping his heavy leather belt off to give me a lashing. Never again would anyone threaten me with belt or whip without paying dearly. I swung my rifle around, pointing it at the centre of the horse's chest. 'Stop right there,' I shouted, gulping back any betraying sign of nervousness. 'We are on Crown land, below high-water mark.'

He pulled the horse in and lowered the whip, knowing that a .22 round into a lively horse, while not seriously wounding the steed, would send him flying. I moved my hand down, cocking my weapon with a loud click, and lifted the muzzle to reinforce the point. 'Don't test your luck, you bastard,' I threatened. He immediately swung his horse around and disappeared at full gallop into the edge of the open forest.

Uncle Stan discouraged us from any further such expeditions by his casual comment later that he hoped we weren't among those fellows who were going across the river to shoot Fairymead ducks. The Youngs were important to him and Aunty Isobel socially and in business. After that we left their ducks alone, contenting ourselves with the river and crabbing gold.

After that day, I knew I needed to learn how to defend myself properly. I returned to Alec Dick, my friend the blacksmith, to take up his long-standing offer of boxing lessons. He kept two pairs of heavy sparring gloves hanging on a nail in the back smithy. Fear of my father and challenging his authority had stifled my fighting instinct up to this point. No more.

I had lived an isolated life at Montville with little time for social occasions and very limited access to the opposite sex. With cousin Jack's help, I had long since discovered girls, particularly the nurses from the general hospital. I have no need to regale you with stories of frantic and fortunate fumblings, my tender touchings and slow familiarisation with the wonders and texture of women. It was a delight for a young man and included Friday roller-skating and visits to the old Paramount theatre. However, it was Aunt Isobel who insisted I take dancing lessons at the rowing club. 'Gordon,' she said, 'it's time to have a bit of fun and break into your hard-earned savings. Order yourself a made-to-measure dinner suit from the tailor just across Bourbong Street in Bundaberg.' She was right, but I could only imagine and delight in my mother's undoubted apoplexy had she known of my spending.

I also started to attend golf club dances with Jack and Guy and met some really nice girls, needing no more persuasion to go to these functions, black tie and all. After the initial avalanche of intimacy, I began to appreciate the finer things that female friendship could bring. I had already seen the power of a true lifelong loving partnership with Aunt Isobel and Uncle Stan and I wanted to find my own sweet recipe.

In the meantime, my father had secured employment as a weigh-bridge clerk at the mill in Bundaberg following the foreclosure on the farm by the bank. My sisters came with my parents to live in Bundaberg and my younger sister by two years, Rua, left home to train as a nurse, I suspect to evade the constant demands of my mother.

In April 1939, at the age of 21, I sat for my second-year sugar chemistry exams and passed reasonably, receiving a certificate stating I was now a qualified sugar-boiler. I left this document of achievement propped up on the mantlepiece at the Kasmaroskis' for at least a couple of weeks. I was now well credentialled and finally beyond the grasp of my parents. I didn't realise the extent to which my ability would transform me, and take me beyond the shores of my country and into the skies.

3

PASSING MUSTER

It was Australia, mid-1939, and the premonition of war was in the air. My cousin Jack had enticed me, when not working at the mill as a sugar-boiler, to join the local part-time militia in Bundaberg with the lure of being part of the supporting Vickers machine-gun unit. To my delight each of us was also issued with a brand-new SMLE .303 rifle, mine having the original packing grease in its chamber and muzzle, and we were encouraged to keep them at home. You can imagine the use the odd spare cartridge was put to for duck and pigeon shooting. I also honed my longer distance gunfire skills with the militia rifle club every Sunday, building my proficiency in crosswind shooting.

I was surprised how easily I adapted to military life and soon rose to the rank of corporal in the militia, training the 21-year-old intakes in standard infantry skills with rifle, bayonet and specialised training with the Vickers. These veteran water-cooled guns from World War I had a range of 4500 yards and could produce devastating plunging fire onto the enemy from an elevated position. Cloth ammunition belts tore at high speed across the breech to pump out 10,000 rounds an hour, a fearsome two rounds a second or more.

The gun itself weighed 25 to 30 pounds, the tripod 40 to 50 pounds and then there were the 250-round ammunition boxes at 22 pounds, plus the 7.5 imperial pints of water for the evaporative cooling system. After an hour you would need to change the barrel to stay functioning and avoid overheating. Hence the need for a six-man team for its operation. It amused me to see crews sometimes fire off a few rounds to heat their gun's cooling water to make tea, a deadly brew tasting of machine oil.

In September 1939, with the close of the refinery season, I became involved in intensive army training that was taking place all over the country. It was during the final route march of one of these three-month militia training sessions that I started wondering about alternatives to army life, the possibility perhaps of joining the RAAF. World War II had just broken out and we were encamped at Enoggera outside Brisbane. The 'chair-bound leaders' at the top had decided that our newly trained force should demonstrate their battle-fitness and mobility with a 43-mile footslog with full packs and rifles.

We were on our way at the first hint of sunrise. The troops stood up well to the first half of the journey, resting ten minutes in the hour. It then started raining heavily as we reached the battle training area. Our unit's task was to protect the flanks with our Vickers, digging emplacements, setting the guns and sorting out drainage issues created by our newly completed reservoirs for water. The rain eventually eased, but we were thoroughly wet and caked in red mud from our endeavours.

This was only the beginning of our trial. At eleven that night our esteemed leaders decided we should pack up camp and make the return trip. While my country upbringing had hardened my feet, others were not so fortunate. With half the return journey still to make, the Vickers' support cart already filled to capacity with the badly blistered and the horses tested beyond good judgement, I felt it my duty to maintain army discipline and authority. Following my training and its blueprint for bastardry, I moved up and down the column like a white pointer shark mercilessly circling its prey, my loud abrasive voice took on a life of its own, echoing along and railing at the ranks.

'Keep in line there, private. You're not on a busman's holiday!' I thundered, calling the step, raging retribution at unfortunate bodies not conforming to this strict order. I was spoiling for a fight.

Then something unexpected happened. In a quiet yet firm voice, the platoon sergeant ushered me back into the ranks.

'Corporal, I'll take over,' he almost whispered as he took my place alongside the troops.

He had spent time in the permanent army and understood his men. I can still picture his calm weather-beaten face. He had a full pack and rifle like the rest of us, yet I saw him take and carry another rifle for one of the unfortunates who was beyond caring. Like a mother hen spreading her wings and gently shepherding her brood back to the nest, he called the step.

'Left, left, left, right, left,' his voice was low and soft and the rhythm impeccable. I swear he sang us all along that road of torture, lifting us, his charges, into the step and the rhythm. As our stride lengthened into standard marching, our heads slowly rose resolute with a new confidence. He took us all home, no more casualties, as if we all floated on the sergeant's feet and spirit. I wish I had got to know him better.

After helping train the 21-year-olds in the militia, I was transferred to the 8th Division AIF training depot outside Brisbane, with a lift in rank to full sergeant. I continued the proud tradition of unlovable sergeants when drilling the troops on parade. I completed a crash physical training course that nearly killed me and I became the company PE instructor, spreading humiliation and physical dismay. Later in my service career, I tempered my approach, applying my sergeant's lesson in leadership to let men's spirit, not abuse, carry the day. I was a fit, healthy and highly motivated young man, looking forward to what war would bring me.

Still needing a bit of family support, I was fortunate at this time to have my Uncle Bernard, my mother's brother, and Aunt Nell living not far from Brisbane over the New South Wales border. I used to take the train south to Lismore to visit them, when I could manage it. A stretcher-bearer in World War I, Bernard had built a life in Lismore with his wife, Nell; he with local government and she with nursing before babies came. In 1912, Nell had graduated as a nurse and enlisted in the Australian Army Nursing Service. In July 1915, she had headed off to Egypt on a four-year posting. Nell was among the few Australian women at the time allowed to go to war. She arrived on the Western Front in the April of 1916, when preparations were under way for the advance at the Somme. She met my uncle while she was working at a casualty clearing station.

Uncle Bernard and Aunt Nell were another example of the love and companionship that came from two bonded as one. They had a warm but simple relationship caring for each other through thick and thin. This probably came from their meeting among the brutality and unpredictability of war. On one visit I prompted them to talk of their hellish experiences of war.

'Tell me how you two met,' I asked.

'Well, Gordon, we were literally thrown together,' Bernard offered. 'I was close to the clearing station, crossing the last stretch of the wooden duckboard track with a badly wounded digger. I heard the "crump crump" of artillery shells, the earth shook and still we pressed on carrying our damaged human cargo. I caught a brief glimpse of a welcome angel of red, white and grey. Then the shell hit. We were thrown off our perch into a bomb crater, seemingly whirled mid-air like spinning dervishes. Splinters of duckboard flew everywhere.'

Aunt Nell couldn't resist taking over the tale. 'I had been told by the badly shaken padre to take cover, but felt it my duty to see the last lot in to safety. I was literally thrown off my feet by the blast and into the arms of your Uncle Bernard. The ditch must have saved all our lives, with even our wounded charge surviving the added trauma.'

Uncle Bernard then further explained that it hadn't been easy for Nell at the front in those early days. Women initially hadn't been welcome, but they soon won the day, bringing a warmth and normality to the chaos of battle and its devastating aftermath.

'Was it really as bad at the front as they say?' I asked hesitantly.

'By the end of it I'd seen enough blood to last a lifetime,' Nell offered softly, as if disturbed by the very thought itself. 'Most of the men coming in had multiple wounds from the high-velocity shells, sometimes up to ten wounds in an individual. It was beyond shocking, and with no let-up. At one time I had to manage a ward with 40 severely wounded men, 11 had lost both legs, another bunch their arms and there were head and chest wounds galore.'

She paused for a moment before continuing. 'And the fertilisers in the soil contaminated even the slightest of wounds.' She shook her head. 'That winter was so cold in the trenches that for every man taken by the fighting, there was one spirited off by the bitter freeze.'

As if to cement the image in my mind, Uncle Bernard continued: 'I willingly left a hard life at home with my father to go to war, but it was nothing compared to the brutality of the Somme. I was lucky to survive. What astounded me was that, even though the hospitals were clearly marked, emblazoned with large red crosses, they seemed to receive no immunity from ground bombardment or onslaughts from the air.'

Aunt Nell added in conclusion, 'Bernard and I had become inseparable after the Somme, almost afraid to be apart again. Like many others lucky enough to return, we just quietly faded back into the community, grateful for the normality of a simple family life.'

I remember Uncle Bernard always eating fruit in large quantities, particularly of the non-citric variety. This somehow counteracted and soothed the burning he had received to his stomach walls from the unrelenting toxic gas residues, as he wearily weaved his way through the carnage porting his battle-scarred wards. He was a solid, rounded fellow with a shiny forehead that almost beamed. He never complained, remaining good-natured and cheery, celebrating every day in the sunshine. Aunt Nell, though presenting a prim and proper image, had a wicked turn of phrase and sense of humour. She was good fun, a straight-talker and a great comfort in her subtle commentary on my less than fortunate upbringing. It was good to have them.

Their stories of mud, trenches and sickening slaughter started to prey on my mind. Maybe I did not want to go to war as a foot soldier.

On another visit, I listened to Uncle Bernard's enthralling description of what for him was a glorious distraction from the horror and turmoil in the trenches.

'I can still picture in my mind these beautiful biplane birds, carrying their insignia in colourful arcs across the skies,' he reminisced. 'These air battles certainly ended abruptly but it was quick and somehow honourable.' Listening to his story, I relished the thought of soaring in the skies, free from the battle below. As war broke out, I was confirmed in my growing intention to leave the army and apply for RAAF entry.

In early 1940 Australia undertook to provide 28,000 aircrew over a three-year period as part of the Empire Air Training Scheme so the RAF could be maintained at adequate air-strength for its fight with Germany. Flying schools were established in Australia, Canada and New Zealand and so I decided to volunteer for the RAAF. Being fit, technically qualified beyond my meagre high school education, and with exemplary coordination skills, I satisfied the selection criteria. I could also demonstrate a capacity for decision-making under pressure. Ready for the challenge, I went down to Brisbane with a cut lunch to sustain me through the selection process of interviews, intelligence tests and medical examinations. I had to prove myself with such simple exercises as catching a ruler before it hit the floor and reading three-dimensional diagrams of cogs and levers. It seemed you needed a minimum of four years secondary education to become a pilot or navigator and those coming from the 'white collar' professions were favoured.

It was a close call but I made it, with my practical skills and experience making up for my limited education. I was told to report to the Initial Training School (ITS) at Bradfield Park in Sydney.

When I learnt that the 8th Division AIF had sailed shortly afterwards, to be stationed in Singapore, I felt a twinge of regret that I would not be joining my compatriots for the fight. This would be short-lived as they would end up being captured as part of the Japanese invasion of Singapore later in the war. Survivors of this conflict were to spend time in the brutal captivity of Changi prisoner-of-war camp at the whim of their Japanese tormentors. Some were sent to the even more notorious Burma railway camp that yielded few up from their track-work trauma. Not many of the 8th Division ever made it back to Australia.

I started my initial three months RAAF aircrew training at Bradfield Park, now known as Lindfield, in October 1940. It was rudimentary with lectures on service ranks and regulations, the workings and hostile environment of weather and the basics of military training. This was the last time we would be required to endure drill and marching, slightly repugnant for those destined to duel in the clouds.

I was amused to receive as part of my 'kitting-up' a relic World War I leather flying helmet. The quartermaster urged me to accept this offering, saying, 'Aircraftsman Second Class, you'll need to take this otherwise you won't satisfy full-kit paperwork requirements.'

I didn't want to upset the applecart at this early juncture even though the helmet was two sizes too small with earpieces pre-dating the invention of electricity, not to mention headphones. I could only fantasise as to the biplane brilliance of the pilot who had worn it with distinction, living to tell the tale through the proud proxy of his headgear.

Every week there was a demanding round of lectures in meteorology, armaments, signalling, navigation and maths. I didn't have the same depth of education as others in our ranks, particularly those with teaching qualifications who found little difficulty with this first stage of training, so there was minimal opportunity for me to have time off, if I was to make the grade. We never entered an aeroplane so I couldn't bring my practical skills to bear. It was all theory and there was the constant threat of being scrubbed and being 're-mustered' because of a failure in a course or because of the mere glimpse of a mental or physical condition. Eighteen per cent of the intake failed to get through at ITS. We ran between classes, dressed by day in our overalls called 'goonskins', and I understandably excelled at the compulsory drill and physical education. I knew this was to be my chance in life. Based on the results, recruits were to be designated for specialist training as pilots, navigators, bomb-aimers, wireless air gunners and air gunners.

There was great camaraderie at the school. We were all intent on living up to the high expectations of us, and there was a very strong will for everyone to succeed. It was as if all thought of competition had been put to one side with an almost spontaneous manifestation of collective help. Morale was high and there was a common positive energy with the enemy the focus. All participants were determined to make the grade, and give themselves the maximum chance at surviving the war. Few of us previously had any understanding that flying involved such a hostile environment, quite apart from the consideration of facing enemy action. 'Scrubber Scott' was the most feared of instructors and imposed the harshest of training standards yet I never forgot his simple words of advice towards the end of training: 'Listen, chaps, take it from me, the best way to survive enemy action is to cast out all thoughts of hope. Any return from a mission over enemy territory should be taken as a bonus. Just concentrate on the job in hand, take each day as it comes.'

During one of the rare times that I could afford to take time off from study, I made my first real visit to the big smoke of Sydney. When I'd first arrived and crossed the harbour en route to the training camp, such heavy rain had been falling that I could scarcely make out the bridge. Now in glorious Sydney sunlight, rumbling across the Sydney Harbour Bridge on the train from Bradfield Park, I traversed this amazing span over the glistening, ferry-stippled waters, trams to the left and trains to the right, the grandeur was everything I had imagined, and a far cry from the small towns of Queensland and the isolation of my youth.

Uncle Stan had captivated us with his story of the great grey bridge's opening on Saturday, 19 March 1932. I remember him explaining in exquisite detail, 'Francis de Groot was a member of a right-wing paramilitary group called the New Guard, and astride a 16.5-hand chestnut horse and dressed in military uniform with sabre swinging, he prematurely cut the opening ribbon.' Uncle Stan continued, 'There was strong resentment at the time of the then Labor Premier of New South Wales, Jack Lang, who had decided not to ask a member of the Royal Family to open the bridge.'

De Groot had defied protocol. I could only applaud his action but not his leanings. The Empire Air Training Scheme had however triggered in me a strong patriotic bond for the empire. King George VI was a man to be admired, not just a monarch. He was the first member of the royal family to be certified as a fully qualified pilot and became Britain's national symbol of wartime resistance, restoring faith in the monarchy after the indelicate abdication crisis of King Edward VIII.

I've had some good fortune in my life, not to mention some inexplicable coincidences. It was around this time that I discovered that Dr John Bradfield, the Australian engineer responsible for the creation, design and construction of the Sydney Harbour Bridge, had been born in Sandgate in Queensland in 1867. Sandgate was also the place of my birth on 27 September 1917. A sleepy coastal town back then, it boasted clean pristine beaches and was a popular weekend destination for thousands of visitors to escape the heat, being a short hour's train ride from the main city of Brisbane and part of the city train network. I suspect my parents had come down from Montville to stay with a midwife to await my birth, a common practice in the early 1900s. Two beautiful, matching, stilted Queenslanders sat side by side with a commanding view out over the waters of Moreton Bay. It was here that I would have taken the first dose of intoxicating sea air deep into my lungs, setting up my love of nature, the outdoors and the pull of the oceans and rivers on my anima. I can only hope my parents had some serene happy times with me in this idyllic haven, far from the imminent and rudimentary rigours of their future farm life.

Bradfield was born in Sandgate 50 years earlier than myself, when it was an even smaller seaside village edging the bay. He was not only responsible for the Sydney Harbour Bridge but also for the ideas of electrification of Sydney's suburban railways and the city underground rail with a bridge crossing. He was also instrumental during World War I in establishing the ITS, where I was training, as the first civil aviation school where pilots trained for overseas service. Bradfield Park was named after him.

I like to conjure up the impact Sandgate had on both our lives, the suburban railway capturing Bradfield's schoolboy imagination as it was constructed in 1882, slowly weaving its way from Brisbane; and the sea air, freshwater lagoons and reed beds fitting together like pieces from a jigsaw puzzle to stir in my blood a love for birdlife and nature. If a boy born in Sandgate could conceive and build the Sydney Harbour Bridge, then it was up to me to build my own pivotal span and engineer my own destiny.

In the city, meandering towards the gleaming harbour foreshore in search of the beautiful gardens that bookended Sydney Cove, I discovered a magnificent statue just outside the Mitchell Library, holding out a sextant and beckoning me in to find out more. It was the famous navigator Matthew Flinders.

As a young airman in training, I was learning about the challenges of navigation, how to plot a position and find your way to a desired destination using a sextant. Flinders used this apparently complex, but beautiful, brass device, which measures precisely the angle between two distant objects, to plot the entire Australian coastline.

On entering the library I was transfixed by tiers of books lining the walls, lit up by the wash of harbour light through the translucent ceiling. I had never seen such a bountiful collection and I unearthed Flinders' own tales of travel, *A Voyage to Terra Australis*, as well as his original maps and some seascapes painted of the coastline.

I discovered that Flinders was induced to go to sea at the age of fifteen after reading Daniel Defoe's *Robinson Crusoe*, first published in 1719 about a character with a lust for the sea who would evade the life sentence of the law. Flinders' father had wanted him to follow in his footsteps as a surgeon. I identified strongly with these extraordinary stories of youthful escape.

In 1798, Flinders, accompanied by George Bass, proved that Van Diemen's Land, now Tasmania, was an island thus providing the small New South Wales colony with a shorter, safer route between the Indian and Pacific oceans. He spent the years 1801–1803 on his voyage of discovery in his 100-foot sloop, a converted 334-ton collier appropriately named the *Investigator*. In this he circumnavigated the entire continent and completed a journey of over 22,000 miles. This distinguished navigator and cartographer proved that Terra Australis was a single entity and not bisected by a north–south seaway.

I was also delighted to find that it was Flinders who suggested the name Australia for our continent; and that he had invented the

Flinders' Bar to counteract the magnetic effect of the ship itself, allowing the accurate plotting by compass of the vessel's course. He was an ingenious and enterprising gentleman who shaped the very future of our country.

His maps and seascapes were truly objects of splendour, the diligent detail impressive. He conducted his surveys ashore and at sea, often from the masthead of the *Investigator* or close to shore in a small boat, recording the features on charts at the end of each day. His trusty sextant would confirm the accuracy of his workings.

There was a whimsical side to Matthew Flinders that struck a chord with me. I liked his turn of phrase, his teasing, playful sense of humour. On the left of his statue as he looks out over Sydney from the library is a beautiful and fond 'biographical tribute' that is immortalised in brass on stone. He wrote of his beloved black cat, his faithful intelligent Trim who accompanied him on his voyages never leaving his side.

Flinders also wrote an essay of dedication to his beloved feline. I imagined he must have had the knack for running a happy ship. He somehow seemed to be preparing me for my future profession steering aircraft to their target through sight readings, charts and the glowing guidance of the stars, not to mention the superintendence of men. We both shared a strong love of nature and exploring new lands. He was my first navigational hero.

Lying below Bradfield Park was a beautiful expanse of bushland. Magnificent *Angophora costata*, Sydney red gums, towered 75 feet into the air, their ruddied trunks often gnarled and crooked, marking a time in history well before white invasion. My greatest comfort during the intense learning at ITS was the honeyed fragrance drifting up from their spidery plumes of white with yellow centres, like clusters of eggs awaiting separation. It reminded me of my bush origins and was complemented by darting coloured streaks of beautiful birds, the rainbow lorikeet, chirping and nattering to each other on their merry way. Kookaburras were my early morning companions, high up in the trees and doing their best to help me laugh off the coming day's endeavours.

Our three months training at the ITS was nearing completion. I am not a religious man, but I will never forget the rousing rendition of 'Rock of Ages' sung by all at our last assembly. Our voices were strong and vibrant and seemed to capture the same positive spirit that Flinders engendered among his men in the exploration of his new world.

The Empire Air Training Scheme had outlined the types of people wanted for the war. They were to have high standards of energy and stamina to cope with long work in high, cold altitudes; a combination of alertness and steadiness; analytical mentality and accuracy in detail; determination, tenacity and courage. Of those originally applying to be aircrew less than one in five had been selected for the ITS course and I was now among the 82 per cent of these who were accepted for aircrew. We had completed the initial phase and were now ready for specialised training.

In late December 1940, I embarked on the MV *Aorangi*, a vessel six times the size of Flinders' *Investigator*, on a six-week voyage for Canada and the second stage of the Empire Air Training Scheme. Recent troopships had been attacked by U-boats so we diverted across the Pacific to Panama to avoid the submarines, then headed north for docking in Vancouver. I was a mature 23 years of age and had passed muster. I had exceeded my educational ceiling and qualified for training as a navigator/bomb-aimer.

4

TRAINING IN CANADA

We docked in Vancouver Harbour, snow-capped mountains framing the foreshore from a distance. Wispy residual steam drifted lazily from the *Aorangi*'s twin funnels, blending eerily with the dismal grey of an icy Canadian winter. Long gone were the tepid green waters, tinged with sky blue, of a sunny and languorous Sydney summer. Travelling nearly 11,000 nautical miles underscored the vast distances and sheer size of the oceans that faced the undaunted aviator or explorer.

It was now February 1941. There was not a glimmer of heat and minimal radiant light. It was colder, much colder than I could have possibly imagined. We felt vulnerable to frostbite and were persuaded that our exposed extremities, such as ears, were in great danger of freezing. To our relief the Royal Canadian Air Force issued us with their standard heavier greatcoats and felt caps with earflaps. We were not reassured by their glib quips that this was a warm day at only 14 degrees Fahrenheit on the old scale.

For the first few days we were royally entertained, experiencing the largesse of local hospitality from the good folk who took us on sight-seeing trips north to Stanley Park, and treated us to unlimited food and much alcohol. Canadians were a welcoming bunch, and laidback just like Australians, always with an easy banter and a joke at the ready to make us laugh. Even their beer, rumoured to be on the watery side, packed a punch like the weather and made us feel right at home.

We were soon on the train for Edmonton via Jasper Pass, reputed to be the highest railway line in Canada, cutting through the grandeur of the Rocky Mountains. The mountain scenery was spectacular, with towering bleached pinnacles wrapped up in white, meeting frozen lakes and pencil pines trying to reassert their verdant vista. I experienced my first close-up encounter with snow, soon to become a familiar part of the landscape.

On arrival at our destination, we found the station wedged either side with house-high banks of snow. We also got our first taste of a miserable three-day blizzard with temperatures plummeting to an inconceivable minus 13 degrees Fahrenheit, certainly fully flapped ear weather and requiring a boost of Johnnie Walker Black Label before we left the heated train. Those Canadians certainly knew how to prepare for the cold.

Edmonton was the sub-Arctic gateway to the isolated settlements of the Canadian north, interspersed with lakes and muskeg, dank and dark green swampland overlaid with a veneer of sphagnum and other mosses. It was here that we were to learn the art of navigation over twelve weeks at the Air Observers School. The first twelve days seemed to drag, as we acclimatised and started theory. Desperately waiting to be airborne and escape from our earthbound icy prison, I was conscious of being far from home. I was haunted at night by the distant thundering of gigantic mile-long trains tracking their supplies to the east. Their locomotive whistles wailed mournfully, seeming to confirm our isolation, the 500 miles back over the Rockies to Vancouver.

I will never forget my first exposure to the mighty Avro Anson Mark I aircraft. My seat was directly behind the pilot so I could see all the action. The clear windowed canopy of the cockpit surrounded me, ushering in the light and the splendour of the Canadian countryside. A network of strutted supports held up the superstructure with two vaulted skylights beckoning my future observations as a navigator.

Stretching out either side of me, the powerful wings were coloured with red and blue insignia circles subtly superimposed on the camouflage paintwork, asserting our wartime purpose. The Anson was nicknamed the 'Faithful Annie' and came into service in 1935. It was the first RAF monoplane with retractable undercarriage, needing the pilot to turn the hand crank 140 times to lift the landing gear and reach the maximum cruise speed of 188 miles per hour. I felt right at home in this, the perfect plane to start my training.

The deep-throated twin 350-horsepower Armstrong Siddeley 'Cheetah LX' engines roared to life and were powered up for my first flight. I experienced a building, joyous euphoria mixed in with a slight feeling of apprehension. I couldn't stifle my bemused brain as it floated in feeble thoughts like, *Was man intended to fly? Could these grinding propellers really initiate movement and lift this mighty beast into the air?* The seemingly transparent shell reinforced our vulnerability to the elements, which had also been lovingly learnt in our introductory but land-locked training on the ground. This was further compounded by the realisation that we were soon to face an enemy intent on attack and the destruction of both craft and crew.

It is impossible to explain the exhilaration of a first flight. The power of two hard-driving engines finally lifts your craft off the ground and you experience the amazing force of the air as it tracks over the wings to take you above the earth's surface, defying gravity. Nothing can prepare you for this and you feel like screaming at the top of your lungs, 'I am flying.'

I will never forget my first flight in the mighty Anson.

The Edmonton Flying Training School allocated us into groups with a trusty bush pilot assigned to teach us novices how to apply our navigational concepts to the real world. He understood every nuance of the weather and the Alberta landscape. Our teacher had regaled us with pride about the Anson's incredible capability. Our training aircraft had gained its stripes during the evacuation of the British Forces at Dunkirk, where it was more than a match for the German Messerschmitts.

He recounted the story of Pilot Officer Phillip 'Pete' Peters of No. 500 Squadron, who, on 1 June 1940, had led a patrol of three Ansons to Dunkirk to support the evacuation. The story goes that, while flying at a mere 50 feet, they were attacked near Ostend by a band of nine Messerschmitt 109s. Peters dropped even lower and throttled back to make his aircraft a difficult target. The other two Ansons had taken the full force of the attack and he ordered them to disengage and return to base. His navigator/wireless operator moved to man the extra beam machine guns that had been added to the windows of what was affectionately called the 'greenhouse' cabin, while the air gunner manned the menacing Armstrong Whitworth–built manually operated gun turret in the dorsal section, that was fitted with a single Lewis gun. Peters immediately turned to the attack and skilfully manoeuvred his aircraft so the navigator and air gunner could give the enemy a solid dose of concentrated fire. They each bagged one confirmed crash and one seriously damaged Messerschmitt. The fight lasted less than ten minutes with Peters' Anson receiving only four bullet holes in the battle and the remaining 109s flying off to avoid further combat. It was a gutsy performance proving the perfection of our training aircraft.

We had lectures in basic navigation for six hours a day, reduced to three when we were flying. There were two navigators per training aircraft and they alternated roles. The 'first navigator' worked at his log and chart and directed the pilot; the 'second navigator' assisted the first with such additional tasks as taking drifts and bearings and keeping weather observations. The daily wrestle was to determine the strength of wind blowing at cruising altitude and its direction, as an undiscovered beam wind could push you well off track. The local pilots always knew exactly where they were and delighted in the dismay of the novice navigator getting lost over the many lakes and small towns that took on a surprising similarity from the sky.

On my first flight I was paired up with a fellow Australian who had arrived a week earlier. He was enthusiastic, talkative and fun. After that, we often talked over a beer in the trainees' mess, just off the aerodrome. The mess was luxurious and beyond anything we had ever seen, with pool tables, a well-appointed bar, unlimited food and a constant air-conditioned temperature of about 75 degrees Fahrenheit.

We remarked on the change in airspeed once the tailwind got hold of the plane, rocketing you along so you lost track of your position. It was so different actually being in an aircraft, at the mercy of the elements, and hard work navigating and staying focused on the chart with the constant vibration and turbulence. It was also difficult to concentrate with the noise and movement of the plane. We now faced the reality of flying.

It was not for the faint-hearted. At 5000 or 10,000 feet an Anson's speed could be halved by a headwind or increased 50 per cent by a tailwind. The skills we'd learnt in the classroom had to be relearnt under the intimidation of the elements. Clear thought seemed scarcely possible under this assault of noise, motion and gravity. Then there was the smell—petrol and oil, a toxic melange of the workings of machinery—lifting airmen into the strata of warfare.

Navigation was a complex art with many traps for new players, including the difference between the compass heading you gave the pilot to steer and the true headings you plotted on your charts. At this point on the globe, the difference between the two was 21 degrees. Get them mixed up and you could find yourself hopelessly lost, much to the amusement of the staff pilot at the controls, who always knew where he was.

There was the constant threat of being scrubbed and sent to Trenton for re-mustering, assigned for lesser duties if you did not measure up.

You needed all your wits about you and an ability to adapt to your environment and the variable wind patterns. We soon started to get the headings right, in spite of the dramatic changes in wind direction, making it back to home base without a hitch. As our confidence built, we made unofficial diversions over the Rocky Mountains, with the pilot flying well below the towering peaks and cruising down the glorious valley over the glistening Lake Minnewanka to Banff.

We added our own little touches occasionally, such as the army cooperation day, when the astonished ground forces out on the prairie were bombed from low-flying Ansons with 2-pound brown paper bags filled with flour, carefully sealed and made up from flour bought at the local store the previous day. Our trusty pilot brought the Anson in right on line over the Canadian ground forces. It was our first experience of aerial bombing and we were truly amazed how hard it was to get the goods close to the target. In a way we were slightly relieved that our efforts had not hit the mark and stirred an international incident among empire forces.

By the time night exercises began, our confidence in our navigation skills had been mightily magnified. Suddenly we were able to decipher the jewel-like clusters of villages and towns, read the winds so that we were unfailingly able to find the path back to Edmonton, its reassuring glow 70 to 80 miles out, drawing us home like homing pigeons sighting the familiar skyline. We started to relax, take time to notice the remarkable beauty of the country and to enjoy some of the undoubted hospitality that was part of the Canadian experience.

I thought I'd found true love in Edmonton. Like all airmen on our course, I was given a home away from home and accorded special treatment by my host family, the Debucs. They were French-Canadians who had established a highly successful wood-milling business in Edmonton. One of the three brothers would always pick me up from the depot and drop me back. I felt welcome and at ease in their company, though they were clearly wealthy beyond my station in life. Their financial success was never paraded and they reminded me of Queenslanders with an easy-going charm that made me feel at home. I got on famously with all the brothers, who all delighted in the Canadian outdoors with the pursuit of hunting and stories of a new form of fishing with fly, rod and reel in the summertime.

The real prize though was Jeanne Debuc, the youngest sister. She was the jewel in the Debuc crown, classically beautiful in the French style with a petite slightly pouting face and short black hair setting off her athletic statuesque female form. I was besotted.

It wasn't just her beauty. She had the easy-going style of her family but she was also devoutly Catholic and this seemed to give her an almost pristine purity that really set her apart from other girls I had met till now. Her belief was resolute, unremitting and provided a certainty for her that, perhaps, I found of comfort at this unpredictable point in my journey.

We got to know each other very well in a short period of time, with her family fully supporting the attentions of this like-minded Australian. Jeanne and I would return from a night out to find a blazing log fire in the living room and not a soul in sight as if they understood the limited time we had to secure a deeper understanding and potentially find a future together. We held many similar aspirations, a longing for the simple life in this beautiful lake- and mountain-studded world, with our universe merely filled with the enjoyment of people and a communion with nature. I was not religious. It was really a blank page in my experience to date. I did not feel apprehensive, but more a fascination for the depth that Jeanne's faith had etched into her very being.

I remember one fireside heart-to-heart we had towards the end of my time in Edmonton. It was clear that we had to work out if there was a future for us on this war-torn planet. While still young, I felt ready for a meaningful relationship well beyond the physical attraction we felt. Certainly religion played a strong role in preventing Jeanne crossing the boundaries of intimacy that we were both eager to traverse. She was a warm, affectionate young woman with doe-like brown eyes. I felt her tender temperament drawing me closer to her beliefs and her way of life. She asked me direct, out of the blue, did I want children and, more to the point, how many?

I was certainly not ready for this next step, but didn't mince words. I assured her of my affection for her, allowing time to order my thoughts, to give due deference to her magnetising question. I explained that, so far, my life had been about bettering myself and finding a meaningful pathway. The idea of children had not really entered my head.

She quietly responded that she understood, emphasising the importance to her of raising her children in the Catholic faith. She could see that I was uncertain about entering into such a definitive contract, that my preparation for war somehow precluded me from any real thought of future and family. It was as if I had been anaesthetised from emotional involvement. Religion was not one of my primary driving forces.

I could already see in her eyes that I had failed the test by not being prepared to make resolute commitment without rational thought or consideration. We kept in contact but I sensed our connection had been splintered. We corresponded as I continued my training across Canada and for some months after I arrived in Britain, but it now seemed that a friendly mix had replaced warmth and affection.

In the end, I believe Jeanne ended up marrying the young and handsome local priest, the two of them being drawn together in the exercise of their good works. On the few church occasions where I had been included, I had noticed her fervent attention to his words, but had put it down to her strong commitment to the church. He had, in the end forsaken his calling.

From our Ansons we could see that the mighty Saskatchewan River was beginning to uncurdle and thaw into an icy flow. The worst of our Canadian winter was surely over. There were many broken hearts among Course 7OH as we left for Mossbank, Saskatchewan, and the bombing and gunnery school. We now headed truly into the centre of prairie country with symmetrical 640-acre blocks of everlasting wheatfields, aligned north and south, and stretching halfway to eternity in all directions. It was to be eight weeks of intense practical training, twenty short flights in the ancient lumbering Fairey Battle, an outmoded fighter-bomber relegated to help us perfect our skills under the Empire Air Training Scheme.

The Fairey Battle was the first all-metal bomber to serve in the RAF and was weighed down by three crew, a bomb-load and powered by a single Rolls-Royce 1050-horsepower V12 Merlin engine. More like a fighter than a bomber. By May 1940 it had become an underpowered defenseless aircraft, easy prey for the Luftwaffe and enemy ground gunners. There was almost a sense of growing German shame in picking off these sitting ducks. This ancient craft had well and truly passed its prime and was retired from front-line service. Nevertheless, we came to respect its remarkable strength and resilience. In trouble, the Battle could land wheels-up on any part of the countryside and then be taken back by a recovery truck, the wheels jacked down and the mud wiped off the underside. Ready to go, good as new.

We were paired up two at a time in rotation for the gunnery section of our training. I was fortunate enough to meet up with a canny pilot, fresh from flying school, who encouraged me in the cunning capability of gaining the maximum number of hits on the tiny target drogue, towed on a long cable by another Fairey Battle. The trick was to wait until the towing aircraft turned, leaving the drogue momentarily suspended, almost motionless. Then let go with a full pan of 50 rounds of the gas-operated Vickers 303, being careful not to collect the towing aircraft itself.

With the aid of my old friend the Vickers, I followed my adviser's instructions precisely, often achieving a remarkable score. I would routinely notch up 17 per cent of hits or more, almost double other people's scores. I also managed to bring many of our pilots to apoplexy as they screamed 'Cease firing!' down the intercom to save their companion aircraft from my apparently undisciplined barrage.

I had a marvellous feeling of freedom during gunnery training. The rear cockpit canopy was slid back, leaving me standing waist-deep in the aircraft with the rest of me totally exposed to the elements, with just a heavy-duty safety harness attached to prevent me being ejected into the slipstream. The Vickers was mounted on the port side of the long cockpit with a suitable stop for the gun, to preclude an over-eager gunner from blowing the tail off his own aircraft. I thrived in this familiar use of weaponry but was never again to man a gun in warfare. After this training, only my navigational skills were required to deliver the payload to target.

By contrast, bombing was claustrophobic. It reminded me of my time in the Babcock boiler. To reach the bomb-aimer's position under the wing centre section in the Fairey Battle, you inserted your body with care into a minute hatch, surrounded by knobs and sharp corners, and crawled forward along a lower deck too confined for sitting, towards a sliding panel in the floor of the fuselage. The aim of your endeavours was to sight through the perplexing Mark VII Course Setting Bomb Sight with its four interconnecting controls. Move one of these related controls even slightly and the others would be thrown wildly out of kilter. Move two and the sighting device would jerk off to one side even more rapidly. Change the aircraft heading and the sighting arm of the bombsight would have to be realigned all over again.

A bomb-aimer's life was not a happy one. Frantic calls of 'Left, left . . . steady, right . . . steady' to get the sighting arm on target were the height of difficulty, entombed in this narrow compartment. You would desperately reconcile the bombsight settings of wind speed and direction with the aircraft heading only to see, at the last moment, the target escaping away to one side of the nose of the aircraft, elusive from the drop. Columns of tall white cumulus clouds abounded over Saskatchewan and were the cause of extreme turbulence. Only the narrow corridors of beautiful blue provided any relief to the hapless trainee. Still, we again somehow mastered this challenging new skill cocooned in the confines of the Fairey Battle, our resolve having been sorely tested. I am pleased to say that Course 7OH passed their bombing and gunnery without exception.

It was just after this course completion that a telegram arrived telling me of the death of my younger sister, Rua Jean. She had just turned 21. This news was shattering. Growing up on the farm, I had not paid her much attention. Women in those days were attributed secondary status and relegated to the most menial and domestic of duties. Women's work was considered of little importance to the not inconsiderable ego of the maturing elder son. In those early years, I really did not know or understand her.

Rua was a vibrant energetic girl with a real love for life. She loved horses and was a very good horsewoman. Her only recreations were tennis and horse riding and there was little enough time for those. I do remember her remarkable capacity to, quietly and without offence, deal with my mother's sharp tongue. She seemed somehow out of reach and able to deftly defer any demands with a 'Yes, Mother' before she dashed out the door for some social occasion. My less than sympathetic mother was left gasping for words, staring after her as Rua offered a questionably conciliatory, 'I'll be dealing with that when I get back.' I suspect my mother recognised in Rua some of the spirited stock that had allowed her to survive her own brutal beginnings on the land.

It was only later when she came to Bundaberg General Hospital to train as a nursing sister that I squired her on a few social occasions. I soon realised that, for a sister, she was really good company. While not beautiful in the classical sense, she had a simple natural allure and captivating charm that made her attractive beyond good looks. Sometimes she revealed a mischievous spirit, with a broadened outlook well beyond the surroundings of a country farmhouse. This caring, companionable soul brought out the best in people coming under her spell. I became one of her magical converts, learning how to replace remoteness with a human warmth and friendliness.

My father's telegram advised in stoic staccato that Rua had contracted pneumonia while serving in the hospital and that this had proved fatal despite all the efforts of the hospital doctors. Pneumonia was still a deadly silent killer in the early 1940s. This 'captain of the men of death' was acquired through contagious bacteria. At that time this could only be treated with serum therapy using sulfonamides with limited antibacterial activity. My dear sister missed out by a year on the miracle antibiotic drug penicillin, which had much greater success fighting pneumonia and was first made available for commercial use in 1942.

The name Rua has Irish origins and means 'dreams and visions'. To me, she had been like the glow from a distant lighthouse, beckoning to all yet keeping them safe from harm.

As I contemplated my own mortality heading into war, I felt cheated that this generous soul would not be there if I was lucky enough to return. How could this blithe spirit be snuffed out, denied her own dreams and aspirations while safe at home in Bundaberg? I was left bereft and searching for meaning.

The last port of call for Course 7OH was a remote air force aerodrome near to a small scattered village called Rivers on the railway line to Winnipeg. We were now on the edge of the Arctic and halfway across the North American continent, a solid 1400 miles from Vancouver. We were at the No. 1 Air Navigation School for four weeks to learn the science, or perhaps the art, of astro-navigation. This involved learning how to plot one's position and proceed using the sun, moon, planets or stars. No clear starry night was to be wasted.

Each of us would climb a ladder to a darkened cubicle in the lecture hall roof, at the top of which an aircraft astrodome was mounted. A Mark IX bubble sextant was suspended from the centre of the perspex dome and was used to take shots measuring the altitudes above the horizon of certain stars, correctly identified from the accompanying star chart. The precise time to the second of each shot and its resultant altitude would be applied back to books of pre-computed navigation tables. Calculations were then made and the end result plotted on a chart. These position lines would all intersect on the chart forming what was called 'a cocked hat', like a triangle, with the centre being the fix and indicating our position. No matter how big the 'cocked hat' of the three intersecting position lines, the astrofix at the midpoint was the position of the aircraft, the holy grail. I thought of the intrepid Matthew Flinders and how he would have coveted this refined form of navigation.

Before we could take to the air again in the mighty Avro Anson, we were required to prove proficiency by taking 50 sextant sights each, for day and night, and recording these in the sight log book, so that accuracy could be verified. If you found yourself nearer to Winnipeg than the aerodrome, it was up to the embryonic navigator to quickly discover and resolve the cause of this sudden worrying displacement. This would later mean life or death for your crew.

To be recognised as a complete air navigator, we were now obliged to fly night exercises for anything up to four hours' duration along a prescribed route, maintaining the aircraft on track through position fixes using the stars. In the air things got harder. The magic bubble of the sextant was the horizon and now became subject to all the acceleration forces of a moving aircraft, dancing around the chamber like a tethered party balloon in the wind. Aligning the sextant with a star was also much more difficult. You had to adjust to the real world of the aircraft, make a practical judgement call in this moving environment, and change the headings of the aircraft in accordance with any new wind velocities calculated.

I completed ground and air training at Rivers and was posted to Halifax embarkation depot for transit by boat to Britain with the rest of Course 7OH. However, after a long train journey covering what remained of the North American continent, and one foggy 24-hour period at the depot, I found myself, with one other member of the course, once again on the train. We were heading back the way we had just come, destination Montreal.

I had been selected to join Atlantic Ferry Command, the organisation responsible for ferrying American aircraft to Britain for the war in Europe. I was to be the navigator of a Hudson aircraft, flying with the regular civilian crew, and this was to be my one-way ticket to war. I had traded the delights of a further ten-day sea voyage across the perilous Atlantic for a nine-hour flight, destination Prestwick, Scotland. This was still not an easy feat in the air and was sure to test my newly learnt navigation skills.

5

MONTREAL AND MEETING BENNETT

It was in Montreal, in the summer of 1941, that I first met Donald CE Bennett. Appointed in the early months of the war as Flying Superintendent of Atlantic Ferry Command, he had a reputation as one of the most brilliant technical airmen of his generation. Bennett trained as a pilot but was a consummate navigator, also capable of stripping a wireless set or overhauling an engine. Later in the war, he would use his considerable navigational know-how to turn around the Allies' dwindling fortunes in the air battle for Europe.

At eighteen years of age, Bennett had ignited in himself a determination to fly that would transcend his parents' meagre expectations and lift him to extraordinary heights. They thought him not to be of the academic calibre of his three brothers, which struck a chord with me due to the way my father had halted my education. Parental presumption had starved us both of early opportunity.

Fellow Queenslander Bert Hinkler had sparked Bennett's imagination for long-distance air travel. 'Hustling Hinkler', as he was nicknamed in 1928, was the first person to fly solo from England to Australia, covering 11,000 miles in fifteen and a half days in an Avro 581 Avian, with a solitary Cirrus engine. This indefatigable aviator travelled from Croydon in Surrey, England, to Darwin in the north of Australia, enduring 128 hours of loneliness, flying solo in an open cockpit at an average speed of 86 miles per hour.

Bennett sat for his first-class navigator's licence in 1934 and became only the seventh man in the world to pass the examination. He wrote his first book, *The Complete Air Navigator*, in 1936 on the slow boat home to Australia, on his honeymoon. It became the standard and remained in print for over 30 years. Let there be no doubt, Bennett was legendary in the orbit of aviation, and also, like me, a Queenslander.

I was about to cross the Atlantic and couldn't believe my good fortune when I was chosen to receive brief additional training in the art of navigation from the man himself. I had it on good authority that he loved working with his men, giving them the benefit of his years of experience and leading-edge knowledge. I met the rest of my crew, who were full-time Ferry Command staff; the skipper was a Canadian flight lieutenant, Jimmy Anderson, and the radio operator an American civilian, Frank Wright, a one-time ham operator. For my benefit, we were now to undertake a short familiarisation flight on board Lockheed Hudson 9087. While we waited to be joined by Bennett, I genially chatted with the staff sergeant in charge of new personnel.

He clearly admired Bennett and, as we waited, was happy to fill us in on the already remarkable achievements of this aviation pioneer. He explained that Bennett was an exceptional airman and responsible for setting a new long-distance flying boat record before the start of the war. He had started his flying career with the RAAF in July 1930 and had volunteered for service with the RAF in England to gain the necessary hours of flying experience, taking to the air in a strange-looking biplane called the Armstrong Whitworth Siskin. These amazing relics were used in World War I.

He then moved to more modern craft, the larger flying boats including the great wooden-hulled, silver-painted Supermarine

Southampton flying boat. This was also a biplane and a heavy multi-engined machine at that, requiring special techniques of airmanship and water handling. He didn't stay long in the RAF. Realising the limitations of service in a peacetime air force, in January 1936 he joined Imperial Airways. He did this to ensure his progress in aviation and, by the time he left this civil service, our flying superintendent had 1350 hours' flying to his credit on 21 different types of land and marine aircraft.

Our flight sergeant pressed on with his yarn about Bennett. In 1937 he received his first modern commands with Imperial Airways in the Short 'C' Class Empire flying boats. They were sleek monoplanes and really gave him his first taste of long-distance airline travel. Bennett was keen to take on any flying challenge and, in October 1938, volunteered to pilot the *Mercury*, a small four-engined float plane that was to attempt the world long-distance flight record. It had just sufficient space for one pilot and a radio operator. No room for a navigator, unlike the Hudson I was about to go aboard.

The seaplane record was held by a German Dornier float plane that had been catapulted off the deck of a ship. They had to pioneer a unique composite aeronautical configuration called the Mayo Composite, where the *Mercury* was carried aloft, piggybacked astride the parent Maia flying boat. The *Mercury* was given the power of eight full-throttle engines to achieve take-off with 45 per cent more fuel in its floats. It was released by a patented separating technique and mechanism once the tandem planes were at cruising altitude, allowing it to carry the necessary fuel load to make the journey.

They travelled some 6000 miles from Dundee on the east coast of Scotland to Alexander Bay on the Orange River in South Africa in 42 hours and 30 minutes. In the end their electric pumps failed and they had to take it in turns to pump 1400 gallons of gasoline by hand from the floats to the wing tank, in order to stay airborne. Though exhausted, they managed to complete this difficult task in enough time to avoid crashing over the desert and make it to a safe protected landing harbour. Bennett navigated his way down the length of Africa with his sextant, picking up positions through the night using only trusty astrofixes. It was one hell of a navigational feat.

The *Mercury*'s average speed was 144 miles an hour, easily the highest speed ever maintained on a long-distance flight, and broke the seaplane record but not the overall record. That trip confirmed for Bennett that long-distance air travel was here to stay.

We then learnt of our flying superintendent's early work with Atlantic Ferry Command. After he was appointed, one of his first steps was to visit Lockheed in America to conduct flight-tests on the Hudson. He confirmed the need to install an additional temporary fuel tank to fill the central fuselage. Only by doing this would the Hudson be able to make the distance to deliver these much-needed aircraft for the war effort.

The story continued. He set about organising the Atlantic Ferry Command to be established at Gander Airfield in Newfoundland, the closest practical departure point for aircraft to be flown into Europe. It was mid-winter 1940 and they now had a few Hudsons ready for transportation. This was to be their first exploratory trans-Atlantic flight, with such a hazardous crossing not having been contemplated before that time. The North Atlantic weather patterns were still not fully understood and could possibly take a heavy toll on their fuel-laden, minimally equipped aircraft. It was certainly not the best time to try this trip but the aircraft were desperately needed for the Allied war effort. Facing the dangers of ditching in the ocean and the hazards of cloud, icing, and the buffeting strong winds at altitude, it was vital to prove that the problem of delivery could be overcome. Bennett decided to lead the first formation of aircraft across, demonstrating how it could be done with his own navigational skills. He had hoped that this would inspire some much-needed confidence for others to make this perilous journey.

They were set to leave Gander on 9 November 1940, but were delayed 24 hours to clear the aircraft of a steel-hard layer of ice on the flying surfaces. With seven Hudsons on this initial trip, Bennett was the first to take off. He estimated a nine-and-a-half-hour crossing to Aldergrove in Northern Ireland, allowing for a helpful 23-knot tailwind. There were two pilots and a radio operator on board each Hudson, no navigator. Bennett was to provide the navigation for the formation.

Before Atlantic Ferry Command, only about 100 aircraft had ever attempted the journey, and these brave bids were all made in good weather. Only half had made it. Not great odds for survival. I thought of my own upcoming journey.

Deep into the flight, due to an area of severe weather, the formation was forced to break up. Luckily, by that time the track was well established and all aircraft arrived safely. Bennett had stood watch, staring out of the control tower, waiting for the last two tardy Hudsons to taxi in and stop engines. The trip was exhausting and proved to Bennett the need to have a navigator on board each aircraft. That was why I was now needed.

That pioneering crossing, this first journey out into the icy windswept unknown, was a brave and extremely hazardous enterprise, particularly in the grips of a bleak winter. It was an amazing feat of navigation for Bennett. He implicitly trusted his own ability and, as I was to learn later, this was a strength that would stand by him throughout the war. He had a reputation for not suffering fools gladly and was sometimes seen as a difficult and arrogant loner, yet I admired his approach.

We were now joined by the man himself. We climbed into Hudson 9087 and prepared for take-off. Bennett was courteous but curt. A tall man of striking demeanour with no hint of any cloud of competence, he struck me as a man of action, highly professional, someone who called the situation exactly as he saw it. Everything he required of his men, he would also do himself. He outlined the task ahead and the navigational challenges of the Atlantic. Under his influence, my knowledge of navigation doubled overnight, confirming the need for confidence, the belief in myself and the inviolable astrofix as the undeniable pinpointed position of the aircraft. He was the consummate master navigator with a deep love of navigation. His imprint on me was like the first impression from an old-fashioned stamp firmly loaded from a brimming ink pad. Respected by all, he was almost revered.

We then had a couple of days free during which my cordial crew made sure I saw many of the sights and nightclubs of Montreal. It was a most fascinating city and my first exposure to a multicultural society. I had ventured a few words of Polish in my time with the Kasmaroskis in Bundaberg, but never been to a place where English was a second language. I loved the timbre and flow of 'la belle langue Française' and revelled in the fact that I was experiencing the largest French-speaking city in the world after Paris.

Over a few balmy summer nights we wandered the local streets to take in the true flavour of Montreal, block after block of duplexes and triplexes wound up together with corkscrew staircases. These majestic, curving balustrades would link the living quarters upstairs with the shops and nightlife entertainment of the cafes and bars below.

I told Jimmy what a novelty it all was for me after my life in Queensland. I was to learn that many of the inhabitants of these fine flats were rural refugees from the villages and farms of Quebec who had come to Montreal seeking work, and escape from the routines of country living. I found my story had been replicated in a faraway land where people spoke in a different tongue yet shared the same human experience.

As we continued our journey of discovery, I came to appreciate what gave Montreal its buzz, its zest for life. Saint Lawrence Boulevard brimmed with the aroma of Italian antipasto, little German sausages, Hungarian goulash, apple strudel, onion pretzels and more.

Montreal at night also drew me in. Hurdy-gurdy men ground out music in front of the all-night movie theatre and street hawkers peddled their wares. The carnival mood was not to be resisted by a young airman, far from home and on his way to do battle for the empire.

I was now Flight Sergeant Goodwin, qualified on my flying log book as observer/navigator. We became airborne on 5 August 1941 and were to fly across to Gander in Newfoundland, a flight of 5 hours and 50 minutes, in Lockheed Hudson 9180 that I would be navigating to Britain. This flight was of immeasurable value to me as it allowed me to become more familiar with the plane, the performance figures indicated in the manual and to plan the route as well as the actual navigation. I was pleased to be able to confirm for myself the actual deviation of the compass against the figures last recorded. These checked out well on the headings flown on this flight and were very close to those to be taken for our planned Atlantic crossing after we left Gander.

I thrived on the feeling of the sheer power exuded by this R-1830 twin Wasp radial-engined beast, decked out in British insignia, and ready for war. The Hudson had a dark green, almost olive hue with a dark earth background completing its camouflage. Though built in America and towed on its wheels over the border to Canada to preserve US neutrality, its mechanical glow reminded me of the very best in British steam locomotion and engineering. The two Pratt and Whitney engines each generated 2700 revs per minute on take-off and delivered a maximum cruising speed of 261 miles per hour. It was to replace the 'Faithful Annie', the Avro Anson, as Coastal Command's standard shore-based aircraft, and was certainly a larger aircraft than any I had trained on. I was about to get a taste of flying and navigation on a large scale.

We spent two days in Gander during which the aircraft was given a full servicing. It was here that I was at last able to try the art of fly-fishing that Jeanne's brothers had whetted my appetite for. My obliging crew borrowed fishing gear and transport, and I was then given some rather hasty instruction and practice in fly-fishing out on the edge of the tarmac. This kind of fishing was entirely new to me and seemed to involve a delicate art and refined skill.

We fished the mouth of a small creek so that long casts were not necessary and I managed to set the fly on the water. My 'Silver Doctor' fly did its job, a masterpiece in glistening silver tinsel, with scarlet floss and gold at the tip, and teal blue and yellow feathers to camouflage the barb. There was no shortage of trout but the difficulty was to get the fly near a bigger fish before the voracious small rainbows grabbed it. I loved this new form of fishing and I vowed to try it again, hopefully in the rivers and lakes of our own alpine expanse, the Snowy Mountains region in Australia, if I had the good fortune to make my return.

By the end of the war, 9000 aircraft were ferried by Atlantic Ferry Command across this treacherous ocean. Crossing the Atlantic was to become a routine operation, foreshadowing the introduction of scheduled commercial air transport services after the war. At the time of my first impending trip, it was still an adventure into the unknown.

6

CROSSING THE ATLANTIC

It was 8 August 1941, and our Lockheed Hudson 9180 was waiting for take-off at the end of the runway of Gander airstrip in Newfoundland. My training in Canada was complete and I was off to England to join the war. We had a journey to make of some 2000 miles over the perilous North Atlantic, between the eastern tip of Canada and Prestwick in Scotland. I had enjoyed great camaraderie and Canadian hospitality from my fellow crew members but, at the end of our trek, I would stay for combat and they would return for yet another foray into the icy climes. Hudson 9180 and many more like her were desperately needed by RAF Coastal Command to protect Allied cargoes in the north-western approaches to the Atlantic.

Long though the Gander runway was, our small airframe was weighed down heavily by the large supplementary fuel tank, courtesy of Flying Superintendent Bennett. This filled the inside of the fuselage, giving us an almost certain chance of making the distance, but it also meant we would be uncomfortably close to the ditch at the end of the runway when we finally staggered into the air. It was going to be touch and go.

My earlier RAAF aircrew training at Bradfield Park in Sydney had already prepared me for the hostile nature of the elements and their impact on flight, particularly over the Atlantic. I was well versed in the variations in temperature, winds and great swirling air currents caused by the 23.5 degree tilt of the planet towards the sun. The thin tempestuous veneer of atmosphere, a mere 75 miles in height, could rupture violently, roiling any craft that dared to attempt passage over its alluring surface. Shimmering unpredictably above the earth, it seemed to have a heartless regard for human endeavour. I was ready for the whims of weather, heartened by the feats of my mentor Bennett, and felt immune to the dangers of enemy action.

We hurtled down the runway and managed to take off, despite the heavy load, and soon reached a cruising altitude of 10,000 feet. We expected our journey to take nine hours and everything was reasonably normal for the first three hours. My position in the Hudson allowed me to gaze out ahead through the front perspex nose giving me a perfect view of the seas below. The twin fins of the aircraft's tail floated gloriously behind and seemed to applaud my elation at being at last on a real operation, part of the war effort.

It was my first flight as a navigation officer, away from the shelter of training, no longer able to have another go if things did not quite go according to plan. My responsibilities were to make sure we reached landfall and took the best route for the economic use of fuel. During the early stages of our journey I became rather frustrated because of the scarcity of astrofixes. There had been a succession of weather fronts on our track and the presence of high cloud obscured the stars. I had not been able to effectively plot our position, nor our progress, and I was very keen to make my contribution on this, my first and only, delivery flight. Jimmy had made three previous ferry crossings and assured me that this situation was completely normal over the Atlantic and likely to improve. I had to bide my time.

And, indeed, things soon picked up. In the ensuing two hours I managed to get two three-star fixes, about 55 minutes apart, and this time the sights did not have to be taken through high altostratus cloud. With these welcome calculations, I felt the lifeblood of my profession come coursing back through my veins. I was now able to log the new wind velocity and confirm the estimated time of arrival. I had the situation under control and felt proud of my contribution.

My nonchalance was soon put to the test. Around this time, just four hours into the flight, Jimmy reported, 'Listen, guys, the port engine's running a bit rough. It's not good.'

Frank attempted to reassure us. 'The ground engineer advised me just before departure that it was fine-tuned and running smooth.'

This failed to give me comfort as I knew the Hudson had its limitations. It was essentially a short-hop aircraft being asked to face the challenge of an Atlantic crossing, like subjecting an overly plump duck to a flight north for the winter. The Canadian mechanical crews were meticulous in their adjustments to the two Pratt and Whitney engines, and would not have missed any evident fault in this gutsy beast. They clearly understood the difficulties and demands that would be made on our aircraft over the Atlantic.

'We'll work out what adjustments we can make to the petrol mixtures for now to see if we can get engine two back in business,' Jimmy said over the intercom. He knew it was vital to set the appropriate throttle adjustments to return the engine to functioning at full bore so we could make our necessary landfall. We worked for half an hour on relentless adjustments. 'No joy, guys, we'll have to shut her down,' Jimmy eventually announced.

The engine was now dangerously overheated. Jimmy then put to me the chilling question, the dread of any navigation officer, 'Gordon, I need to know if we have reached our flight plan PNR yet.' This was the Point of No Return where we were better off keeping going than turning around.

It was my first real excursion into the unknown and I was already being tested. I was elated that I had managed to make the two recent astrofixes to confirm our position through the cloud cover, which had momentarily lifted to give us our chance. I felt proud and confident of my technical ability. 'Thirty minutes to PNR, Skip,' I stated clearly, after a last reassuring glance at my calculations. There was no room for error, no time for re-checking my fixes. This was not a training exercise.

'Thanks, Gordon, we're heading back!' Jimmy resolved. As if confirming his commitment to the decision, he immediately swung the aircraft through 180 degrees. 'I now need our course to Gander and an ETA.'

'Roger that, Skip,' I responded.

The decision was well founded—it was much better to head for a known aerodrome with weather we had already experienced than carry on to Prestwick into unknown winds and weather with a 'duff' engine. It made no sense to tempt fate, even before my war service had begun. Had we been forced to ditch in the cold Atlantic, we would only have been able to survive for a short time, even if we made it to the dinghy.

Our return to Gander was not easy. We were losing height most of the time because we were flying on just one engine. To offset this, every so often Jimmy would restart the defective engine and run it until it started to overheat again. This nerve-racking exercise gained us several hundred feet in altitude but carried the terminal risk of engine fire. After a further four hours of this fine balancing we limped back into Gander after a total of 8 hours and 25 minutes of flying. I was surprised at my relief in making it back—not just for my own safety but because I was determined to make it to the war. I hadn't come all this way to be cheated on the last leg.

'A job well done, you guys,' Jimmy affirmed as we touched down on terra firma.

The mechanics worked on that engine for another week off and on, before pronouncing our aircraft serviceable again. We were in no hurry. The mess at Gander had an international flavour and was first class for food and drinks at any hour of the day. Apart from the American civilians, the rest of the aircrew were mostly old air force hands. They gave me some idea of the war ahead. Plainly enough, it was to be no holiday jaunt.

I also learnt of the exploits of Giovanni Caboto, or in English John Cabot, a lesser-known navigator of the fifteenth century. Leaving from Bristol in the south of England, his crossing of the Atlantic ranks as one of the greatest voyages of exploration of all time. Cabot covered 2200 miles in this epic journey, facing treacherous seas in a boat three quarters the size of Flinders', and had done it 300 years earlier. His single vessel was a small three-masted caravel, a mere 78 feet in length.

On the morning of 24 June 1497 this brave soul and his modest crew of twenty landed at Cape Bonavista, just north of Gander, to 'discover' the New World. They were the first Europeans to set foot on the continent of North America since the Vikings. At this time, Christopher Columbus was still exploring the Caribbean islands. Giovanni is said to have uttered the words 'buona vista' to describe the site of his landing. He marvelled at the pristine beauty of the cape, with its rocky shores and pebbled beaches extending out into the bay, framed by distant looming icebergs. These towering white ramparts floated eerily among myriad islands, cloaked in dense green forestry.

He had only the use of a compass and an astrolabe, a medieval navigation instrument which allowed mariners to calculate their position north or south of the equator, and could only be used if the skies were clear. This brass circular device, nearly the size of a man's head, was suspended from the left thumb with a central sighting piece, the calibrations etched into the circumference and not easy to use on a rolling ship. Latitude came from a fix on the sun or Pole Star, and was the only certain means of navigation. Compass needles swung wildly in rough weather and were subject to deviation caused by the earth's magnetic field. Fifteenth-century navigation was really a hit-and-miss affair and Cabot would have needed to use his intuitive skills to overcome the variation in his instrumentation, not to mention the icebergs drifting south from Greenland's glaciers and the North Atlantic drift.

Thankfully, the crew and I had avoided ditching in the watery wilderness of the cold Atlantic Ocean this time so, unlike Cabot, I would not have to face the turbulence of the ocean's boiling surface, the whims of the currents and ice flows.

We taxied out for our second try for Scotland. Although chastened by our aborted attempt, I was surprisingly ready to take up the battle again to get to war. We were at the tail of about eight aircraft waiting for take-off and Jimmy throttled back to give our charge, and its Mark III engines, one last rest as we were again at maximum permissible take-off weight.

The Hudson directly in front of us prepared for the fight for flight. I could smell the fumes as the streamlined craft powered up for the difficult task ahead. It moved out onto the tarmac and started its forward course as we went through our own last routines with a casual air belying the nervous anticipation resting in the pits of our stomachs. We watched it gather speed and prepared to follow. The grind of the Hudson's twin propellers at maximum thrust grabbed our attention as it struggled for take-off down the runway. The noise was both deafening and alarming. It was already three-quarters of the way to the imposing barrier and there was not the slightest sign of lift-off. Its airfoils seemingly were being denied Newton's third law of motion, thrust being complemented by the simultaneous reaction of lift.

It was too late. Even full brakes could not now stop the collision, the impending doom. The pilot, knowing that he was not going to make it, swung his aircraft around as it reached the ditch at the end of the strip. His Hudson began to ground-loop, collapsing the under-carriage, which was notoriously weak under this sort of treatment. Fractured metal ruptured the wing fuel tanks igniting the Hudson into a ball of fire. The flash of the blast painted our ruddy cheeks with the pale wash of horror. It was a grim reminder of the hazards of my new occupation, punctuated by a black mushroom cloud tinged with burnt orange. I had not been ready for eyewitness explosions or the idea of accidental death before even getting into combat.

It was only seconds before all three of the crew burst out of the rear door of the blazing plane, seemingly spewed out by the force of the fireball. One of the men even had the time to grab a small bag of his own effects on the way out. We could only marvel at their skipper's quick reactions and the crew's anticipation of escape. Flight Control directed our return to the tarmac to top up our fuel. It took only half an hour to smother the fire with foam and for the wreckage to be bulldozed from the runway. It signalled the dispensability of planes, crews and valiant effort that were to become the fodder of warfare.

Soon we were on our way again with what ended up being a relatively simple departure. Although I was not of a religious bent, Hudson 9180 received our unanimous blessing as we finally separated from the safety of dry land and soared into the void for our second attempt. Our faith was restored and I felt a powerful feeling of optimism for my pilgrimage into the conflict ahead.

It was only in the latter half of the flight that we encountered unreasonable and unlikely headwinds. We were flying without en-route radio aids and the dismal Atlantic weather once more greatly restricted our access to astrofixes. It seemed a miracle that we made landfall only 18 nautical miles from my aiming point on the west coast of Ireland, with Hudson 9180 falling well short of the 2000 plus miles needed to make Scotland. The headwinds had sapped our fuel supply, denying us our original destination.

'Where's best to set down, Gordon?' Jimmy queried, knowing we would not be making Prestwick.

'Skip, suggest we land for refuelling at Aldergrove aerodrome, near Lough Neagh,' I said.

I calculated that if we had continued our previous journey with the 'duff' engine and headwinds of this strength we would have ended up in the Atlantic, well short of Ireland. I felt a sympathy for John Cabot toiling over the watery surface in his small ship. It also confirmed my lesson from mentor Donald Bennett: the cool assessment of risk at a moment of crisis was the secret of survival.

After taking on board the vital gasoline, we completed the final leg and landed at Prestwick on the west coast of Scotland. I had been a small and temporary cog in the large wheel of Atlantic Ferry Command to get Hudson 9180 to join the war effort. I wondered what would happen to her. Would she serve her crew well in Coastal Command and survive with them or would she finish up at the bottom of the Atlantic, leaving the crew floating hopefully on a life-raft?

I was surprised to discover later in the war, that Hudson 9180 was possibly responsible for the surrender of German submarine *U-570*. After our arrival, our much-loved Hudson had been consigned to the British Hudson Squadron 269 for service as a maritime patrol aircraft, operating from Kaldaoarnes in Iceland.

U-570 had been sent on its very first patrol in late August 1941 as one of sixteen U-boats to attack a large concentration of Allied merchant ships in the North Atlantic, south of Iceland. On 27 August 1941, this U-boat had been spotted and had spent much of the morning submerged, travelling at a laboured 8.7 miles per hour beneath the heavy seas. Many of its novice crew were suffering from acute seasickness and several were severely incapacitated. The boat decided to surface at around 10.50 a.m. in broad daylight, and was immediately detected by the radar of 269 Squadron, which had been summoned into action by a previous Hudson patrol sighting.

On surfacing, the U-boat captain had climbed out onto the bridge and, on hearing the approaching engines of our Hudson, skippered by Squadron Leader James Thompson, had ordered an immediate crash-dive. Our aircraft reached the beleaguered submarine before she could fully submerge and dropped its full load of four 250-pound depth charges, with one landing and detonating just 10 yards from the boat. The power of the blast almost rolled the vessel over, knocking out its electrical power and damaging the craft. The air became contaminated and the inexperienced crew believed it to be chlorine gas, which was the deadly mixture caused by sea water combining with acid leaking from the battery cells. There was panic and the captain resurfaced with ten German sailors bursting out onto the deck to escape the gas. The sea was choppy and heaving and prevented the demoralised German sailors from manning their anti-aircraft gun. They raised the white flag fearing further attack, although the Hudson was now devoid of charges.

By early afternoon, the gathered Hudsons were low on fuel, returning to Iceland after being joined by a long-range Catalina that was able to circle the stricken U-boat and hold it in check for thirteen hours until Allied ships arrived. The British command then insisted the German crew secure the submarine to stop it sinking before they would take them to safety. Further, if they attempted to scuttle *U-570* then the anti-submarine trawler HMT *Northern Chief* would open fire and not rescue survivors from the water. Three sailors from the trawler HMS *Kingston Agate* then battled through the rough seas in a life-raft to attach a tow line. Only then were the German crew taken on board the British vessels.

The ships began slowly sailing to Iceland with *U-570* under tow, with a relay of Hudsons and Catalinas constantly patrolling overhead vigilant for U-boat attack. The depth-charge damage was found not to be critical with the water leakage coming merely from an unseated valve that was easily fixed. A more experienced crew could have submerged and escaped. The Germans had also failed to destroy many useful papers and copies of encrypted signals, of great value to the British Enigma code-breaking effort. Even the boat commander's handbook was recovered.

U-570 was converted for use in the war by the British as HMS *Graph*, Squadron Leader Thompson was awarded the Distinguished Flying Cross for his brave feat, and the attack and capture of this U-boat was used to great effect for rallying war propaganda by the British government. Our mighty Hudson had again proven her worth.

7

INTO WELLINGTON WARFARE

We had safely made Prestwick in Scotland and my arrival was duly rewarded with a welcome three days leave and a rail pass south. Bournemouth was my destination, an English holiday resort on the coast at the opposite end of the British Isles set up as a reception unit for overseas aircrew. I was then to start in earnest the intense, final leg of my wartime operational training.

Traversing two-thirds of this realm, from Ayr Bay in the north to Poole Bay in the south, I marvelled at the cavalcade of green countryside, melded and stitched together by some quaint little villages and larger industrial towns. England was all that I had imagined, a lush panorama of grass and greenery, underscoring the red arid land of my origin. August in England was still warm but more like a Queensland winter than summer and so I made the most of my days at large.

I was still in contact by mail with Jeanne but I could feel our bond fading fast. I wrote one last letter to cut her free, then joined my mates for a spree. The ladies of this fair land, though not of the nutted complexion of Australian girls, were delicate, pretty and lots of fun. I made the most of my three days of freedom and put aside any thoughts about being in the air again, this time in the thick of the action. I was a month short of my twenty-fourth birthday and looking for a good time.

Water always gave me a feeling of spiritual release. It was hard to resist and the weather down south still inviting, so one day a few of us ventured onto the gravelly beach, so different from the hot white sands of home. I remember diving in from the shore, Queensland style, hoping to paddle out, revelling in the liberation of exercise after my confinement in plane and train, and to embrace that sublime floating feeling. I was gripped by an immediate crushing sensation on my lungs, the cold of the sea like a vice on my torso. I could barely make it back to shore, crawling from the water on hands and knees, suffering from what I considered to be acute hypothermia. I had thought the ocean was supposed to be reasonably warm, considering the time of year and it being at the lowest latitude for this luxuriant landscape. I could only imagine what it would be like swimming to a life-raft out in the North Sea.

After my few days respite, I was on my way to 27 Operational Training Unit at Lichfield, Staffordshire. I put on hold any thoughts of the lovely ladies of England and entered into the remarkable exercise of forming a crew. It was a task of complete trust by all concerned, where six souls somehow self-selected each other to take on one of the most onerous and risky odysseys of our lives. All of the potential crew members were assembled one morning and told to sort themselves out into crews. There would be no changes after 1800 hours that night.

I was fortunate to meet up with a fellow Australian from the bush, Pilot Officer Arthur Doubleday. He and his mate Jimmy Breen were two pilots looking for a good navigator. I didn't take much persuading as they both had reputations as exceptional pilots, coming out of their Canadian training. They would be the greatest of assets at the helm of a Wellington in the thick of battle.

Next to join our retinue was Flight Sergeant Geoff Carter, another Aussie of more mature years, a novelty in the assembled throng at 30 years of age. Geoff had been a commercial traveller and would become 'the old man' of the crew and our wireless operator/air gunner. We Aussies seemed to stick together at the start of our first venture on this perilous journey of war and another Australian, 'Chappie' Chapman, followed as our front gunner. Pilot Officer Bert Walker became our rear gunner. He had left his jeweller's shop somewhere near Leeds to ply the trade of cutting down the enemy rather than precious gemstones. We joked he was with us Aussies to provide a bit of local colour.

We were now committed to the full training program of navigational cross-countries and bombing on the range at Cannock Chase, which was an area of outstanding natural beauty in the south of Staffordshire, comprising rolling open heath and woodland divided by deep valleys. It seemed reprehensible to be practising our skills of aerial destruction in this tranquil place. We also practised air-to-air firing and other gunnery exercises, air photography, formation flying for the pilots, and high altitude flying and the use of oxygen. Virtually every operation would be 'on oxygen', coping with the mask and performing our duties until the apparatus became just a normal part of our lives in the air. We also mainly flew at night, which was an adjustment as the majority of our training had been in daylight hours. My position in the crew was described as 'observer' which involved both navigator and bomb-aimer duties, including the responsibility of identifying our best way in to the target.

We had a further 53 hours of training together, mainly during daylight, on the 220 B Wellington Mark IV, which was the aircraft we would be using. The six of us started to build a strong sense of admiration and interdependence. Also emerging was the sardonic and subtle sense of humour, characteristic of Australian mateship. Geoff became the resident comedian, always with a joke or questionable yarn to tell. I hold him accountable for encouraging my own whimsical turn of phrase, always looking for the lighter side of life to keep things on an even keel.

The Vickers Wellington was a fascinating twin-engined, long-range medium bomber that drew upon the geodesic construction devised by Barnes Wallis in his earlier work on airships. Designed in the mid-1930s at Weybridge, Surrey, 'the Wimpy' utilised American Pratt and Whitney radial engines that had a somewhat higher turn of speed. The aircraft paid the price with a reduction in its range, the distance it could travel to the target. It was strong and light for its size with the capacity to carry a heavy bomb-load. The fuselage was built from a number of crosshatched aluminium alloy beams, giving the plane tremendous strength and the capacity to sustain damage and still support the remaining structure across the body of the aircraft. Wooden battens were screwed to this frame, which was covered with Irish linen, treated with 'butyrate dope'. This was a non-flammable, colourless and syrupy liquid derived from rancid butter. I was never tempted to try the taste.

Wellingtons could absorb a great deal of punishment and still remain airworthy. Even with huge areas missing, their naked frames dramatically exposed, they could still return to base. There is a story told of Co-pilot Sergeant James Allen Ward who climbed out of the fuselage, in flight, and kicked holes in the fabric of the wing for hand- and footholds. He then made his way along the wing to the burning covering of the starboard engine and smothered it. His aircraft and crew made it back home and Sergeant Ward was awarded the Victoria Cross.

At about this time, shortly after crewing up, Flight Lieutenant Jimmy Breen was given his own command and replaced by Pilot Officer Jimmy Falkiner. Our second Jimmy came from a well-known Australian grazing family who ran cattle and grew wheat out west in New South Wales on the Hay Plains.

My last step towards real warfare was to be posted with Arthur, Jimmy, Geoff, Chappie and Bert as one of the first bomber crews in RAAF 460 Squadron, which was then forming up at Molesworth in Huntingdonshire. It was the first time Australians had been put together in one squadron and not just allocated as part of the normal RAF retinue. I can still picture clearly in my mind flying north from there, through driving sleet and snow showers, on to our permanent base at Breighton in Yorkshire. It was a cloudy day in January 1942 and the land below glistened, resplendent in white with the dark hedgerows crisscrossing the fields like a patchwork quilt in monochrome.

Here we completed a further 35 hours of intensive flying training and slowly adjusted to local life in Yorkshire. In our limited leisure hours we ventured into the two local pubs of Bubwith, a little village almost encircled by our cold, draughty and uninviting Nissen billet huts, created as part of our wartime station. Here we started to decipher the broad brogue of the locals and, in exchange, regaled them with the raucous voices and laughter of young Australians far from home. We joked that they should appreciate a visit by the colonials since our land had been 'founded' by one Captain James Cook, a Yorkshireman born in nearby Marton, who made the first recorded European discovery of Australia's eastern coastline. The famous navigator and cartographer was one of their own.

On 12 March 1942, the battle order at RAF Station Breighton heralded the crews for the first operation of No. 460 Squadron RAAF, RAF Bomber Command. Twelve months since the start of my RAAF training in Canada, I was finally to set out on a real operation in a Wellington Bomber on my first tour of duty over enemy territory. I will never forget entering the briefing room as part of our band of six. Filing nervously into the Nissen hut allocated for the briefing, we discovered that our first target was to be the German North Sea port

of Emden. A huge map hung on the wall at the far end of the room and broadcast the dangers ahead. Shaded red areas seemed to scream out the anti-aircraft defences for each major and minor target across Germany and Occupied Europe. Our target for the night, Emden, was indicated with a blaring red marker. As we prepared for our first onslaught into the Ruhr Valley, Germany's industrial powerhouse, it was clear that the enemy would be ready as there was considerable red shading in what became known as 'Happy Valley'.

As our commanding officer, Wing Commander ALG Hubbard, DFC, walked into the room, we all stood up. He took his position by the map and invited us to be seated. There was a buzz in the air as he called the roll of captains for the night's operation. He was a man of medium height, curly brown hair, but solidly built exuding a quiet confidence. He had been in England for many years but his Australian accent would not be denied and broadcast his origins.

'All right,' he continued. 'Would you give us the gen on the weather please, Met?' The meteorology officer turned to the map with his long pointer and outlined what was undoubtedly the critical factor for bombing success. He explained to we expectant crews, 'There is a high centre over the Bay of Biscay, and a depression just off the north coast of Norway with an occluded front over southern Norway . . . cloud will be scattered.' He continued to outline the depression's location and its make-up through and surrounding our target. He summarised what we were to expect from this area of low pressure, wind, cloud and rain: 'You will encounter slight turbulence when climbing through cloud, and icing conditions will be moderate to heavy, but clear inland above 5000 feet. Weather over target will be 10/10 cloud, and headwind component less than 10 knots both directions.' He continued to give full temperature data and conditions at base on return, including visibility.

The intelligence officer was next up and gave us the detail on Emden. It contained the usual port facilities, U-boat construction yards and was an important transhipment centre for vitally needed

Scandinavian iron ore. We were told to aim for the heart of the town. Our bombing height was to be 15,000 feet and our bomb-load was to be six 500-pound general purpose bombs. He explained that while we were attacking Emden, another force of 68 Wellingtons would be attacking Kiel. He spelt out all the detail and then summed up what we were to face and possibly didn't really want to hear. 'The defences are strong, you can expect heavy searchlight concentration. Flak is also pretty well concentrated. You may encounter reasonable night-fighter opposition, although it is probable they will concentrate on the main force attacking Kiel.

'Take-off will be 2030 hours, and as Met has already told you, weather over the target is 10/10, so it is essential you're bang on course all the way.' Finishing, he asked, 'Any questions?'

There was silence as we all came to terms with the brutal reality of combat in the air, several hundred Germans 4.7-inch guns defending the target plus about 500 light 40-millimetre anti-aircraft guns. The knots in our stomachs had grown tighter. The air control officer now told us the height to rejoin the circuit on return, the call signal for aircraft radio recognition, the 'letter of the day' squadron code and other information for our return to base.

After wishing everyone good luck, Wing Commander Hubbard finished off, 'Well, chaps, this is the moment we have all been waiting for. This is the squadron's first operation, the climax to the months of training you have all put in. As our first squadron in Bomber Command you have a big responsibility to set the standard. I know you will not fail.' We felt an air of excitement and apprehension at the task ahead, but somehow privileged to be selected as the 'lucky bastards' to do the first op. The briefing ended and we were joined by our mates who had not been 'so lucky'. Good-natured banter was exchanged between the combatants and non-combatants which helped to relieve the tension.

We were on our way to avenge the attacks on London, Bristol, Coventry, and other centres in England that had been blitzed by the

Germans. We felt no remorse. As darkness gathered, we went outside into the chill night air and on to the Parachute Section to pick up parachutes and our flying kit, then out to our Wellingtons. I will never forget the roar as the Pratt and Whitneys opened up all around the airfield and we began to roll our Wimpies around the perimeter track to the runway for take-off. The remaining squadron members lined the runway and their cheers and shouts seemed to catapult our laden bombers into the air with ease. We were on our way to war at last.

We were fortunate to be joined on our first jaunt to Emden by Flight Lieutenant Oakley, the Officer Commanding A Flight, 460 Squadron. Arthur was to act as second pilot and benefit from the experience of our leader on this initial occasion. We had barely made it over enemy territory when the variable pitch control of one of the propellers started acting up. We had no choice but to return to base, after jettisoning our bomb-load off the Dutch coast. It was an anti-climax with a mere 2 hours and 30 minutes of flying time after all our training, but at least we had got 'one up on the board'. My flying log book read:

Operation 1 abandoned. Var. pitch U/S.

I had once again endured the problem of engine trouble on my maiden voyage, but I still had a further 29 operations to face to complete my tour.

When the rest of the squadron returned we learnt that heavy cloud formations had made it impossible to pick up the landmarks. Most of the bombing was haphazard with the run in to target depending on dead reckoning, the cloud cover preventing astrofixes. They had to rely on their ETA calculations from initial take-off and then be guided by the thickest part of the flak, no doubt thrown up by the enemy over the most prized piece of the target. Even the flak fizzled out once the squadron got close to target. A clever tactic by the Hun, some thought. Only one aircraft claimed to have hit Emden and two others attacked the adjacent town of Oldenburg. The remainder let their bombs go over what they thought to be the city area, and hoped for the best. The squadron's first operation, while having been satisfactorily executed, given the weather conditions, was negative in results achieved. Effectiveness over the target was the issue. This was to be a common theme in the early days of Bomber Command.

The very next night we were sent out again. Operation No. 2. Leaving close to 7.30 p.m., with the sun just setting on the horizon behind us, we were chased by its crimson glow as we headed out over the English Channel. This was an eerie experience, one we were to get used to, as our operations have been described by better authors than myself as 'chased by the sun' and 'a journey into night', with thanks to Hank Nelson and Don Charlwood. It was to be our baptism of fire with Arthur now at the helm and Flight Lieutenant Oakley acting as the number two pilot. The twin engines of Wellington Z1384 hummed problem-free and so we were certainly on our way into war this time. Our destination was Dunkirk on the French coast, a return journey of four hours. As we approached the coastline, there was only the hint of a dusky half-light.

As we were running in to our target, it was now almost pitch black, when suddenly, out of nowhere, came a strange and frightening blue shaft. It seemed to pick out our aircraft and hug it mercilessly with its cobalt light tracing our travel, its lethal beam cutting through the grey ground haze. Then between 10 and 30 searchlights hit the cockpit, their illumination brighter than daylight. We were confused and not really prepared for this blitz of light, which almost blinded us with its intensity. These extremes of visual and auditory experience marked our first night raid. From dark to light, from the quiet drone of the radial engines to the tumultuous shattering sound of exploding flak about our very vulnerable Wellington, we had engaged with the enemy.

'Taking evasive action,' Arthur calmly commented, not showing any hint of the surprise dogging the rest of us.

'You've lost the blue light, Skip,' Oakley confirmed, as our Wellington appeared to fall out of the sky, leaving the deafening thunder of explosions and brilliant eruptions of luminescence suspended in the air above us.

'Get us back on track, Gordon,' Arthur requested as we levelled out, returning to friendly darkness.

'Roger that, Skip,' I responded. I had time to identify our position through dead reckoning and a faint visual outline of the coastal fringe. I then confirmed our path back to Dunkirk and the target.

I learnt later that we had experienced only medium flak and that we had only seconds to escape the murderous searchlights as they coned into an intersecting apex that would have been our end. I can still feel in my bones, Arthur thankfully throwing our plane into a session of violent acrobatics, tearing our captured craft from their deadly tentacles. The blue master light was radar-controlled to direct the searchlights to their target and allow them to pinpoint our height and exact location before the release of the barrage of heavy flak. These concentrated belts of searchlights, which clustered around any target of significance over France and Germany, were to become, for me, the epitome of the enemy and would decide our fate in the many operations that lay ahead. My flying log book entry was again the master of understatement, using red ink to indicate a night mission, recording:

Caught in S'light cone. Medium amount heavy flak. Ground haze.

It belied the terror we had all felt in finally making it to war.

We made it back from Dunkirk without further incident. Others were not so lucky. Five aircraft from 460 Squadron had joined this operation and only four returned. I will never forget the announcement that Sergeant JFD Cooney and his crew had been shot down, becoming the squadron's first battle casualties. You expect death in war but not the loss of a familiar group, the gap in the aircraft line-up, the faces never to greet you again in a friendly drink with a bit of banter in the sergeants' mess. It reinforced the brutality of war. Even though our bravado continued, with a toast to mates lost, the loss of any airman was something I never got used to, and will never forget.

8

FINDING JOY

Our raid on the Lens area on 28 March 1942 was actually part of an operation of the greatest significance. Although we were involved in the dubious propaganda exercise of 'nickelling', the dropping of leaflets, we were the diversion for the primary force which was to attack Lubeck, a major port in Germany. It was Bomber Command's first massed strategic bombing and helped build our battle momentum. A total of 234 aircraft took part, the prime objective being to destroy the heavy stocks of equipment awaiting shipment to the German armies on the Russian front and in Norway, before the winter ice melted. It was a taste of what was to come.

There were many old wooden houses in Lubeck and these were ignited by the first wave of aircraft, creating a navigational and bombing beacon for the main force following. Using a total of 144 tons of small bomb container (SBC) incendiaries, the advance fire-raising aircraft demonstrated the value of starting a conflagration right at the aiming point and the ensuing bombers were able to drop 160 tons of high explosive accurately, causing 200 acres of devastation in the town. An SBC contained multiple small 4-pound explosive incendiary bombs (up to 236) that spread on impact, creating more sources of fire at the target than a larger single incendiary could.

The central power station was destroyed, together with many warehouses and factories, and the main railway workshops were badly damaged. Bomber Command had now replicated the Germans' destruction of the English town of Coventry early in the war. This set the scene for what would become known in Bomber Command as 'the Pathfinders' to ensure prior effective marking of the target for concentrated attack by the main bomber force.

For Operation No. 7 we had been to Cologne on our first night-time visit to the land of the Third Reich. This assault on the enemy in his home territory commenced, in earnest, on 5 April 1942. My flying log book entry was an all too common one for our future experience over German targets:

Large cones of searchlights, flak intense, accurate.

Accuracy of bombing continued to be the problem.

Our previous four operations had been about distributing messages of hope to the French populations of Lille, Lens and twice to Le Havre. We showered pamphlets over the population centres and joked as to the questionable benefit of this activity, suspecting that only street sweepers would make use of them. We also wondered whether we had created a glut of toilet tissue that would impede future French toilet roll manufacture. Our front gunner 'Chappie' would have to leave his post defending the aircraft to feed the bundles of pamphlets through the aircraft's flare tube. The drop was normally done at about 12,000 feet above sea level. To carry out the task, he would be off his much-needed oxygen and, as a result, exhausted by the enterprise, not to mention the increased risk to all of us of an undetected enemy attack.

The questionable value of this activity was further compounded, on one of these 'missions of tissue', when we were trapped in a large searchlight cone for four minutes with heavy flak bursting all around us, our lives on the line for pamphleteering. We later joked it was us who needed the tissue on that occasion, as we all felt that our lower stomach contents had only just been held in check during this violent and terrifying episode.

Enemy action was not the only hazard we faced. The stunning cold at high altitudes often froze equipment solid making it unable to function and the mere touch of it to bare skin brought injury. Most Wellington Bombers were inadequately heated, with hot air only emerging reluctantly from a solitary outlet, with the result that one crew member sweated profusely while the majority froze. The air gunners had electrically warmed oversuits, boots and gauntlets, but these were notoriously unreliable. It's hard to describe the deeply penetrating continuous cold of a six-hour operation in a thinly wrapped aircraft. You relied on your clothing and flying suit to keep you warm and fight the freeze, the like of which none of us had ever experienced before.

My log book entry on 8 April 1942 merely read:

Aircraft iced up west of Elbe river – severe electrical storms.

We were on our way to Hamburg, Operation No. 8, and had encountered an intense cold front lying directly across our track as we approached our target from the coast. There was no way around the weather, so we were trying to climb over it. Heavy flak was bursting in the cloud all around us, like incandescent tubes sparking to life after slow ignition. It was too close for comfort and obviously radar-directed. Long gone was any mollycoddling by the CO, we were well and truly on our own.

'I can't see any way ahead through the cloud, Skip,' I confirmed from my position below. As bomb-aimer I was in the belly of the aircraft, not strapped in because I needed to be able to move around so I could identify our route in to the target and also to find a way through the icing cloud.

'Roger that, Gordon. I'll have to take her a bit higher to dodge the flak.' Arthur spoke with relative calm, knowing we were at the absolute ceiling for the aircraft and now experiencing severe turbulence with our wings icing up rapidly. All the cloud tops were still above us.

'Good god,' Arthur gasped, his first real sign of emotion in our time together. The aircraft had stalled and was literally falling out of the sky.

I was positioned in the nose and so had no restraint to protect me as we plummeted downwards. I was pinned for most of the fall to the fuselage roof. It was like I was hovering overhead, watching the unfolding scene and enduring the strange sensation of gravity reversed in a falling aircraft.

The aircraft ranged through some 8000 feet before Arthur regained some control. 'Come on, you mother,' he muttered through clenched teeth. 'Jettison bombs now,' he barked.

'Bombs away, Skip,' Jimmy Falkiner uttered in a somewhat garbled tone. At that moment, as Arthur levelled out, the floor came up at me very rapidly. I instinctively put my right arm out. The top end of the humerus bone would never be the same again but I kept my whimper of pain bottled inside.

'Nice work, Skip. Splendid flak evasion,' I offered, in as steady a voice as I could muster, to somehow counter the extreme throb of my shoulder.

'I must confess I don't want to go through that again. Keep your eyes peeled for fighters, chaps,' Arthur reinforced over the intercom. He was meticulous in his demands upon his crew to minimise the risk. He never relented for a moment, his country upbringing building into him a sheepdog determination to cover every possibility for movement by the enemy. In private though, he confided to me a somewhat fatalistic approach to his own chances of survival. Our bomb-load gone, Arthur turned back for base and, fortunately, on this occasion, there were no further incidents. We now appreciated the dangers of aircraft icing up and why such emphasis was placed in briefing on these vital cloud conditions. I remember feeling intense relief and a zest for living as our Wimpy flew in over the Yorkshire moors and we could make out the beckoning lights of the Breighton strip. It was always good just to make it home.

During this tense time, humour proved to be our salvation. The pranksters took our minds off the futility of a fight with the odds stacked against us. Their shenanigans took many forms and were to reach epic proportions in the ingenuity and sheer effort put into pulling off the subsequent ruse. These mischievous miscreants were unofficially tolerated by the ruling hierarchy, who I think recognised their value in keeping up the spirits of young men at war.

I now happily relate the 'keg incident', which the flight sergeant in question dined out on for weeks to come. He had the good fortune to be standing outside the sergeants' quarters when a lorry driver arrived and sought directions to the officers' mess. He was delivering an 18-gallon keg of beer, a gift from the group captain at the parent base as a goodwill gesture to his fellow gentlemen of rank at our base. Our flight sergeant cleverly discerned what the valued cargo was and, with great presence of mind, assured the lorry driver that his destination had surely been reached. The precious liquid was rolled into our mess and a pleasant party was held with frequent toasting by the assembled sergeantry of the esteemed group captain.

Towards the end of the month, on 24 April 1942, we were one of three crews from 460 Squadron forming part of a force of 125 aircraft raiding the Heinkel works and Neptune shipyards at Rostock and this was our chance to inflict first-hand a similar fire-raising attack as had been achieved on the Lubeck yard. The operation was a complete success with the destruction of three-quarters of the Old Town of Rostock. The port and storage works were extensively damaged, and almost a third of the Heinkel works were wrecked. The people working in this town for the war effort were without water, gas and electricity for eighteen days. Aircrews reported seeing the fires burning from 100 miles away, leading them straight to the target. Subsequent attacks over the following two nights were also easily guided by the fires still burning. The Germans weren't ready for an attack of such a scale and we encountered minimal flak, night-fighter or decoy-fire defences.

This was the last of the 'easy runs' as in a matter of hours the Germans remedied their complacency. Up to this point they had assumed that targets like Rostock, far from RAF bases, on the Baltic Sea were too remote for attack and enjoyed natural safety cover. Bomber Command was now a significant force to be reckoned with. My flying log book for our raid on Rostock read:

6 S.B.C. 4lb Incend. Photo. Nickels – Vis excellent. – Fires started. – Flak, negligible, inaccurate.

It was Operation No. 12 and we felt well and truly blooded for warfare.

To this point my relationships with English girls had been of a casual nature. I was well aware of the air force conviction that airmen who had serious attachments flew more carefully, thus inevitably 'inviting the chop'. Marriage was certainly well off the agenda.

My skipper, Arthur, had met Phyll Buckle on his arrival in England. Like me, he had made a recreational sojourn down to Bournemouth before the beginning of battle and was smitten by a beautiful English rose at a local dance. Arthur saw Phyll again and again after their first meeting but was conflicted. He was convinced that he would not make it through the war. Phyll was a tall and intelligent, statuesque woman who had a responsible job with Imperial Chemical Industries (ICI), and was firmly committed to a future and a lifetime with Arthur. They clearly loved each other but the war was getting in the way.

As we were waiting to be called into the briefing for the next operation to Rostock, Arthur had opened up that he and Phyll were having some troubles. She wanted to get married and he wanted to leave it till after the war. They'd been arguing about this a bit lately and it was making them both unhappy. Arthur felt they needed to get back to enjoying themselves with not too much thinking about what was to come.

He really wasn't one to beat around the bush. My skip's strong country origins demanded that you simply got on with life. The outback was an unsympathetic mistress and his family's wheat and sheep farm at Coolamon in the north-west of New South Wales could produce a harsh and unforgiving environment, tough on cattle and farmers alike. This was the vocation he would face on his return, one that may not be suited to his beautiful flower of English heritage.

He asked that I join them for a date, thinking it might settle them a bit, maybe get things back on track. Phyll had a close work friend, Joy Turner, who she would invite along to make up the four. We would meet up with them the next Saturday on our weekend leave in London for a few drinks and a meal. I was only too happy to help out.

Having made it back from Rostock, we headed off on leave in Arthur's rattler, an old MG TA sports car in glorious British racing green with heating that was even more non-existent than in our mighty Wellington Z1384. We wended our way through small Yorkshire laneways before heading down the main highway to London. We reached the Queens Head pub and entered through the low-hanging doorway, stooping as if to accentuate the greater height of humans, particularly of the Australian variety, compared to those gracing English pubs in the sixteenth century.

'Gordon, I'd like to introduce you to a good friend of mine, Joy Turner,' were the words that seemed to float from Phyll's mouth, as I gazed at Joy through what seemed to be a hazy mist, somehow beautifully suspended in the pub. She was petite with beautiful blue–green eyes that seemed to beam out a confidence and kindness that were the foundation of her very being. I felt both transfixed and comfortable at the same time.

I offered my extended hand, relishing the touch as we made initial contact. My Australian accent seemed to ring out my simple origins as I met this delightful and sophisticated London girl. We talked all night and the success of our meeting seemed to do the trick, releasing Arthur and Phyll to return to their own simple formula of love for the moment, free of responsibility. I felt no doubt, as Joy and I parted that night, that I myself had found someone special, with none of the constraints of religion or rationality.

ICI made armaments and was also doing research with the American DuPont Company into nylon and plastics. Due to the importance of the work being done, staff had been evacuated from London to Welwyn Garden City in Hertfordshire. The ever-functional Nissen huts, in all their World War I half-moon glory of cylindrical corrugated steel, had been set up around the plastics factory for the office staff to work. Joy and Phyll not only worked in the same section at ICI but also shared a room in an old boarding school called Lockleys nearby. They had both somehow got leave that weekend: Phyll to see Arthur and Joy special leave to visit her mother in hospital. It was very unusual for these two girls to be given weekend leave at the same time. Even in my doubting brain, I felt that our meeting was ordained by higher forces.

As Arthur and I were about to depart, I explained to Joy that our crew were on leave in London for the weekend, and that the next evening we planned to see a film called *The First of the Few*. If she would like to join us I would leave a ticket for her at the box office.

To my joyous surprise she said she would love to come and I took her down to get her train from Piccadilly tube station. I could not account for the strong bond that seemed to have formed between us after such a fleeting connection. It was as if wartime had spurred a concentration of feelings, an intensity of emotion to counteract brevity, a love possibly to be cut short.

The next evening, the film was almost over and there was no sign of Joy. Could I have been mistaken in my eager interpretation of our short-lived meeting? To my wonder, Joy appeared belatedly out of the black-and-white languor of the cinema in the closing scenes of the show. I felt an immediate relief and comfort again in her presence. As I took her back to the station again to catch the train to her parents' place in Wimbledon Park, she explained that on her way to the film, just as her train was about to cross Putney Bridge, the air-raid alarm had sounded and the train had been forced to stop with all lighting expunged to erase any welcoming beacon for enemy bombers. There would be no crossing of the bridge during an air raid, simple movement also inviting destruction. She had been stranded there for more than an hour before the all clear had sounded, releasing her.

That brief tantalising meeting left me wanting more, so I asked Joy if I could see her the next day, the very last day of my London leave. She explained that her mother needed her again at the hospital during the day. In the evening, she had promised to take her two cousins, Joan and Doris Court, to a local dance and they were looking forward to it immensely. As they could not go alone, would I like to come too? It was a clarion call to action.

I was to meet Joy and her cousins at Wimbledon station, taking the District line. Somehow I got my tube lines muddled and ended up waiting at South Wimbledon station. Joy dutifully arrived at the original meeting place only to find that there was no Gordon Goodwin waiting for her. She patiently watched one more train come and go and then decided that I must have changed my mind. It was only the romantic fervour of her younger cousin Joan that kept our dwindling prospects alive. She did not want to believe that this budding love affair with an Australian air force navigator had come to nothing and said she'd go to South Wimbledon station in search of this Australian in uniform.

I will never forget Joan coming up to me, beaming with the joy of her find. 'Are you Gordon?' she asked with a cheeky bravado that warmed my heart. We returned straight away to the right station and I enjoyed a splendid evening dancing with Joy and her cousins.

In between dances, I learnt from Joy a little more of her family circumstances. Her mother had been experiencing bouts of illness since her only brother, Derek, had been killed training to be a Spitfire pilot for the Battle of Britain in September 1940. He had hoped to help in this critical turning point of the war where a mere 5000 brave pilots turned back the onslaught of the Luftwaffe, demonstrating that Britain's airspace could not be the domain of, nor dominated by, the Nazis. At the time, Joy was working out of London as the personal assistant to the chief chemist of ICI. As the only living child, she felt extremely guilty at being away from home at this time when her parents, and particularly her mother, needed her.

I felt perplexed at her circumstances and wondered at the chances of her taking seriously a liaison with a far-away colonial whose chances of war survival were questionable and his country of origin so distant. I also reflected upon Arthur's view that the midst of war was not the right time to start a serious relationship. But any rational thinking seemed to have been overtaken by a strange instinct and feeling, a bond not yet formed. I was now the willing captive of a surprisingly powerful attraction.

All too soon, it was time for her to take her cousins home and for me to go back to the Regent Palace Hotel, returning to base the next morning. Joy also was to return with Phyll the following day to her wartime job with ICI at Welwyn Garden City.

We left each other that night with no real commitment but yet an underlying connection that was to weather many storms. We both somehow knew there was more to come.

My tour of operations continued as I now tried to dispel thoughts of this English girl who had captivated me. Operation Nos. 14 to 16 took us on heavily defended missions from Kiel and Warnemunde naval bases on the Baltic Sea to Gennevilliers, back close to Paris, putting to peril the Rhone motorworks.

It was in the middle of May that the RAF decided that, with the current casualty rate in Bomber Command, it could not afford the luxury of two pilots per aircraft and so Jimmy Falkiner then moved on to skipper his own crew, leaving us with a crew of five. I had flown with Jimmy on no fewer than 49 occasions, either on training flights or operations. We had built a strong bond, an unspoken comradeship. He was not an imposing man, in spite of his shock of red hair. His country providence had created a softly spoken gentleman, slow and steady but not without intelligence. His measured approach to combat had been the author of his survival. He had learnt well with Arthur how to duel with the enemy, avoiding flak and fighters alike.

In his next command Jimmy faced some difficult encounters with enemy fighters and bravely fought off many onslaughts by Junkers Ju 88s and Messerschmitt 109s. While we had the good fortune to complete our tour in the Wellingtons, he was not so lucky. He had four good months in the Wellingtons before he and his crew were retrained on the four-engined Halifaxes, which had a tendency to develop rudder stall and 'spin in'. The rudder of the triangular tail fin would lock in an extreme position, sending the plane into an unrecoverable spin. Jimmy was one of two crews to 'spin in' while training, killing all aboard. He was a brave man and sorely missed. Soon after Jimmy's demise, Bomber Command withdrew the

Halifaxes and re-armed the squadron with Lancasters. It was too late for my good friend and a bitter twist of fate that aircraft flaws, not the mastery of warfare, should be his undoing.

My war continued with our second raid on Cologne, Operation No. 17, on the night of 30 May 1942. This would prove to be the lynchpin for Bomber Command, prising out its moment in history, its first 1000-bomber raid to destroy a whole city. The plan was to remove the focus on precision bombing aimed at individual targets and instead attack whole urban areas of Germany to thwart the war effort and establish, once and for all, the pre-eminence of warfare in the air. So began the controversy of Allied civilian attack that remained with Bomber Command until June 2012.

9

COLOGNE, HARRIS AND 1000 BOMBERS

Cologne was ablaze even before we arrived. As a result of our attacks, 45,000 people would lose their homes, at the mercy of 12,000 individual fires burning out of control, similar to our earlier exploits with the port of Lubeck and the town of Rostock.

'No problems in finding the target tonight,' Arthur mused as we headed in to drop our load. The city glowed like a homing beacon, already having received 'the treatment' from our earlier squadrons.

'I think Commander Harris will be happy with this little exercise,' I responded knowing that on this historic mission, Bomber Command had finally realised its objective. Air Officer Commanding-in-Chief RAF Bomber Command was Arthur Harris's full title. Commonly known as 'Bomber' Harris by the press and affectionately called 'Butcher' Harris by his men, 'Butch' for short, he was simply known as Bert by his contemporaries. He was determined to assemble a 1000-bomber strike to prove the decisive nature of mounting a major offensive to neutralise a large industrial city, its factories and workforce. He also believed that air offensives would now replace military operations on the ground as the determining factor in warfare. The hard slog of soldiers in marching boots would give way to the artful manoeuvres of flying machines.

We seemed to glide in to the target, the noise of the exploding munitions below drowning out the frightening bombardments of flak, which were becoming increasingly more accurate as each mission unfolded. Noise was indeed the most memorable sensation experienced in any operation.

'Three minutes to target, Skipper,' I offered to keep things on track.

'Roger that, Gordon, let's get in and out fast. This glow will work both for and against us,' he added reassuringly.

We hovered tantalisingly over the burning city for what seemed like an eternity, until our payload was released and plummeted to the buildings below, immediately adding to the inferno.

'No need for a second run tonight. Let's go home, chaps,' Arthur signed off.

I responded by providing the course to safety, avoiding any flak hotspots along the way to our base. We had certainly given the Germans something to think about on this momentous occasion.

Cologne was the last raid of the month of May 1942. With 1000 bombers in action for the first time, the enemy had to endure one aircraft with its deadly cargo over the target every six seconds. The effectiveness of saturation bombing was proven beyond doubt in this watershed of bomber warfare. Large-scale raids could now be planned with precision.

The RAAF's 460 Squadron had certainly made its contribution by providing eighteen aircraft. Our very own Pilot Officer Arthur Doubleday, titled as one of the 'originals' of the squadron, rated this landmark raid as the most successful operation we had carried out. Intelligence reports told the tale of 600 acres laid to waste, half of this in the centre of the city. Over 250 factories were either destroyed or badly damaged. These included the Humboldt Deutz submarine engine works and the Gottfried Hagen accumulator factory, both

making vital components for all manner of warfare engines. Adding
to the devastation, the Nippes railway workshops had been gutted,
curbing the movement of German armaments. Extensive damage
had also been done to civilian property, greatly slowing any possible
recovery.

In spite of the concentrated efforts of 120 searchlights and 500
anti-aircraft guns thrown into action to thwart the efforts of the 1000-
strong attacking force, there was a total loss of only 40 aircraft, none
from 460 Squadron on the first of these raids by Bomber Command.

Aptly named, Bomber Harris had been Commander-in-Chief of
Bomber Command for only three months. Before he took over, the
bomber force had been too small to make a significant impact on
the enemy's forces. Thinking at the Air Ministry in the early 1940s
had been stagnant and stultified. The air force, to this point, had
only been considered of value tactically in attacking warships at sea
during daylight hours. This made them sitting ducks for fighters
and flak.

It was not until the summer of 1940 that the Allies started bombing
German industry on land, but the scale of the offensive was too
small, and was carried out by day to avoid navigation by night. The
impact of these efforts had been negligible on the vital German war
production from synthetic oil plants, aircraft works and factories
making aluminium.

When Harris took over, Bomber Command was poorly equipped
with only 378 serviceable aircraft and a meagre 69 heavy bombers. We
were suffering devastation from the weather, German defences easily
deployed in daylight, insufficiently trained crews and, most importantly,
no radar navigation aids. The solution came to this great man as he
watched part of London ablaze from the roof of the Air Ministry in
1941. The words he used were, 'They are sowing the wind.' While he
was referring to the blitz before him by the Germans on the much-loved
capital, in his mind was the earlier devastation of Coventry, where a

concentrated Nazi bombing attack had completely razed 100 acres in the centre of town. The day after the attack, war production had been conclusively cut by two-thirds for this major industrial centre, known for its invaluable light-engineering capability, churning out a great range of weapons and war equipment.

This blitz on Coventry was a lesson well understood by Harris, even if it was an opportunity missed by the High Command. He appreciated the strategic importance of neutralising a whole production centre, disrupting its output for months by dislocating transport, destroying civilian homes and keeping the workforce from the factory door. A second attack would further exacerbate the situation, making immediate recovery at some level of effective production almost impossible. Bomber Harris was convinced as to the value of a concentrated strategic bombing attack from the air.

No longer could a power subordinate its whole air force to supporting the land operations of its continental army. This leap of faith, 1000 or more bombers acting in concert for night assaults, defied current conventional thinking, and gave Harris the foundation that would help to win the war in Europe. He got to work bringing about this blueprint for ruination, like a farmer seeding his crop then setting it off with fertiliser. This concentration of bombers over a target in as little time as an hour and a half would bring major German cities to their knees, including Berlin. They would truly reap what they had sown.

At this critical time, Churchill needed to boost British morale. The country's military fortunes were at their lowest ebb and he was desperate to strike back at Germany itself and inflict some of the misery on its people that they had inflicted on the world. It was pivotal to strike Germany and retaliate for the Luftwaffe bombings of Britain, starting the long road back for an Allied victory in Europe. Bomber Command, under Butch Harris, provided the means to help turn this tide. The move to night bombing re-established the momentum, with the now highly trained crews easily able to find their targets by night.

Also, at this time, the Russians really needed our help to divert German fighters away from the ground attack on the Russian front. The Axis onslaught had to be stopped at the watershed Battle of Stalingrad. With Harris's bomber offensive beginning to take hold, the German fighters would have to remain in Germany to defend the homeland. By January 1943, the Battle of Stalingrad would see the complete surrender of the German 6th Army, with only 90,000 survivors from an originally 300,000-strong force. Mass air attacks, such as our second on Cologne, truly set the scene for a war now to be won outright by air power, and regained the initiative for the Allied attack.

At this point, even though the destruction wrought on cities in Germany did not measure up to the significant losses of aircraft and aircrew we'd already sustained, a new level of air warfare was initiated to stem the losing battle. Only the weather and its unpredictable patterns could stand in the way of this determined new strategy. It was the War Cabinet, not Harris, who took the decision to carry out area-bombing on whole industrial cities where there was the potential to kill women and children. Churchill himself supported this unpalatable decision, which was not taken lightly. War was not for the faint-hearted with humanity becoming the poor cousin to survival and freedom from domination.

We logged two further operations of note, which were under the codename 'Gardening'. Both took place at the shipping channel off Terschelling Island, stretching parallel to the Dutch coast. We had to drop a large magnetic mine from low altitude at a much-reduced speed. On striking the water, a wedge-shaped piece would shear from the head of the mine, arming the device. The mine would then deflect horizontally in the water and settle peacefully on the sea floor awaiting the unsuspecting vessel above. Not all of the firing mechanisms were set to explode at the passing of the first ship, mine-sweeper or submarine. They would merely advance one notch towards detonation for up to nine or ten notches. It was like a clockwork lottery, making it difficult for the enemy to confirm that any particular channel had been cleared for a passing convoy.

Bomber Command's 'Gardening' has been credited with the destruction of a very substantial tonnage of enemy shipping. It quite often took place in conjunction with a major raid on a city not too far away. As a consequence, we experienced only occasional angry bursts of light flak, as the enemy appeared to have more to deal with elsewhere.

All too soon we were back at Emden, where we had started our tour of duty. This time we made it to the objective, recording many large fires. Learning from earlier attempts to blow up the impenetrable submarine pens, enclosed in a protective casing that could not be breached, we had turned our attention to burning out the surrounding city. The technicians and workers who survived the fires would no longer have homes and so would not be able to carry on their work in the factories and military installations. On this run we were again coned by searchlights. In a blinding assault they sought, locked on and singled us out for annihilation.

It was our trusty comedian and wireless operator, Sergeant Geoff Carter, who would save our skin on this occasion. He opened up on the port side with his single Browning set amidships, menacing the enemy through the triangular side window that looked more like an inverted chapel portal than a gun support. His concentrated bursts were resolute and lasted over three minutes. He shot out two of the three searchlights from a height of 2000 feet, one blue searchlight being seen to explode. The coruscating light vanished under his onslaught.

In June 1942 we made three concerted attacks on Emden with my flying log book recording the devastation:

6 S.B.C. 4lb Incendiary. 3 S.B.C. 30lb Incendiary. Many large fires. Moderate to intense light flak, light heavy. In S'light 3 mins. Photo.

The trip back from Emden sticks in my mind as a testing time, a protracted feeling of vulnerability. We wanted to get home, but the winds and the weather played their part in extending our torment. A headwind of 50 to 80 miles per hour cut our groundspeed to a dawdling 130 miles per hour, seeming to suspend us in the air, easily open to further attack. Relief finally flowed as we touched wheels to tarmac.

A few days after Operation No. 23 to Emden, we went out on a further 'Gardening' operation that, equally, was by no means peaceful. This time it was Operation No. 24 to Saint-Nazaire, on the coast in German-occupied France, the north bank at the mouth of the Loire estuary. Three months earlier the Allies had mounted one of the most successful and daring raids of the European conflict. Three destroyers and sixteen small boats left Falmouth, Cornwall, on 26 March 1942. Using an obsolete destroyer, HMS *Campbeltown*, that had been packed with delayed-action explosives, they rammed the Normandie dry dock, taking it out of action for the remainder of the war, denying the enemy a safe haven for the repair of large vessels on the Atlantic coast. Since that decisive raid, fourteen large fortified U-boat pens had been constructed at Saint-Nazaire and the roof of this rectangular monolith, buttressed in brooding concrete, was dotted with extensive anti-aircraft weaponry, defying further Allied attack.

The enemy was well and truly prepared for our visit to Saint-Nazaire and intent on avenging their previous hammering with light but intensive flak coming at us from the adjacent shores. It was as if we had entered a shooting gallery. Fortunately, we could keep our distance from this perilous crossfire as we only had to lay our mine in the outer section of the harbour entry. The eerie shadow of the pens loomed large in the distance. I will never forget the arcing tracer bullets seeking us out on our approach. They glimmered like a perfect line of fireflies, seeming to bounce off the glistening surface of the moonlit ocean, as we prepared to lay our mine as instructed, flying straight and level and at low altitude. Though vulnerable and a sitting duck, we were far enough away to elude the enemy.

Pilot Officer Bert Walker saved our bacon on more than one occasion. As our protector and air gunner, he inhabited the very extremity of our fighting machine at the aft of the aircraft. It was the loneliest position in Bomber Command. His attention to detail, as a Yorkshire jeweller, appeared to have honed special skills for spotting the approach of enemy fighters. With a few bursts from his intrepid synchronised Browning .303 machine guns, ranged four abreast, he could warn off an attacking night-fighter. A long-range accurate strafing from Bert could discourage the assailant from continuing his run, or at least throw him off his game, spoiling his line-up on our craft.

A good rear gunner was critical for a crew's survival in a Wellington bomber. He could literally save you from certain disaster. Vigilance was the key, even if you had dropped your bombs with great precision and were on your way home from another trip to Happy Valley. The shudder through the aircraft of the rear gunner's trusty four opening up would coincide with an immediate warning over the intercom, 'Fighter at four o'clock.' Bert could often amazingly hit the mark on the Messerschmitt 109's first approach with a burst of 120 rounds, dealing with this infernal warplane as it projected from its nose a devilish white light that danced on and off our camouflaged Wellington's skin, lighting up the exposed mosaic of brown and green.

We relished Bert's vaulted cheer as he caused the port wing of the fighter to burst into flame, then completely disintegrate under his barrage. 'Got you, you bastard.' The rest of us would roar into life with whoops of delight as the fighter plummeted away beneath us. Sometimes it had not even fired a shot.

We now were on our third and last run in the 1000-bomber raids for Commander Harris. Bomber Command didn't have enough resources to sustain regular operations at this strength so they were using training crews and their instructors as well. Inexperience had been added to the potent mix of massed attack. For us, it was Operation No. 26 to Bremen and we were only four shy of the 30 required to complete our first tour.

On this fateful night, the whole of Germany was blanketed by a cover of stratocumulus cloud. I had no way of identifying any helpful landmarks looming up from below and, even when we crossed the coast, I was denied the regular, reassuring visual fix of our position on approach into Germany. To further add to our woes, all radio aids were jammed and useless; plus the forecast wind velocities provided to us in flight planning were not remotely like the actual winds. Our experiences with wartime navigation would eventually lead to a new understanding of the meteorological machinations of our planet. Super wind streams, with power well beyond those experienced in the air to date, could play havoc with any bomber force mustered for mass attack. We weather experts in the air were to discover a new phenomenon and could then teach the weather gurus on the ground a thing or two.

I had been on 'dead reckoning' virtually since leaving base and, while I knew we were now well inside enemy territory, I had not had the slightest hint or opportunity for a position fix. I then did what all Bomber Command skippers detested with every fibre of their being. My words to Arthur were measured, distinct and carried an urgency that would leave him in no doubt as to the necessity.

'Skip, I need three two-minute astro-sights.'

He knew I would only call for this in dire circumstances. There was no such thing in normal operations as flying straight and level, even when not yet across the enemy coast. A good skipper had his aircraft weaving through 10 or 15 degrees either side of his course, anything to ensure that the pattern of flight was irregular. At the same time, he would be moving his aircraft up and down through several hundred feet in the vertical plane, defying the temptation to keep us in the purely horizontal. Arthur was expert at this variable medley of movement and it had got us this far in our first tour of duty.

My request to take astro-sights would mean we would have to lock onto a predictable course and it could make us a sitting duck for radar-predicted enemy battery, or fighters homing in for the kill on our seemingly motionless aircraft.

'Roger that, Gordon,' Arthur responded without hesitation, knowing we were clearly silhouetted against the fluffy translucent glow of the white stratocumulus below, precisely in the area where enemy fighters would be most active.

I took the astro-sights and my request was quickly vindicated. We were so far north off track, in winds of a force not yet appreciated, that I needed a 30-degree alteration in our course to ensure our challenging journey was not wasted. The city suddenly emerged from the mists below as a wide orange glow of fire beckoning through the breaking layer of cloud. We bombed the fires relentlessly. My flying log book noted:

8 S.B.C. and 4lb Incendiary. 3rd 1000 Op. 10/10 Sc.

But I had no real confidence that we were near the aiming point prescribed at our briefing. There was no way of checking, but we felt satisfied that we had at least made it to target.

Turning for home from the drop, it was Bert who made the call that would again keep us from harm. We were at a height of only 2000 feet just off the German coast when a Junkers Ju 88 came in from 500 yards on the starboard quarter. It was one of the best German night-fighters, twin-engined and very fast with strong forward-firing offensive armament. I caught a glimpse in the moonlight of the cannon and machine guns blistering from its metal nose, flashes of its grey–green, sleek tubular body with a touch of red and yellow markings on the tail and engines. It was a fearful foe.

'Corkscrew to starboard, now!' rang out over the intercom.

Arthur sprung into action and both rolled and dived our lumbering Wellington steeply to the right, minimising the time this enemy predator would have to range us in its sights. At one and the same time Bert opened up with a prolonged burst at 25 yards. As we dived away, he kept at it, firing again and again. We relished the telltale thudding strikes on its wing and fuselage followed by an explosion, and an immediate flash of fire. Never to return, the Junkers Ju 88 dispatched itself to the sea below like an Australian gannet, with wings dislocated for ultra-high speed, diving deep into a school of baitfish.

Bert had fired approximately 1500 rounds in the combat with no stoppages. The dreaded jamming of his guns would have taken us out of action and out of the war. With minimal damage to the starboard elevator and flap of our Wellington and no crew injured, we counted ourselves lucky yet again. The Junkers Ju 88 would be added to the enemy tally on the fuselage of our aircraft, a grim reminder of battles survived and vulnerabilities not yet discovered in our defences.

We prepared for landing at Breighton base.

'Well done, chaps. A great operation, one to be proud of. It's a privilege to fly with you,' Arthur congratulated us all, now we were out of harm's way.

He finished his brief commentary with, 'Nice work with the fixes, Gordon, we were well off the mark.' But he had a special thanks for our saviour Bert, 'Good to have you back there, Bert, my old son. That Junkers was on us so fast I thought it would do for us.'

We could feel Bert's facial glow radiating through the aircraft. As 'Tail-end Charlie', he was subject to the most violent movements of the aircraft and would have keenly experienced Arthur's dramatic pitch as he spiralled our craft away from the fighter. Yet he kept on shooting. Bert performed his miraculous duty while squeezed into a cramped metal and perspex domed cupola, with so little legroom that he had to place his bulky flying boots into the turret before climbing in himself. He would have this housing constantly rotating, scanning the surrounding blackness for any grey shadow that could instantly become an attacking enemy night-fighter. It was his uncanny knack for this, matched with methodical checking quarter by quarter, that denied the enemy our scalp. Others were not so lucky and 20,000 air gunners were killed, often with their whole crew, while serving with Bomber Command.

In spite of his strong Yorkshire heritage, Bert, in our eyes, had become an honorary Australian.

On our return from Bremen, Operation No. 26 now completed, I received my commission as pilot officer. It was 26 June 1942. Arthur and Bert insisted on a drink at the officers' mess at Breighton to celebrate my newly found gentlemanly status. I felt a little hesitant at forsaking the rather riotous company of my fellow sergeants, knowing I would miss their happy badinage of life. Nevertheless, there was a war to be won and it was time to move on up. Any sensibility for moral correctness was now but a distant thought. My experience of a larger, more brutal world had changed me in a surprisingly short period of time.

10

SEA RESCUE, LAST OF TOUR

During my time at Breighton, I met up with a fellow navigator from the Air Observers' School in Canada who had just been reassigned to 460 Squadron. He seemed a little disheartened and I learnt that he had been a little busy—engine trouble over the English Channel followed by a dip in the ocean, not something to be recommended. He had been the sole survivor of the sea rescue.

Just before our operation to Bremen, we had been involved in an almost five-hour sea search, flying out over the North Sea in broad daylight, close to enemy territory and greatly exposed to attack. I had begun to feel sea rescue operations were pointless as we had not sighted anyone in any of these operations. There had been many stories, however, of the nightmare of escape from a sinking aircraft and the long tenuous wait for possible rescue. We also had the grim reminder of regular dinghy drills for abandoning aircraft in the event of our own possible aqueous ending.

I was soon to hear further 460 Squadron stories of survival in the sea, against the odds. One bomber had suffered coning by searchlights in the target area of Essen and been repeatedly pounded by flak with the starboard engine taking a direct hit, leaving the lumbering

Wellington to jettison bombs and limp off for home on its remaining engine. About 17 miles north of Cromer the port engine misfired and they were forced to ditch in the North Sea. Drifting down to a difficult landing, skimming the sea's surface in a surfeit of spray, they came to a shuddering halt, bending the propellers. The landing was brutal.

With fifteen seconds from ditching to sinking, the bomb-aimer got out pretty smartly through the astrodome hatch. Kitted up in his Mae West life jacket, he gratefully squeezed himself through the opening. On the way out he managed to pull the dinghy release, to drop the small life-raft from its stowage compartment on the wing, in the nacelle behind the port engine. If he made it out, this would be his only refuge. The aircraft filled with water almost immediately and, on exit, he inflated his vest and found himself floating back on the surface towards the tail. He was only just keeping his head above the salty ocean, as he was hauled down by the weighted mass of his flying suit. Kicking off his fur-lined flying boots, he gave himself a bit more buoyancy.

He called out to the rear gunner, a young boy on his first operation, but got no reply. Through the pitch black, he could see no movement inside the dimly lit turret. The tail was the last part of the fuselage visible above the surface and was gone before he could do anything. The Wellington slipped forever beneath the cold and forbidding waters. He had thrashed around in the moonless ocean for what seemed like an eternity. Suddenly he spotted a dark object wallowing in the heavy swell a couple of waves away on the crest and set off with every ounce of strength he could muster. He knew he didn't have long to escape the freezing sea.

Swimming towards the greying outline, he discovered to his joy that it was in fact the dinghy. He was surprised at the sheer effort needed to haul himself aboard, the yellow craft enveloping him, getting him out of the cold water. From somewhere in the blackness, through the ruckus of the winds and the sea, he heard a cry for help. Eventually he was able to haul in a crewmate, who had suffered heavily on the impact of the crash, with a broken collarbone and severe bruising. They kept calling out for the other members of the crew, but to no avail. They drifted in the sea for the rest of the night, rocking up and down over the heavy waves battering their tiny craft. They were bitterly cold and chilled to the bone.

Just before dawn they heard the approach of an aircraft and were on the verge of firing off distress signals, when it screamed overhead seemingly at a height of about 10 feet. The swastika and black crosses were easily distinguishable and emblazoned the menacing visit from a Messerschmitt 110. The Messerschmitt miraculously missed them in the darkened swirl of the ocean. Hours passed and, as daylight came, they could see searching friendly aircraft flying all about them. It was not till 10 a.m. that an Anson, a familiar Faithful Annie, swept over their dinghy and indicated their position to a high-speed launch, which picked them up a couple of hours later.

Through such stories, I came to appreciate what it must be like waiting to be rescued. I changed my tune. Sea rescue was now imbued into my very spirit, not only as a worthy task but one worthy of the risk.

Further 'Gardening' and a redeeming sea search to 0325E latitude in the North Sea off Holland for a downed Wellington from 460 Squadron got us to our Operation No. 29 to Wilhelmshaven, a protected harbour that provided North Sea access for the German fleet. The target of our two 1000-pound bombs and three 500 pounders was the docks, where there was obviously something afoot that our navy didn't like. We joined in a total force of 285 bombers, including thirteen from 460 Squadron, and obtained reasonably good results with heavy damage done to the armour plate and engineering works of the Deutsche Werke ship-building yards, two naval barracks being hit and many warehouses and ships' stores set afire.

Our upcoming Operation No. 30 should have been our final operation to complete our tour but our last sea search wasn't to be counted in the normal tally of operations as it had not been classified as over enemy territory. We still had one more operation to go.

The thirtieth operation was a nightmare. It was part of a series of raids on Duisburg, on the French–German border near Essen and in the heart of the Ruhr Valley. It was heavily defended by the Germans and the weather conditions were shocking. We took part in the third raid. The first raid had gone badly but the second raid, to our relief, had caused heavy damage to Niederrheinische Hutte, Krupps and Thyssen steelworks with the target having been yielded up by the foolishness of the Germans. Someone had left the flare path lights of the Duisburg aerodrome on, which had not only elegantly illuminated this landmark but also easily identified the nearby industrial targets.

We were not so fortunate. I remember my frustration as bomb-aimer lying in the belly of our Wimpy as we tried to pick a pathway to target through the weather, the cloud packed in tight. My eyes strained through the bombsight as I did not want to have to instruct Arthur to go round again. This would certainly not have been welcome in this hotspot of enemy hatred and just one mission away from our tour completion. Out of nowhere, the clouds parted momentarily and my reward appeared miraculously below. I released our bombs with a slightly more exuberant than usual, 'Bombs gone!', triggered the photo flash for a photo of the aiming point and checked the selector switch for any 'hung up' bombs. We were on our way home. My flying log book duly recorded the discomfort on this our next to last operation to complete our tour:

intense, accurate heavy flak, visibility poor. Photo.

Following this third consecutive raid on Duisburg, we learnt that two crews from our squadron had 'Gone for a Burton'.

'Gone for a Burton' referred to Burton on Trent, the home of a very substantial brewery in the county of Staffordshire in England. Burton Ale was usually advertised on a billboard in two parts. The first had two men, one at either end, carrying a ladder, with the second panel showing the same ladder minus the man at the end. The caption underneath recorded that the worker had deserted his mate for beer, leaving him holding the ladder. 'Gone for a Burton' became the RAF's, and indeed the RAAF's, slang for 'buying the farm' or 'getting the chop'. It was a whimsical way of registering when mates had been shot down and were not going to make it back. It was perhaps a way to cope with the diabolical, the dangers and unpredictability on every operation.

Normally the squadron would lose one crew out of our strength of eighteen aircraft per mission. Duisburg brought us the burden of two. Posted missing with their crews on this night were Squadron Leader Leighton and Pilot Officer CH Burgess. Leighton had an exceptional reputation as an airman and was a very popular flight commander, and Burgess was a pilot of great experience. This was further compounded on 460 Squadron's following mission to Hamburg, when two more 'old hands' didn't make it home. We had not been called on to fly on this one.

Jimmy Breen had flown with us as co-pilot in our early days with the squadron. He would always be one of us even though he had been given his own command very early in our tour. He was a reticent fellow, perhaps reflecting his earlier legal training. Just before the war, he had returned to his property near Narrandera and tried to balance the life of a country solicitor with managing the family farm. Like many of us, flying had delivered him a release. Pilot Officer JF Breen and Flight Lieutenant VF Keyser had both been lost with their crews on the Hamburg raid, a stunning toll of four aircraft and familiar RAAF family faces in just two operations. The odds for bad weather and 'buying the farm' seemed to be mounting against crews of extended experience, as we approached our last operation, No. 31, to Saarbrucken.

Nothing was said as Arthur gunned the engines ready for take-off. As with our first operation to Emden, we had more than token support to make sure we followed 460 Squadron's motto 'Strike and Return'. Group Captain Blucke was occupying the co-pilot's seat, together with the potential spirit of Jimmy Breen, an indomitable force for survival on this our final operation. If we returned, we would be the first crew from the squadron to complete a tour without injury or loss of a crew member. Arthur made no pleasantries or philosophical commentary. He merely repeated his standard fare. 'Keep your eyes peeled, chaps. Let's make this a good one'.

Blucke was the station commander at this time and an unusual man with pencilled moustache, short in stature but not of spirit. He craved to be part of the action and had been a successful pilot in his own right before assuming ground responsibilities. He would often accompany crews on an operation and is rumoured to have even acted as rear gunner on one sortie, happily taking instruction from the commanding sergeant at the helm. He said he would not miss our last operation for the world. I was pleased to learn later in the war that Harris had given Bobby Blucke operational group command responsibility that would satisfy his desire to be in the thick of battle.

It was just an hour before midnight on 29 July 1942. As we gained height above Breighton, grinding our way to 260 miles per hour cruising speed and a height of 20,000 feet, I allowed myself one momentary thought, one perilous visualisation. The break of day and all non-flying crews and ground staff lined down the runway celebrating our return. Then it was back to business and plotting the course to Saarbrucken. Abandon all hope.

Our target for this fateful night was the industrial and transport hub of the Saar coal basin and this was one of the few German centres left that had yet to be raided in force by the RAF. It was situated next to the French border at the heart of a metropolitan area where most of the people of Saarland live. Tonight, 291 Allied aircraft would target these industrial facilities for the first time with the objective of destroying buildings, homes and civilians. The Coventry formula was now fully in play.

I remember the bright moonlight flickering over the River Saar with its twelve bridges crisscrossing the winding artery. Flak and enemy defences for us were negligible. On approach we had clear visibility and I guided Arthur down to 7500 feet, before holding the bomb release button tightly down and watching as our full load of incendiaries plummeted away. The aircraft would lift as it unburdened itself of these 6000 pounds of pyromania with the enemy's name written all over them, courtesy of our ground crew. They prepared and armed our aircraft with meticulous dedication to duty, and somehow kept our aircraft flying. They were as much involved with the delivery of our cargo as we were and had a heartfelt involvement with each bomb, inscribing them all with a personalised and somewhat irreverent message for the Fuhrer. I watched as the railway yards took a battering below, courtesy of us all. It was a dream run compared to Duisburg.

Still, Arthur refused to let us count our chickens. As we turned for home, he kept us in focus with a cool, 'Gordon, I need the best plot to get us home. Stay alert, chaps. This isn't over yet.' We could still see the fires at Saarbrucken burning from 60 miles away, glowing in the distance like 31 candles sealing our tour completion.

Abandon all hope, I again reminded myself.

I was painstaking in plotting our passage back to Breighton over Luxembourg then Belgium, carefully avoiding close proximity to any enemy targets that might bring us into contention for fighter attack. Of the 291 aircraft involved in the night's assault, nine of our compatriot bomber crews had been lost. We were beginning to pay a more firmly entrenched price for warfare now. However, in this, our first raid on Saarbrucken, we had extracted our due with 400 buildings destroyed,

300 more damaged and the sacrifice of more than 150 people. My flying log book for Operation No. 31 duly read:

Saarbrucken – 6 S.B.C. 4lb Incendiary. 3 S.B.C. 30 lb. Flak negligible. Photo obtained – Bombing height 7,500 ft.

My vivid memory of this journey, this last of tour, was the sunrise behind us in the east as we headed for home. As we crossed the early, glassy stretches of the North Sea, the red glow from behind seemed to be etched into the green of the Yorkshire coastline. Riveted into my brain forever was this brilliant reflection and I marvelled at how magnificent it was to be alive, still on this planet. It had been a dream operation and I found it hard to abandon all hope. I started to think of a future and Joy and wanting some life at home beyond the war.

There was a rousing cheer as we landed back at Breighton. We were heartened to see the welcoming committee, the superb ground crews and everyone who was not in action there to bring us home. Group Commander Blucke added the defining statement over the intercom as we came in for landing. 'Well done, chaps. You are the first crew of RAAF 460 Squadron to complete a tour totally unscathed. Australia would be proud.'

We had maintained the illustrious military traditions of our homeland and the tremendous reputation of our fellow countrymen who had fought and died with RAF squadrons during the first two years of war. I found it hard to believe that it had been less than five months since we had flown our first operation. Our initial flight, cut short, for Emden seemed a lifetime away. It was 30 July 1942 and I now had 475 hours' flying under my belt.

There is no doubt that RAAF 460 Squadron accustomed itself to the harshness of operational flying much more quickly and effectively than most squadrons, building up a great fighting spirit. Minimal losses of only two crews in the first six weeks of operations were in contrast to an incredible work rate, 124 sorties on thirteen different targets. The squadron's maintenance efficiency reached the highest standards right from inception. This outstanding support from our ground crew was never surpassed by any other squadron in Bomber Command and greatly contributed to our first-tour survival rates. The best description of these comes from rough raw statistics put together by Rob Davis in his webspace *RAF Bomber Command 1939–1945*. Out of 100 airmen, 55 were killed on operations or as a result of wounds, 3 were injured and survived, 13 were taken prisoner, 2 were shot down and evaded capture, leaving 27 who survived a tour of operations unscathed. This was not something we dwelt on at the time but it puts into perspective the risks involved in taking to the air in a Wellington Bomber in 1942. It was certainly not for the faint-hearted.

Australian Prime Minister John Curtin visited 460 Squadron at Binbrook in England in April 1944. He was proud of this Australian Squadron and later announced the squadron's only surviving aircraft, Lancaster Bomber 'G for George', which made 90 operational sorties between December 1942 and April 1944, when it lastly bombed Cologne, was to be taken home to Australia. This scarred piece of machinery, 30 tons in all, had acquired significance from a charmed and long life in the company of young Australian men. It is now on display in the Australian War Memorial in Canberra and is a fitting tribute to the bravery of all those who served in RAAF No. 460 Squadron, flying in these vibrating mechanistic monsters at work stations that were harshly utilitarian, laced with the smell of glycol, the mighty engines pounding in their ears and in temperatures sometimes below freezing. It is a relic of flying times past but a significant memento of airborne conflict for all Australians.

11

THE DIRTY DUCK, ROYALTY AND RADAR

'My shout tonight at the Dirty Duck,' Arthur cried out as we left the debriefing after our successful Saarbrucken operation and took in the euphoria of our final days of battle in a Wellington bomber. The town of Bubwith had two pubs and to this point the Black Swan was the favoured meeting place for our crew. Here we passed our valued leisure hours talking of girls and home. I'm not sure who came up with this canard christening but needless to say Australians away from their native land are always after a bit of fun. The other pub, the Seven Sisters Hotel, was neatly nicknamed the 'Fourteen Titties' and I need not pursue further explanation.

Once we were clear of the review of our last mission, Arthur made a point of going straight down to our prized ground crew and ensuring that they would join us for our celebrations in getting Wellington Z1401M through the unthinkable 31 operations over enemy territory. It is said that we had really only borrowed our aircraft for these excursions, our revered aeroplane always 'belonging' to its ground crew. They checked every rivet and kept this throbbing beast alive, ready for the fray on each and every outing into uncertainty and the forces of wilful enemy destruction. Aircraft would be switched if there was any hint of a problem, with my log recording the change of aircraft number.

We all arrived close to opening in a warm crush of mates, ready for an unforgettable night of celebration. It seemed every available member of 460 Squadron not on active duty that night was there. We poured into the lounge bar with this remarkable feeling of comradeship regardless of rank. There could be a mixing of like duties where an air gunner would meet up with other gunner pals to compare notes and experiences. Sergeants and officers sometimes got together at their respective messes, but we generally always socialised as a crew. Even though there was a spread of different ranks in our crew—sergeants, flight sergeants and officers—the most important thing was that 'we were all in it together'.

You can imagine our surprise on this momentous occasion when the new barmaid bellowed out, 'Officers only in the lounge bar, please. The rest of you lot into the public bar.'

Not a grumble or even a solitary sound of objection was uttered by the assembled throng. It was as if we were all carried on a cloud of contentment and nothing could dampen our evening of pleasure. All the non-commissioned ranks immediately departed for the public bar. Then, to a man, the officers set down their pints and followed them, leaving the lounge totally deserted and the barmaid with a startled gaze of disbelief.

The men now packed the public bar and we almost started breathing in unison just to ensure that enough air could reach our lungs in this tight squeeze of festivity. Relief soon came when the senior flight commander nipped upstairs to have a quiet word with the pub's owner who, at the time of this downstairs debacle was quietly enjoying his supper, oblivious to this breach of unwritten protocol. Extensive apologies were offered to all assembled and the barmaid put in her place. She was not seen again at the Dirty Duck after that memorable night.

A great time was had by all. Thinking back, our talk that evening was not about operations, close shaves or the devastation wrought on our enemy. It was the simple things: home, a recent walking trek, a fishing trip anticipated. It was as if we wanted to reflect on the normalcy of living and not dwell on the horrendous odds we had faced in getting to this point. While we were certainly grateful to be alive, we felt the need to celebrate the experience of living, and in doing so we would somehow help to repay the immeasurable debt owed to our not-so-fortunate compatriots. My thoughts briefly returned to my ramblings through the Blackall Range, rifle in hand, and my simple fishing exploits in a flattie on the Burnett River with my cousins. I was two months short of my 25th birthday and had now completed my first tour of duty.

Before we all went our separate ways, Arthur organised a celebratory dinner for the crew at a restaurant in London. The German bombing of this vibrant capital had eased a little, sufficient to allow Phyll and Joy to return to the city for their work with ICI, located in an office in the precinct of Buckingham Palace. Now that our first tour was completed, Arthur and Phyll finally resolved to get engaged. He had relinquished his mantra of no survival in favour of Phyll's plea for marriage and children. He told me simply, 'Gordon, I can no longer deny the lady I love a future. She says we are both not getting any younger and can't leave having children till after the war. Even if our life together is short-lived, we need to carry on and believe in ourselves.' I was tickled pink to see the change in his intentions and again started thinking of Joy and a future beyond the here and now.

'I'm sure you've made the right choice,' I said. 'She's a lovely girl, strong of spirit and one you need to keep by your side.'

'What about Joy?' he quizzed me in return. 'Should I ask Phyll to invite her to our dinner?'

I hedged nervously, not having had any meaningful experience of affection to this point. 'I'd love to see Joy again,' I said. 'Do you think she'll want to come?'

Arthur read me like a book. My confidence in the sky was in marked contrast to my mastery of women, particularly where growing feelings were concerned. 'Why don't I ring Phyll and ask her to invite Joy to come along as my guest, so you can be sure of seeing her again?'

The plot was hatched and I was overjoyed. This last-minute invitation however meant that Joy would find it difficult to find a hotel room for the night, as it would be too late to catch the train back to Wimbledon Park, especially if there was an enemy raid. London hotels filled up quickly and she was fortunate to locate a room not too far from the Regent Palace Hotel where the restaurant was and the crew were staying. However, this took time and delayed her arrival.

Love was not to be denied and she appeared at the doorway, a quietly confident vision, happy and relaxed in spite of trying circumstances. She slipped into the waiting chair beside me and I felt my heart swell with a burgeoning feeling of contentment. I knew I had found the girl I wanted to be with. Conversation flowed easily and we joked and enjoyed the crew's camaraderie, at ease in each other's company. We toasted Phyll and Arthur's engagement and I felt the certainty of a young man not yet worldly wise, but nevertheless smitten with what I knew would make me happy.

I walked Joy back to her hotel and we chatted simply. I told her about my time on the farm and starting out in Bundaberg, finishing with a subtle sell of my country of origin. 'The skies are blue every day and Brisbane, the capital of Queensland, is a great place to live, warm all year round and close to beautiful sunny beaches that ring the still waters of a lovely bay, called Moreton Bay. It's by no means the size of London but people are friendly.' She herself had mainly experienced life in the British capital and in Welwyn.

She asked about my life in Australia and what it had been like coming to a war far away in Europe. I explained that country living could be a bit confining and that I had always been hoping for a chance to get away to the 'big smoke'. I had been glad to have my chance to see the world, and added, 'I feel alive in the experience of war, even with the odds stacked against me. I somehow believe that things will be okay.'

We talked of Arthur and Phyll and the difficulties they were having about commitment. Joy asked if I shared their concerns and I sensed in her a gentle exploration of the possibilities of our future. I proffered, 'They say that any commitment can put you at risk, take your eye off the ball, but I can't seem to hold back and want to give way to whatever could be possible.'

She seemed to understand, offering her own experience of risks taken every day in the midst of this war. She herself had already had a couple of dices with death. Working at ICI in the country, she had heard a plane go over and then turn back. 'You wouldn't believe it, I assumed it was one of ours and raced out the door waving.' It was a German fighter bomber off track and it came right for her, firing, no doubt intent on her death. She dived indoors just in time and a fusillade of bullets passed just inches over her head.

Another time she had returned to ICI at Welwyn and was staying at Lockleys boarding school in a small guestroom overlooking the kitchen. It was a rural area seldom reached by German bombers, so she was surprised to be woken by the sound of bombs exploding. Recognising the noise from her time in London, she slid underneath her bed as they had all been trained to do. Suddenly there was an almighty crashing noise. As she rolled out, Joy stared into an enormous gaping hole between her bed and the wardrobe. She peered through this gash in the floorboards to find the kitchen had virtually vanished. There sticking out below was a huge bomb, fortunately unexploded. A German bomber passing overhead had dropped his bombs, wanting to unload after missing his intended target. Four thousand pounds of deadly explosive had passed through the floor of her room and careened down through the kitchen before lodging in the cellar. Had it detonated, she would not have been here.

'You were very lucky,' I confided, feeling a growing respect for this calm soul. I remember feeling a little shocked at her revelation. To this point, I had not really appreciated what war was like for civilians.

As we reached her hotel, we paused by a dimmed lamppost, its light deflected down, shielding any possible enemy signal to the heavens. A simple kiss filled me with a tenderness beyond the physical. Our sharing with each other, on this quiet summer's stroll to Joy's lodgings, of our thoughts and dreams had secured a potential lifetime bond. We parted with a vow to write regularly and to make the most of every moment.

Pilot Officer Bill Brill was one of the originals of 460 Squadron and another of Arthur's good friends from the country. Both were raised on the land in the Wagga Wagga district, Bill coming from Grong Grong and Arthur from Coolamon, and they were both educated at Yanco Agricultural High School. They joined the air force at the same time in 1940 and then proceeded through the same training courses together, finishing up as starting members of our squadron.

Bill had a habit of getting into tight spots, much to Arthur's dismay. He would talk of standing his kite first on one wing and then the other, on its tail then on its nose. He was the master of manoeuvre and taking evasive action with his stolid machine. Always one to push the boundaries, he often found himself running into a forest of searchlights and dense flak. Bill was known to sometimes bellow maniacally as he looked up to see a piercing blue beam cutting a track in the sky a few feet above them. He would laugh and scream, 'Missed us again, you bastards!' On approach to home base, Arthur's and Bill's simple drawl over the radio would break up the formal calls between tower and pilots. 'How are you, mate?' would be exchanged over the airwaves as these two friends checked on each other.

Bill was the first from the squadron to be decorated, winning his Distinguished Flying Cross for his bravery in the assault on Gennevilliers at the end of May 1942. On this raid he had made two bombing runs over the target, coming in as low as 1500 feet to confirm the aiming point before dropping his load. The weather conditions were appalling and he encountered very heavy flak and searchlight opposition, and was severely hit on his first run. Undaunted, he came in again but his rear protective turret was now unserviceable, his hydraulic system shot and the release unit for his 1000-pound bomb damaged. It just hung up under the aircraft with the bomb doors still precariously open. He flew like this all the way back to England and, with the bomb and doors hanging dangerously down, was forced to make the most delicate of emergency landings at White Waltham Airfield, west of London and far from home base at Breighton. His plane was declared unfit for flying and ditched.

Arthur and I were next after Brill to be decorated from 460 Squadron for what was termed 'act or acts of valour, courage or devotion to duty whilst flying in active operations against the enemy'. We had been the first in the squadron to survive a tour of duty and were to be suitably rewarded. Arthur was to receive the Distinguished Flying Cross as a commissioned officer through the tour and I the Distinguished Flying Medal.

The face of this oval decoration bore the bare-headed effigy in silver of a resolute King George VI. Above the medal was displayed a rectangular ribbon with striking stripes of white and violet set at 45 degrees. Clasping the base of this flag of diagonal sliced purple, at either corner, were the outstretched wings of a bird and from this was suspended, at its centre, a symbolic bomb for warfare. This harbinger of destruction then dropped down to hold the marvellous medallion. On the reverse side, the medal displayed Athena Nike in all her Greek glory, worshipped as the goddess of victory in war and wisdom. She was seated on an aeroplane, a hawk rising from her extended right arm and supported beneath by the words 'FOR COURAGE'. All this was encircled in a laurel wreath of victory.

We were informed that we were to receive our medals from King George VI himself at Buckingham Palace that month. We were to meet royalty. Not only did this great king bear the wings of a flyer on his left uniform sleeve, but he was a man greatly revered by all for his commitment to country and empire, including we far-away colonials. He held the British together through the anguish of war and was an inspirational figure, making key speeches over the airwaves even though he faced speech difficulties. He had a keen interest in the war at a strategic level and provided moral support for the British people, visiting severely devastated bombsites and munitions factories with his wife, the queen. King George and his good lady remained for most of the time at Buckingham Palace during the war, undaunted even though it was bombed nine times. Furthermore, they visited the site of the last V-2 bomb to fall in the East End of London at the conclusion of the war in Europe.

I will never forget stepping forward to receive my medal from the king. It was a cold grey morning in August 1942 and the Grenadier Guards were lined up in their red and black blaze of glory, their eight gleaming buttons of brass punctuating their tunic fronts. Somehow Joy and Phyll had managed to slip away from their work nearby to join this amazing ceremony that reflected all the pomp and tradition of the old country.

The king asked where I was from and when I said, 'Queensland, Your Majesty', my answer brought a beam of delight to his face that seemed to lighten and release him momentarily from his chosen burden of duty. He recounted a marvellous trip he had there as Duke of York in 1927, when the Duchess and he visited such places as Beaudesert, Gatton, Toowoomba as well as Brisbane and its suburbs.

He found our people to be warm and friendly and very genuine. They had a delightful time. I managed a simple reply of, 'I remember well your visit, Your Majesty, I was nine years old.' This great king was destined to be the start of a new era in British royalty, where there was an easy mixing and involvement with the people.

We took tea in the palace grounds after the ceremony and, with my fresh tale of the king's Queensland experience, conversation among we four moved to a possible life in Australia. Phyll had already made the move mentally and was contemplating what it would be like at Coolamon as a lady of the land. Joy listened intently and was at times open-mouthed at the anecdotes of a country boy from Queensland, the rudimentary stories of life in the Australian bush, its mighty rivers and soaring temperatures and humidity beyond English comprehension. She somehow never seemed daunted by the prospect.

I learnt more about her younger brother, Derek, and how he had been killed. He was a trainee fighter pilot on his qualifying solo flight in a Tiger Moth, with no weaponry on board, out over the North Sea. At a mere eighteen years of age he had all the pluck and daring needed to take on the Luftwaffe in their future raids on London and their attempts to destroy England. He was the bright spark of the family with a chirpy personality that made him always fun to be with. Joy and Derek had always been close, but he had a particularly close bond with his mother whereas Joy seemed to listen more to her father.

Derek was returning to base after completing the required circuits, bumps and manoeuvres when a German fighter pounced, locking on to his tail and shooting him down in cold blood. These vultures would circle high up over known British training aerodromes, awaiting the return of their unsuspecting prey below. Their aim was to target the vulnerable rookies and make sure that they would never distinguish themselves in the air in a real Spitfire. The German didn't care that Derek's Tiger Moth, a relic of World War I, was unarmed and underpowered in comparison, its cockpit and pilot exposed to the slipstream and the elements, its flimsy superstructure inviting destruction. There was now no honour in warfare, it was only about winning.

Derek's death had had a devastating effect on Joy's tight-knit family of four. However, I could see Joy was determined to keep her family functional and together. She displayed a capability for taking on hardship and a resolute determination to make things work, no matter what the circumstances. I admired her bravery and I desperately wanted her to start contemplating life with me in a far-away country, assuming we had the good fortune to survive a few more years in this one.

When I look back on my first tour of operations, I wonder if it had all been worthwhile. It was an almost impossible task of directing bombs to targets in a night-bomber in a blacked-out landscape without any adequate navigational aids. This essential failure of destruction would become the stimulus for Bomber Command's accelerated development of aircraft, bombs and, above all, navigational aids and techniques. It would culminate in the pivotal bombing campaign of late 1943.

This breakthrough would come in slow incremental stages. As early as December 1941, Flying Superintendent Bennett had been invited to the Air Ministry in London while in charge of Atlantic Ferry Command. This seasoned aviator and strategist had been asked by the Directorate of Bombing Operations for his expert advice on how to ensure that more Allied bombers and their bombs actually reached their targets. Bennett had been prescient in his suggestion for the use of 'fireworks' to mark the target. This revolutionary thinking may not have been heeded by the old guard in control, although an astute Arthur Harris was the Deputy Chief of Staff of Bomber Command at that time.

The bombing offensive, since the start of the war, had progressed through three stages by the completion of my first tour of operations. The daylight stage, with but a handful of aircraft—Whitleys, Wellingtons, Hampdens, Battles and Blenheims—pitched Bomber Command against precision targets of the naval variety. The spirit of the crews was excellent but they had not received proper war training. Their aircraft were poorly armed, badly equipped and too slow for the challenging daylight duties appointed to them. Losses were extremely high and the damage achieved not worth the price of valuable lives and flying resources.

The RAF soon moved to night bombing but was ill prepared for this new form of attack. They had to overcome the difficulties of night flying and night navigation. The British Government also saddled the RAF with a sort of 'sportsmanship policy', not allowing blanket bombing to neutralise a whole enemy city. The gloves came off when the Germans bombed London and left no doubt as to their intentions and mode of warfare. Our night force was further constrained by being confined to attacks on coastal targets and nickel raids on German cities, paper warfare of the questionable kind.

Once true retaliation came into play, Bomber Command was allowed a free hand heading for Cologne, Bremen, Dusseldorf and other major enemy industrial cities, our bombs now lifting roofs off factories and civilian houses alike, leaving roaring fires behind to add to the carnage. These infernos could be seen from the enemy coastline. Our spies reported that, in spite of our efforts, little damage was being caused. This was not believed until a method was invented for taking photographs by night. The results of these photographs at the beginning of 1941 set the scene, proving that only 3 per cent of Allied bombs were indeed landing within 5 miles of the target town. This could not be ignored.

By the autumn of 1941 things had begun to change for the better. There was a great drive on efficiency and accuracy. Attacks were now planned in detail. Crews had to practise their skills and become expert at working at night. Up to this time, an average crew was hitting the target once per tour, a good crew managed twice and a poor crew never reached it at all. We could not hope to win the war at this rate and the fault seemed to lie in the last 20 miles to the target.

The raid on Huls, close to Essen, on 7 December 1941 tells the story. The synthetic oil plant located in this city was a tantalisingly small target left standing after many attacks. Careful planning and organisation were needed. The three best crews were chosen from each squadron and they were armed with a maximum load of incendiaries. They were given a time to be on the target and this was to be two minutes before the main force.

Fortunately that night was clear with a good moon and snow on the ground to reflect the light. Navigation was easy and good map reading and visual identification guided these expert crews to the oil plant. With incendiaries released, patches of fire lit up the target for the main force behind. Subsequent photographic reconnaissance confirmed the factory had been devastated. Maybe they had listened to Bennett after all.

By the time of the famous 1000-bomber raid on Cologne on 31 May 1942, similar planned attacks had been organised where 1700 tons of bombs were lifted and an outstanding 30 per cent of this immense bomb-load fell right on target. On average, in all operations conducted, there had been a doubling of effectiveness through planning to 7 to 10 per cent of bombs lifted being delivered to the target. Even with this planning, not to mention the vagaries of the weather, wastage was still far too great.

The RAF had three major combat commands based in the United Kingdom: RAF Fighter Command charged with the defence of the UK, RAF Bomber Command operating the bombing offensives against the enemy, and RAF Coastal Command for the protection of Allied shipping and the attack on enemy shipping.

At this time, England was suffering from the height of the U-boat menace, which threatened vital shipping supplies. A large part of the combat commands' limited aircraft production was being put into heavy bombers for Bomber Command. It was desperately needed for Coastal Command. The spring of 1942 saw a crossroads for Commander-in-Chief Harris with the need to significantly raise the level of destruction being wrought on the Reich. He had to prove the 1000-heavy bomber raids were the determining factor, paving the way for the annihilation of the German war machine. Otherwise these limited resources, demanded elsewhere, would be reallocated.

There was a critical call for new and effective radio and radar devices to allow greater navigational precision so we could zone in accurately on the targets below.

After my first tour, I was rostered for a one-week course at the RAF training base in Upper Heyford, Oxfordshire, in the use of 'Gee', a radio pulse system by which the navigator could fix his position using three transmitting stations in England. The Gee transmitters set up a vast radio grid over those parts of Europe within range, just 400 miles from the closest transmitter. The aircraft's navigator had onboard equipment to analyse the incoming signals and produce a reading to fix position on what was referred to as a Gee map. The system was only accurate to within about half a mile from the transmission path, with precision falling away as you approached the maximum range of 6 miles from the path. It was first introduced in early 1942 and was only really effective over Britain and the adjacent North Sea, as after six months it had been jammed over the Continent. It did, however, make a major contribution to the success of the first 1000-bomber raid on Cologne in May 1942.

I completed four cross-country flights in Wellingtons using the new aid, before returning to 27 Operational Training Unit, where I was to carry out navigation instructor duties. I continued with one flight a month to keep my hand in at practical work and spent the rest of my time as a lecturer on the various aspects of navigation. I wondered if my father would feel any pride in his son taking on the mantle of teacher and imparting his learning, exacted by a mere five months of horrendous warfare. I discovered in myself a flair for teaching and a finely tuned technical brain.

The relentless search by the boffins for new devices to beat the darkness had achieved some success. The device called H2S or 'Y' was developed and first used to locate and mark a target on 2 February 1943. Once again, the target was Cologne. H2S was a ground-echoing radar set carried in the aircraft itself, with no range restrictions over Europe and a coverage of a 10-mile radius below the track of the aircraft. A radio wave was transmitted downwards from the aircraft, with the amount of energy reflected back from a given point on the ground depending on the terrain. Water reflected almost no energy back, open country a small amount and built-up areas much more. While it lacked definition over many types of terrain, coastlines were clear as a bell. This allowed the navigator to accurately fix the position and then, based on this plotted landfall, set a course for target. He still faced unpredictable winds and weather, plus the difficulty of pitch darkness hampering visual identification methods. The further inland you flew, away from the certainty of the coastline, the more the accuracy of navigation could be affected.

On the upside, this equipment in its limited form was able to operate regardless of the weather and independent of any input from ground stations. Comparisons could be made from the responses on the H2S cathode-ray screen to our maps and photographs on board to help establish our position. While it was impossible to jam the system, the Germans found a means of homing their night-fighters in on its transmissions and so it had to be turned on and off to obtain periodic fixes on the way to target. It is of note that Churchill's scientific adviser is rumoured to have been responsible for the name H2S, which is the formula for rotten egg gas. When somebody asked him what he thought of it, he said, 'It stinks. Call it H2S.'

More was still required from the scientists to turn the tide for accurate navigation and effective bombing, right on target. With the sponsorship and support of Arthur Harris, Commander-in-Chief of Bomber Command, the stage was now set for the arrival of Don Bennett and the formation of Pathfinder Force.

12

ESCAPE, BOFFINS AND THE MOSQUITO BOMBER

Pathfinder Force was formed in August 1942, under the leadership of Air Vice Marshal Don Bennett. The best squadrons in Bomber Command were picked—No. 83 Squadron from 5 Group, No. 7 Squadron from 3 Group, No. 156 Squadron from 1 Group, No. 35 Squadron from 4 Group and finally No. 109 from 2 Group—those that had been at the top of their game in the preceding months of warfare. The whole of Bomber Command was then canvassed for the best volunteers to add to this illustrious group. This new skilled force was to lead the way in future attacks, a concentration of effort with no aircraft acting independently. Bennett would provide the formula, including better planning and coordination.

After successfully organising the Atlantic Ferry Service for the supply of aircraft for the Allied war effort, Bennett soon found himself back in the RAF assuming command of No. 77 Squadron, No. 4 Group, operating within Bomber Command. He had limited time here to demonstrate how to deliver bombing efficiency and improve the minimal results that were being achieved but his flight commanders loved the conspicuous non-conformity of their Australian leader. They admired his ability and how he always flew with them on operations.

I had been appointed Navigation Instructor at 27 Operational Training Unit at Lichfield in Staffordshire and here I enjoyed a welcome respite from the pressure of combat, training my fellow aviators in the art of navigation. I was to formalise the valued knowledge learnt from the heat of battle. By late March 1943 Pathfinder Force was a totally distinct and separate group with Bennett, promoted to Air Commodore and the first Air Officer Commanding No. 8 Pathfinder Group. Bennett liked to spend time with his men and while at Lichfield, I heard Bennett's story about a special mission to destroy the German battleship, *Tirpitz*, which was at Aasfjord, Norway. I have drawn upon Bennett's own account in his book, *Pathfinder: A War Autobiography*, written ten years after the war to tell the tale.

It was not long after he had taken command of No. 77 Squadron that they were given this special mission. The British had already tried to bomb the ship several times, but it was well protected by other German cruisers, destroyers and two flotillas of mine-sweepers. The Admiralty had calculated that, with the ship lying just 50 feet from shore, they could roll spherical mines down the steep sloping banks of the fjord, under the bottom of the ship and blow it in.

From my experience this task was clearly a little challenging. The accuracy of a drop from a four-engined lumbering bomber was difficult enough but they would also have had to contend with the highly organised and intense enemy defences of the fleet, plus the limitations of a night attack. The thought popped into my head that possibly fools were in charge.

There were four Halifax squadrons detailed to do this job. Two bombing from a high level to cause a diversion and Bennett's squadron and another taking the run in to deliver the payload. They were equipped with five mines each weighing 1000 pounds, forcing the bomb bay doors to be left open.

They set off before dark on the night of 27 April 1942 for the long journey north. The weather was perfectly clear. They hit the coast at an angle, ran up to the chosen island immediately north-west of Trondheim, and then turned towards the target. Intelligence advised their flight path was free of enemy defences, giving them a good track in across the island. Suddenly their peaceful twilight erupted in flames and smoke as they crossed the coast. Artillery came at them from every quarter. They were hit many times with the Halifax shuddering under the barrage. A cry over the intercom of 'I'm hit' came from the tail gunner.

It was imperative to remain calm and focused. There was now only time to follow exactly the laid-down attack procedure. They ran across the datum point at exactly 2000 feet and Bennett started the stopwatch to time the release of the mines. He descended the Halifax at the prescribed rate, exactly on course and with the right air speed. As they neared the *Tirpitz* the further might of its German defences was unleashed. Not only a blaze of gunnery from the *Tirpitz* but the whole flotilla surrounding it opened up once more. The starboard wing was now burning fiercely.

Down to 200 feet exactly, the stopwatch screamed it was time for the release. Out of nowhere, appeared a white haze protecting the *Tirpitz* from their bomb-aimer's searching eyes. There was no time for release as the ship's superstructure finally loomed out of the mist, the battleship's funnel and aircraft catapult visible below. The prize passed beneath them too quickly.

Bennett plied the wounded Halifax around for another try, hoping he could hold the aircraft in the air. Flames billowed from the starboard side and the undercarriage came down of its own accord. The machine was now highly unstable, and the flap had begun to trail. With the plane off-balance and flames ever-mounting, he lined up with the battleship's position and went in for a second run releasing the bombs at the best possible moment, knowing they had minimal chance of pulling off the original optimistic roll to the hull of the *Tirpitz*.

Immediately turning east towards neutral Sweden, it was a struggle to keep the Halifax in flight for a chance at clearing the 3000-foot mountains, rising steeply. Trying desperately to climb the labouring craft, it soon became evident that they would not clear the mountains. Bennett banked the Halifax back west and gave the order 'prepare to abandon aircraft'. He directed the flight engineer to help the wounded tail gunner and did his best to keep the plane steady, ready for the crew's departure. Only then did he give the final order, 'Abandon aircraft, jump, jump.'

With all his strength, he held the wheel hard over to port and throttled back the port outer engine. He struggled hard to keep the plane in the air, lifting the nose and applying full port rudder. Through all the turmoil he had not had time to put on his parachute. The flight engineer Flight Sergeant Coglan reappeared through the cockpit door confirming that the tail gunner was conscious and that he had got him out. He had risked his own chance of escape coming back the full length of the aircraft to check on the skipper. Coglan found Bennett's parachute down in the fuselage and clipped it firmly on. With no heroic words he gave him a slap on the back and went out through the escape hatch.

Bennett stayed at the helm as long as he could to allow Coglan to get clear. The aircraft lost altitude rapidly. Holding the wheel hard over to port, he eased himself out of his seat and prepared to jump from the blazing Halifax. At that critical moment the starboard wing folded up and, without hesitation, he shot himself like a missile out through the open hatch directly below, pulling the ripcord the very moment he was clear. The parachute seemed to grab the last of the remaining air, opening with a suck and hauling him back towards the sky. Not long after, he struck the snow with a jolt, the soft cushion of powder saving him. The Halifax burst into flames nearby, far too close for comfort.

He was now in enemy territory, 50 miles shy of neutral Sweden, the high icy mountains denying him passage. Norway was under firm

Nazi control with the local police keen to do their bidding. He heard the sound of German voices and the barking of dogs echoing up the mountain slope.

He moved low and fast, floundering through the snow drifts, flat out for a few hours. Clearing the sparse snowscape, Bennett hit a streaming torrent that cut the mountainside neatly in two, its steep, iced-over banks denying any safe access. He had no choice but to go upwards into a copse of closely clumped trees, to try to get around the top of the stream. Suddenly, out of the void lurched the face of a man, just 2 yards away. They both stopped abruptly in their tracks. The weathered brown mask of a man slowly materialised into the familiar figure of W/T Operator Sergeant Forbes, one of his crew and a fellow desperate.

Armed with a trusty pole, they managed to withstand the surge and waded cautiously across, clambering up the icy banks with the help of some overhanging branches. Ploughing waist deep through the softened snow, they were exhausted and started to hallucinate. Some relief was gained from their 'escape tins', containing a ration of three barley sugars a day and five Horlicks tablets; also a rubber water bag for melting snow and a tiny map of the area on a silk handkerchief. Bennett put this simple chart to good use, enjoying the uncomplicated challenge of navigation on land.

By midday on the first day, the elements had become their major enemy. Forbes had a flying jacket for warmth but unfortunately Bennett had not managed to suit up in his thermal gear. His body was fast giving in to the cold. They decided that a return to civilisation and their captors was the only option.

Using the miniature map, he plotted a course for the railway line to the north, following the tracks to a small town that beckoned them with its lights. Knocking on the door of a solitary house, they were confronted by a terrified twelve-year-old girl who recoiled into the house to alert her parents. Coming to the door her father was reticent, non-committal, impossible to read. They had no choice but to ask for food in English, knowing that this gave the game away. This unlocked a broad grin on the face of the Norwegian who later explained his caution. There were German provocateurs in the district not only looking for the English, but also trying to trick any unsuspecting supporters.

They were fed an enormous meal of stew, probably meaning meagre rations for the family in coming days. The kitchen stove brought their frozen limbs back to life. The next night a young Norwegian came to lead them to safety in Sweden. First stop was a tiny mountain cottage where they were allowed to snatch two or three hours' sleep before setting out at dawn on skis for the high mountain plateau. Their brave guide pointed to distant ridges 5 miles on, it was Sweden, and then promptly skied off back down to his house, knowing the threat of constant border patrols and discovery.

Little hummocks of stone, protruding through the snow, came into view. These confirmed the border between Norway and Sweden with two colours on each side of them declaring the separation of nations: escape and danger. They made their way down and by nightfall were in Swedish custody. At the internment camp they were delighted to find two of their crew, including Flight Sergeant Coglan. He had been convinced of Bennett's death, certain that he could not possibly have made it out of the aircraft in time. Bennett was delighted at his disbelief.

After heavy negotiation with the Swedish Foreign Office, Bennett managed to secure his release to England. Before leaving, he had had interesting discussions with the Naval Attache. He revealed that the British Admiralty had received vital information on the defences of the *Tirpitz* battleship which would have changed the approach of the attack and yielded a much better chance of success. It had not been considered worthwhile to pass this on to the Royal Air Force.

It was also discovered later that it had been known by our intelligence for months that the *Tirpitz* generated its own smoke screen when under attack. This made Bennett's original task complex beyond belief and again belied the realistic planning of their masters. I sympathised with Bennett's reported cynicism and distaste for the barriers sometimes created by supposed partners in the war effort, the territorial bluster by some of the 'old guard' top brass.

Bennett had shown himself to be a man of immense capability, with the know-how to lead the Pathfinder Force. He was determined to equip his Pathfinder Force with the very best in radar navigational aids necessary to locate, identify and clearly mark targets for the following Bomber Command force, referred to as main force.

From his arrival in July 1942, Bennett set the boffins free to innovate. At his behest, these corduroy-trousered scientists and fireworks experts from Armament Branch, came up with some marvellous inventions.

The radar device 'Oboe' was quietly being developed at 109 Squadron. This saved time and achieved the impossible, a radar device that could be contained within the aircraft itself. Inventor RH Reeves and his brilliant young colleague, Dr FE Jones, had then transformed this into a satisfactory system. One navigator thought the note of the set in the aircraft sounded like an oboe and the name gradually became associated with blind bombing.

Oboe was a major breakthrough. It was operated in conjunction with two separate ground stations. The first station was called 'the cat' and ensured that the controlled aircraft flew along an arc, taking it directly over the target. The pilot would hear dots or dashes of radio pulse if he strayed either side of the perfect track, otherwise a continuous tone would be emitted from the Oboe component in the aircraft. It was of modest size and could easily be fitted even to the fast, high-flying Mosquito Bombers.

The second ground station was known as 'the mouse' and followed the track of the aircraft around its arc, sending a signal for release of the bombs or target markers, based on the bomber's airspeed and weapon ballistics. It was near perfection in bombing technology.

Oboe was first used operationally to effect on 12 March 1943 to lead the attack on the Krupps Armament Works at Essen. This elusive quarry had never been seriously hit before and 368 aircraft had been lost in prior attempts. With the aid of Oboe, markers were now able to go down accurately over the factory. Under the older radar system, H2S, only 47 per cent of the bombs found the target. At Essen, thanks to Oboe, 83 per cent went down on the aiming point and the Krupps Works was completely written off. A good raid was now defined by when 90 per cent or above of bombs found the right aiming point. At last Pathfinders had the guidance systems to make the difference.

It was the fireworks that captured Bennett's imagination though. During September 1942, soon after his appointment, he explored the limits of existing techniques for illuminating and marking a target. The increasing range of pyrotechnics employed drew upon the accumulated knowledge and experience of centuries of British firework manufacture and could not be matched by the enemy. Bennett identified how to best light a target from the air with incendiaries to allow visual identification and then how to deliver effective Target Indicators (TIs) to guide the main force right to the target.

Flares were needed in bigger numbers, including the development of the hooded flare to shield the bomb-aimer's eyes for target location on the ground, and a barometer fuse to open up the flare at the right altitude. TIs were known as high-powered candles and came in the colours of the rainbow, plain red, plain green, yellow and white, and produced ejecting stars in the same or different colours. The 'floater', the 'multi-flash', the 'red spot' and the 'smoke puff' were numbered in this beautiful array of firecrackers, with a splendour that would bring terror to those below, awaiting the onslaught of the bombers.

No. 1 TI bombs weighed 250 pounds and were filled with 60 candles which ignited in freefall. A burster charge in the nose of the bomb case was designed to explode, hurling the candles into the air to descend. They either ignited instantly, ignited on impact, had a delayed action, or a mixture of all three. The big league comprised 1000-pound weapons which released up to 200 candles in various combinations.

The 4000-pound incendiaries that ignited with a distinctive pink flash were affectionately known as 'Pink Pansies'. They were used as target markers for the first time on the raid on Dusseldorf in the Ruhr Valley near Duisberg on 10–11 September 1942. Coloured flares were also used; red to mark the west of the town and green to mark the east. The different colours and their purposes were laid out at the briefing before the raid. The main force flew between the reds and the greens and dropped their bombs on the Pink Pansies.

The town of Dusseldorf was obscured by a dense pall of smoke from a large area of fire, but the aiming point could still be clearly seen all the way from the Dutch coast, courtesy of the pink afterglow. I had last visited Duisberg in July 1942 on the second to last operation of our tour, where we had experienced poor visibility and intense and accurate heavy flak. I can only imagine the relief we would have felt on approach to have the target clearly marked to allow a speedy exit from the turmoil. This new array of ingenious devices was a credit to Bennett and his boffins, now setting the scene for the great bombing offensive to come.

Bennett again demonstrated his incisive thinking by recognising the value of the Mosquito Bomber to the Pathfinder Force. It was called the 'timber terror' and was light, fast and deadly with twin Merlin engines and a top speed of almost 400 miles per hour, nearly twice that of British bombers at that time. It was built predominantly of wood, the wings having two spars with double plywood skins on the top, and single underneath. The fuselage was beautifully constructed with a sandwich of balsa between two ply skins, built on spruce stringers. De Havilland had cleverly chosen wood for manufacture to take advantage of the surfeit of carpenters, piano-, cabinet- and furniture-makers available. They had not been needed for the metal airframe construction used for the bulk of other war machines of the air. The Mosquito remained the fastest aircraft in Bomber Command until well after the end of the war.

The renowned Mosquito Bomber could carry a 4000-pound blockbuster bomb called 'the Cookie' to light up a target. It was fitted with the compact Oboe system and had a greater flying ceiling, enabling this curve-of-the-earth device to operate at greater range from stations in England which emitted the signals. The Mosquito was very effective in getting in early to mark the targets, being then potently backed up by the heavy Pathfinder squadrons. It was also brilliant as a 'light night striking force' for use in diversionary tactics, attacking different targets from those intended for the main force. The mere presence of the Mosquito over enemy targets fostered a dread of what was to come, throwing the enemy defences into chaos and drawing the German fighters away from the main stream of bombers.

The Mosquito was said to have been capable of hitting a single building and was responsible for some famous raids requiring pre-cision bombing, including destructive raids on Gestapo headquarters in Oslo, the Central Registry in The Hague, and Shell House in Copenhagen. The first Mosquito squadron to bomb Berlin in early 1943 effectively disrupted a parade where Hermann Goering himself, head of the Luftwaffe, was due to address the esteemed gathering. This very effectively disproved Goering's boast that no enemy aircraft would fly unscathed over Berlin. Another squadron came back in the afternoon and gave the parade, now being addressed by Dr Goebbels, the same treatment.

Bennett had an undeniable passion for both flying and the Mosquito Bomber. True to form, he made it his business to carry out his own assessments of the success of certain raids. No aircraft skipper in Pathfinders could be sure that Bennett was not down there over the target, several thousand feet below, piloting his very own Mosquito.

On arrival back at base for debriefing, the crews would find Bennett there waiting to hear their version of events, having already returned ahead of them at nearly twice their speed.

Pathfinders began a new era in bombing. Markers falling from the sky in bursting red, yellow, green and white cascades now heralded the abject certainty of blanket bombardment. A new phase of relentless enemy destruction was about to be unleashed. Whole towns prepared to vanish, as the intensifying roar of 2000 or more aero engines radiated from the far horizon, signalling the impending choking rubble and blistering fires to come.

This was all leading to what was termed the first great offensive of Bomber Command from March 1943 to March 1944. A new resolute force now ushered in a myriad of Allied bombers, right to target, with unearthly pools of light in reds and greens eerily illuminating the deserted streets below. Courtesy of Don Bennett and his boffins, fireworks would now take on a new and ominous meaning for the enemy, forewarning oxygen-sucking firestorms of bellowing flame to tear through their cities and drive away all hope. Hamburg was to provide the perfect setting for such a storm.

13

THE REGENT PALACE, HAMBURG AND MARRIAGE

After our last meeting at Arthur's end of tour celebration, Joy and I started writing to each other at least once a week. Correspondence took on a whole new meaning, the innocence of new love found. I encountered a genuineness I'd never experienced before, and I felt comfortable revealing my innermost thoughts and feelings. Although I was now based at Lichfield in Staffordshire, far from Joy and London, we started to devise plans for meeting and exploring what could come from this tenuous wartime relationship.

It was an uncanny feeling not to be on operations. I felt the strange pull of the need for excitement, counterbalanced by the joy of waking in the morning to once more experience sunrise just out of bed. It was an adjustment to not be anticipating another journey into the air and the return crossing of the North Sea, grateful to make it home unscathed. I was now supplementing my newfound expertise of navigation with the unenviable skill of teaching, finding ways to hold the attention of men bound for warfare on a dry and highly technical subject, now the central thrust of Bomber Command. This expertise would have to be second nature for my students, instinctively usable in a crisis situation as it could make the difference between destruction and survival for their crew.

I prepared for my lessons as I would for battle, making sure every angle was covered, every potential question covered with a detailed answer. I needed to be proficient with the latest technology, understanding not just the theory but the intricate workings of Gee, H2S and Oboe. I had to be alert to unpredictable weather patterns and wind strengths and quickly make adjustments so there would be no surprises on approach to the battle zone. In my experience, all was sometimes not revealed at the pre-operational briefing and the consummate navigator had to have his wits about him and be ready to modify his ideas and calculations if the evidence presented itself.

I was to spend a stimulating nine months at Lichfield, more time than I had spent on my first 31 operations in a Wellington Bomber. Time passed quickly, but I missed the action in the air, although I loved teaching and being able to be with Joy on the ground.

Joy and I got to know each other more through our enlivening stream of letters. However, time was running out in the delicate matter of a courtship to be conducted appropriately. The Regent Palace Hotel became the place where we could meet for a rushed weekend of normality snatched from a city enduring the turmoil of war. Known as 'the people's palace', the Regent had been created to give the working-class community a taste of opulence. It had a warm glow of luxury imparted by its pale reddish yellow facade, and offset by a contrasting green slated roof of deep aquamarine. Located on an imposing triangular site, it loomed over the surrounding district like the proud bow of a grand ocean liner, asserting its presence over this most fashionable and exclusive part of London. I found it to be a place of solace and welcome respite from the confused world of conflict that I now found myself in.

For Joy and me, at the Regent there seemed to be no question of propriety or what others would think, the war delivering a freedom of action where you had to live for the moment and hope that it could last for an eternity. We enjoyed the Regent's glorious public rooms, its circular lounge lined with creamy apricot marble flecked with grey. The shallow dome was lined in rich walnut and lit up by a sparkling chandelier. It reminded me of the Wintergarden Theatre in Bundaberg, an art deco cinema that gave me my first exposure to the exciting world of film. Joy and I relished our indulgent afternoon teas seated with chairs and tables in the Rotunda Court. We were lured in, on occasions, to try its remarkable offerings given the rationing restrictions of the times. We really preferred the more traditional fare of The Queens Head pub in the heart of London's West End, with its cosy upstairs restaurant offering local real ales and pub food.

I was constantly confounded by the open and gentle nature of my confidante and mate. She had a practicality and a gift for clear thinking that would become one of the many bonuses of our life together. While I am sure Joy's parents knew of our meetings, they somehow chose not to make comment, trusting that their daughter was best able to judge what was right at this moment in time. We talked of many things together including having a family but agreed it was something for later.

This was where Joy displayed a concise but practical approach to the delicate matter of child prevention. She never hesitated to raise the topic in her letters and proceeded to outline a proposed solution. She would consult with Phyll's doctor, who she said was supportive of couples being able to decide on the right time to start a family. As it turned out, Phyll and Arthur were now to throw caution to the wind, as they had set a date for their marriage later in the year and were now intent on having children. Arthur was certainly one to follow a decision with determination and he knew Phyll wanted children, irrespective of their wartime circumstances.

For us, family was for after the war and Joy proceeded to organise the most effective method of contraception at this time, the diaphragm. This was not really an area of expertise for me, mere males often making 'live for the moment' decisions, either using less reliable male methods of protection or letting nature take its course. This way we could enjoy each other's company and our moments together without needing to think of the consequences of the immediate arrival of small progeny. The potential for a shortened life was a reality for both of us.

As a civilian, Joy faced the relentless barrage of the V-1 'buzz-bombs', unmanned winged weapons of revenge, that were sent out randomly to terrorise London and the south of England and win the war for Nazi Germany. One ton of high explosives travelling at a maximum of 400 miles per hour where the engine would eerily cut out, signalling a devastating descent. The advent of the V-2, the world's first rocket, towards the end of the war was even more terrifying, as it travelled at a terminal speed of 2386 miles per hour and could not be seen or, more importantly, heard.

Joy and myself both also recognised and accepted my inevitable return to battle.

In April 1943, I was nominated for the three-month Staff Navigator Course at Central Navigation School at Cranage, Cheshire, which included air work as well as advanced navigation on the ground. I passed the course at the highest level in spite of my early lack of formal education. I truly thrived on this material, the war delivering me the gold pass of navigation. I was well prepared for the next stage of my journey into warfare.

I had just completed my course at Cranage when I heard the amazing reports of the Battle of Hamburg. This should have spelt the end of the war. Such was the devastation with 75 per cent of this glorious and historic city destroyed that, for the first time, German civilians doubted the wisdom of their leaders. Firestorms travelling over

100 miles an hour were created by the bombing, such that a bicycle or a human seeking better shelter could literally be blown across the street with the force. I was sorry to miss this milestone in the chronicle of aerial battle.

Hamburg was located on the Elbe River in northern Germany and was the largest port and commercial centre of Germany, and ripe for Allied destruction. Also located here were the first German opera house and the founding centre for the piano instrument manufacturing of Steinway. While touched at the wreckage being wrought on this temple for classical music that I would come to love, there was no room for remorse. There was no going back, both sides were hell-bent on survival by supremacy, no matter what the cost. The end of this war could be the only reckoning.

Bennett regarded the Battle of Hamburg as the greatest victory of the war—land, sea or air. Bomber Command's first raid was on 24 July 1943 with a force of between 700 and 800 four-engined heavies attacking, all primed with a big load of bombs. Smoke from the blasts reached a height of 20,000 feet and the results were beyond belief. The bombing was accurate and soul-destroying. Two follow-up raids occurred on 27 and 29 July with the aiming point tracking the line of devastation across the city.

According to Bennett, on the intervening nights a few Mosquitoes were sent along to Hamburg to keep the pot boiling, to ring out the alarms and make the city's frightened people frightened once again. In the eleven days of the Battle of Hamburg, the Pathfinder Force and its attendant light night striking force of Mosquitoes flew a total of 472 sorties, with a loss of thirteen aircraft. An exceptional result.

The key to the low casualty rate was the neutralisation of fighter opposition thanks to a marvellous technological breakthrough known as 'Window'. During that summer losses to radar-directed night-fighters had become intolerable. Prime Minister Churchill personally intervened, overruling dissent from Home Security and Fighter

Command, and declaring majestically, 'Let us open the window!' The Window device consisted of bundles of narrow metal foil strips which were pushed down a special chute by the wireless operator and flight engineer at intervals during the run over Germany.

In the short term, Window brought chaos to enemy defences, causing the Germans' normally penetrating searchlights to wander across the sky like drunken men. The metal strips gave excellent radar reflections and simply thwarted the Germans' attempts to predict the position of our bombers above. They couldn't tell the difference between the Window and the aircraft. Night-fighters consequently failed to locate the bomber stream and Hamburg's 56 heavy and 36 light flak batteries were desperately firing blind box barrages.

Window provided a brief moment of triumph for the bomber in its duel against the fighter. There was a fear though that this new innovation would provoke a similar response from the enemy, and they would find a new deadlier means of controlling fighter defence. This was, in fact, the case with the Luftwaffe creating new squadrons of single-engined fighters. These were vectored into the bomber stream over the target by radio running commentary, based on information being fed in from observer posts all over Germany about the bombers' direction and changes of course. We had the edge during the Battle of Hamburg but it was short-lived.

Bennett believed that if our political leaders had made the approach, the beleaguered Germans may have extended peace feelers as their northern populations were now in panic and loosened from the forbidding grip of the Gestapo by these violent winds of uncontrollable fire. The German people had been ripe for capitulation.

Max Hastings, in his treatise on Bomber Command, which traces the development of area-bombing, best sums up the demise of Hamburg in his description of the initial coordinated assault on the night of 24 July 1943. He appropriately chronicles the attack as the most perfectly orchestrated since the war began. The raid was an overwhelming success with 306 of the 728 aircraft dropping their bombs within 3 miles of the aiming point. Vast areas of Hamburg were devastated for the loss of only twelve bombers.

He goes on to describe the raid on the night of 29 July 1943, detailing the 22 square kilometres of the city that had been engulfed in the fantastic firestorm. As the fires reached incredible temperatures—100 degrees centigrade or more—they sucked in the air and bellowed themselves into hurricanes of flame and smoke that tore through the heart of Hamburg amid winds of 150 miles per hour. Over 42,000 Germans were estimated to have died and one million refugees fled the city.

With this exceptional Pathfinder Force now making such a difference, I started to consider returning for another tour of duty.

Pathfinders now formed the spearhead for accurate bombing, with navigation becoming the primary thrust for Bomber Command. Following my successful course completion at Cranage, I was asked to form the 93 Group Navigation Instructors' Course at Tilstock in Shropshire, close to Wales.

The school had to be established from the ground up and I was to teach the teachers. Many of the group instructors in navigation had little more than a good education and had completed a tour with Bomber Command. There was much to be done to bring them to standard with a very strong emphasis on effective lecture technique. This had been my strong suit at Cranage and maybe I had something to thank my father for after all. Teaching must have been in the blood and his collection of books had helped keep this alive in me.

Located at the RAF base 3 miles south of the village of Whitchurch, Tilstock airfield was now used as an Operational Training Unit for the instruction of pilots and crews. We were allocated two Nissen huts, sheltering beneath beautiful green oak tree foliage next to the aerodrome. Our new classrooms were graced with wide window portals ushering in the dappled light. I must confess to lapping up the questionable smell of spent gasoline of the Whitley, Stirling and Halifax aircraft using the airfield. It was a constant reminder of the war I was missing.

I managed to get some time in the air flying during my fifteen months away from active duty. I flew in Wellingtons and the luminescent, light-filled Avro Ansons that reminded me of my early training in Canada. I even had a further five cross-country flights with Arthur, as he was based nearby in Lichfield, conducting pilot training. It was great to be in the air with him again and on our last air trip together in a Wellington III he was full of talk of his upcoming marriage.

During my training at Cranage, the training aircraft we used was again my favoured Avro Anson and we had some memorable excursions out over the Irish Sea in search of the Isle of Man. I was amused at the name of our pilot, Sergeant Whereat, thinking that a man with this nomenclature should have been a navigator. I had 27 flights in all between tours, with a more or less equal balance in flying hours between day and night flying. While totally focused on getting the school at Tilstock up and running, I was only able to carry out two daytime Anson flights but I kept my skills honed for my return to action.

On 14 August 1943, I attended the joyous event of Arthur and Phyll's marriage at Beckenham in Kent. I knew that Joy was to be a bridesmaid on this superb day. The sun was shining and anything seemed possible. The week before I had secured an antique English engagement ring at a little old jewellers in the country village of Whitchurch. Joy had a love for jewellery and so I made every effort to find a ring that she could treasure. The ring had caught my gaze in the shop window as

I plied the narrow streets on a break from the base. Earlier, I had compared the extremity of my little finger to Joy's fingers when holding her hand and I used this to check the ring size. I didn't haggle with the man, even though he was kindly and somewhat charmed to learn of my origins. Money held no sway in the decision.

As I watched her transfixed at the service, the ring sat warmly cocooned in its red velour-lined box in my pocket. The ancient walls of the old church gave me a feeling of certainty. Joy was genial, calm and very assured in her support for Phyll. She was the girl for me.

After the reception, Joy and I travelled back to London and arrived at our usual haunt, the Regent Palace Hotel. I could hardly contain myself but waited until we were alone together in our room to ask Joy to marry me. I sensed an unquestionable love and yet a hesitance. I could see Joy was torn. I have never forgotten her words.

'Gordon, with every feeling in my heart I want to accept. I find it hard to think of leaving my mother so soon after the death of Derek. She is not very well at the moment.'

I understood the enormity of her decision not only to leave her family but England and all her friends. Joy agreed to keep the ring but she needed some time to talk to her parents.

She talked first to her father. He was a generous soul who had faced the difficulties of both the Depression and World War I. He had taken up the simple trade of leather-finishing handed on to him by his father. He was a clever man with a wry turn of wit and a love for sports. In his youth he had been a star soccer player and centre-forward for Wimbledon Football Club. He was also a bit of a larrikin and liked to chance his arm in a gamble. He and Joy had a close relationship that had come from his real collaboration with her in her education as he used this opportunity to better himself. She listened to him. He clearly shared her enthusiasm for this adventure to a new and distant land.

I was invited to Sunday lunch and knew this was an important day in my life. Joy met me at the station and we had a leisurely stroll to her parents' house in Wimbledon Park. She explained that her father had taken her to the pub the previous Sunday. He left her in no doubt that her mother was his responsibility. Even though they had lost Derek, she could not take this burden on herself. 'You must live the life you want and leave your mother in my care,' he said.

'Gordon, I want to marry you with no conditions attached.' It was only at this point that she drew her left hand from her pocket and I noticed she was wearing the ring. It fitted perfectly.

She explained her earlier hesitance, that her mother had been living like a hermit since the death of her brother. She had refused all visitors, until Joy and her father convinced her to finally meet me. This had brought some normality back into her life. Her dearest mother had cleaned the house from top to toe, washed the curtains and saved up their meat coupons for weeks to buy a small roast and a very small chicken. We walked arm in arm towards her parents' simple terrace house, chatting easily about our life together. I was welcomed warmly by her father. Although her mother gave me a slightly saddened knowing look, she sealed her approval with a warm and affectionate hug. They made a huge fuss over my gift of a tin of Australian peaches, a delicacy rarely experienced in the war years. I always admired Joy's father and appreciated his generosity in giving up his daughter to a life far away. On my next leave we had a lively engagement party when Joy and I set a date for our marriage, 20 May 1944.

Having spent three months establishing the navigation school, in early October 1943 I passed control to my able deputy and sought a return to active duty with 8 Group, Pathfinder Force. I had now reached the rank of squadron leader. I had been blessed with a period of respite from battle and I counted myself extremely lucky to have found Joy. I understood the risks we both faced but knew that I had to get back to battle to use my newfound expertise and join my mates in the sky.

14

BACK INTO BATTLE

My return to the war in the sky was chilling. I had been heartened to be approached, while staying at the Pathfinder Training Unit at Upwood, by an acclaimed RAF pilot, Squadron Leader Philip Patrick, who, like myself, was starting on his second tour and needed a good navigator. He'd already organised the rest of his crew, most of whom had served with him in his first tour in Stirlings. Philip had heard of my reputation and that I was planning a return to battle. His reputation as an outstanding pilot was legendary and I had no hesitation in gladly accepting. I arrived at our new squadron, Pathfinder Force (PFF) No. 7 at Oakington, near Cambridge in December 1943, and the Battle of Berlin had already been raging for four months.

A few crews then at Oakington were on their third tour in Bomber Command by this time. I remember hearing of one crew in particular, an American crew from the Eagle Squadron of the Royal Canadian Air Force (RCAF). The pilot had just completed his 100th operation in Bomber Command and could opt with his crew to call it a day. The rest of the crew had completed between 97 and 99 operations. Only the bomb-aimer on 99 was determined to get his century. So, in order to avoid him 'inviting the chop' by flying with a strange crew, his buddies all agreed to make just one last trip. It was to Berlin. This time the crew did not come back. It was ominous.

This bomb-aimer was a real character. He produced more aiming-point photos at the moment of bombing than anyone else on the squadron. His photos were always on the mess noticeboard and they stayed there for quite a while after he went, a brutal reminder of how the odds can catch up with you. His formula for success was always to operate on a pint of best bourbon and have another pint handy for the return flight; well, he wasn't driving.

At our first meeting at the training unit at Upwood, I fondly remember Philip telling me over a quiet drink, 'Gordon, I cannot forget my first trip before captaining my own aircraft. I was with a bunch of Canadians and they never stopped talking through the entire raid. It nearly drove me potty. I vowed that with my own crew it would be different. There's no need to natter, you just keep the airwaves filled with comments relevant to the job. Concentration on the task at hand and focus are all that are needed.'

Unlike Arthur, Philip was not fazed by flying while having a family. He had joined the RAF on 3 September 1940, exactly one year after Britain had declared war on Germany. He had married Olive before the war and had a young one-year-old son Ian. He seemed able to keep the necessary perspective and just take each mission as it came. This was comforting for me as I now wanted more from life with Joy, particularly as I was about to embark on my first return operation over Germany. Philip had completed his first tour with 149 Squadron on Stirling aircraft, the first of the RAF's four-engined heavies to enter service. The Stirlings were prone to attract much of the heavy flak over the target, as they had a much lower maximum flying ceiling, at 12,000 to 14,000 feet with full bomb-load, than the Wellington bomber.

It was common for other aircrew at the briefing for an operation to respond with a low cheer when the briefing officer reported that

Stirlings would also be on that night. It got me thinking that not only was Philip a bloody good airman, but he was also lucky. Surviving a full tour in Stirlings was a good omen. His crews believed in him. Maybe I would return to Joy.

At Upwood, we had a couple of three-hour cross-countries in a mighty Lancaster as a crew shake-down and all had gone well. It was here that I had met Philip's crew, three of whom had followed him from his first squadron: sergeants Lee, Sage and Brown. First was Wally Lee, a distinguished flight engineer also posted to the Operational Training Unit as an instructor after his first tour. I had heard from Philip of Wally's undoubted skills as an engineer. He was a wizard at keeping a Stirling in flight, particularly on the long hauls. These beautiful four-engined bombers were not that simple to operate, a bit different from a Wellington, with fourteen petrol tanks and an extensive hydraulic system. The Stirling was great once in the air but getting it up and landing again were a bit tricky. You needed a good flight engineer.

It had been well known around the traps that Wally knew his stuff. Most trainers at Upwood had sussed out the reputation of their cohorts. Wally had first joined Philip at Lakenheath in Suffolk. He joked that Wally used to call it 'Foresakenheath' as it was like the end of the world, in the middle of treeless heath country, far from humanity and any really pleasant English countryside. It was a truly godforsaken place. Wally loved the Stirlings but was glad to leave Lakenheath. He knew of my reputation and responsibility for navigational training at Bomber Command. With a one in three chance of making it through your second tour, we'd need the best to survive over Berlin.

Wally was a nuggety fellow with a tight-curled head of hair suggesting a close link to the originators of the Brillo pad. I felt happy in Wally's company. Not only did he have complete mastery of his job, but the ideal temperament for the work ahead. He was calm under stress and yet had a quiet sense of humour that could defuse any tension.

Warrant Officer Johnny Sage was our wireless operator. 'Sagey' was the wise man of the crew and had achieved his rank by the completion of a gunnery course (wireless operators otherwise could not gain their sergeant's stripes). He had moved up from there. His job was to receive messages and pass them on to the crew. Every fifteen minutes he would receive a coded transmission from base with vital information to assist the navigator or pilot. If an airfield had been put out of action, we needed to know where else to land. Johnny would only send a transmission if we needed to make an SOS, as we risked giving away the position of our aircraft.

He had joked that you could always tell a wireless operator by looking at his left boot. The rubber of the sole would be partly melted as it got a good roasting from the heating duct meant for the whole forward cockpit. Our two gunners, Jimmy Brown and Jim Smith, always chorused in unison, 'Half your luck, you bastard. Give us a good dose of heat any day.' They were confined to their turrets for the whole flight, spending their life in the freezer. We had a surfeit of Jimmies. Jimmy Brown was rear gunner and married, from Perth in Scotland. He had proved his worth on Philip's first tour, saving them from many scrapes. Jim Smith was mid-upper gunner with a neat pencilled moustache. He had copped the shortening of his name to ease the confusion. I made up the Australian contingent and was to carry the 'banana-bender' tag as this is what the north of Queensland is known for, apart from sugar cane.

Warrant Officer Alan Drew was assigned to our crew as bomb-aimer, until we were able to more permanently fill the position. He served with us on a number of our earlier missions. He had also qualified as a navigator and was of great assistance to me.

Philip had arrived early at Oakington and had a daunting start to his campaign. Coincidentally, he had been called on to fly his first mission to Berlin on the same evening as the ill-fated Canadian Eagle Squadron Leader. He was to fill in with another crew, whose skipper had been taken ill at the last moment. It was the night of 2 December 1943, when 458 aircraft were dispatched, of which 425 were Lancasters. It was to be Philip's first flight over Berlin and it was a baptism of fire.

The raid had been planned at maximum effort, with as many planes as possible, as it had been one of the last two Berlin missions before the moon was to rise. If there was to be strong moonlight or predicted unfavourable weather, then missions would not be planned. It had already been a very hectic first half of the non-moon bombing period, with major operations carried out on seven of the ten nights. Take-off was in the late afternoon and the force faced difficulties from the outset with a towering front of cloud over the North Sea. Nearly a tenth of the aircraft suffered from bad icing as they tried to climb through the cloud and were forced to turn back by their malfunctioning, noncompliant controls.

Philip made it through with real skill and determination, managing to overcome the increasing weight and drag on the performance of his plane and its aerodynamics, to make it to 10,000 feet but no higher. Bad weather continued over Holland and Germany, with the variable winds scattering the bomber stream and hampering effective navigation. Adding to this, German fighters had been brought to maximum strength to defend their capital. Since the spread of the bombers was so great, Window failed to create the necessary diversion to effectively defend the formation against the fighter offensive.

On this occasion, the bombing of Berlin was a complete failure. With variable winds pushing them south of the track, both Pathfinders and main force aircraft were late to target. The markers weren't released on target and the marker aircraft ended up 15 miles south of their intended position. The three towns that they had based their radar echoes on to identify their position were the wrong ones.

The Germans were also able to identify early that Berlin was the target. They initiated a prolonged period of attack on the straggled stream, like the Spartans at the narrow pass of Thermopylae fending off the Persian hordes as they made themselves vulnerable to the concentrated onslaught. The main force casualties mounted still further when the aircraft, mistakenly bombing south of Berlin turned their aircraft over the solid defences of Berlin after completing their misguided drop. That night the only saving grace for the Allies was that for the first time six 8000-pound monster bombs, bulging from the extra-large bomb bays of special Lancasters, made it to the streets of the city below, giving Berliners first-hand experience of huge and catastrophic bomb blasts.

Bomber Command lost 40 aircraft that night, 37 were Lancasters.

On his return, Philip took us aside to give us a first-hand description of what it had been like over Berlin. It certainly got our attention. The last twenty minutes to target had been horrendous. The sky was aflame with fighter flares lighting the bombers up like the main attraction at the circus. Every few minutes a bomber would explode, either side of his aircraft, as he and his crew tried to keep their eyes riveted to the objective. Philip saw two Lancasters from the same squadron collide. An exploding Lancaster created a huge fireball in the moonless sky, the roiling yellow and orange penetrating the dark and sending out waves of heat and destruction. He described his disbelief as their port wing sliced through the ball of fire and somehow, miraculously, remained unscathed. At the debrief he had heard of a valiant air gunner on his first trip to Berlin, whose top turret was frighteningly just brushed by the belly of another Lancaster. He had refused to fly again.

'The Big City', as Berlin was nicknamed, was immense and progress over it excruciatingly slow. The concentration of fighter flares kept their plane forever illuminated, suspended in this cauldron of hell. The defence of Berlin was heart-stopping, unlike anything Philip had ever experienced.

For me, Philip was clearly the man to be with. He was a reticent, understated character, a true Scotsman born in Edinburgh in 1915. His cool reserve made him a natural for keeping his wits about him when under unrelenting attack. His inherent good looks gave him a confidence that somehow counterpoised his slighter build. We were both experiencing a receding hairline that we happily blamed on the challenges of air-force uniform hats and headpieces that, when constantly worn, didn't allow our follicles to gain sufficient oxygen. A poor excuse, particularly as we were still in the second half of our twenties. His hair was sleeked jet black and mine a curly brown with a rather sweeping cowlick, perhaps a token of my rural origins.

Philip had an uncanny knack for flying and a strong streak of determination. I suspected his ability came from his love of cricket, his early schooldays as a resolute batsman defending his wicket. He had a firm yet delicate touch on the controls and was always able to guide his aircraft through the most ingenious manoeuvres, as if he was guiding the ball with a deft glancing blow down to fine leg. He matched his love of cricket with his love for Australians, who he felt also appreciated the finer points of the game. Philip's crews stayed loyally with him through multiple tours. He believed strongly in mutual trust in one another's abilities, that your life was literally in the hands of your crew.

He was a good captain with the ability to exert enough authority, yet he had that unique capacity to keep everyone happy. At the end of his first tour he was assessed by his wing commander as an 'above average' heavy bomber pilot and awarded the Distinguished Flying Cross for his troubles. By the time he reached 7 Squadron at Oakington his rating had moved to 'exceptional', a rating very rarely given. We were fortunate to have him.

We were about to embark on our first operation and Philip's chilling account of his flight over Berlin had helped prepare us for the task. Effective navigation and diagnosis of wind patterns were now mandatory for getting a concentration of bombers on target and, indeed, for our survival. Philip had only a day to recover from his ordeal and we were lucky, almost spared by the sacrifice of his previous mission. The target was switched from Berlin to Leipzig, a large and important city, nearly as distant as Berlin though. It was known for German aircraft production and, to date, had been hardly touched by Allied bombing.

There was to be a clever twist in the strategy this time. The bomber stream flew out on the familiar route across Holland and Germany, as though to attack Berlin. When just 80 miles from this city, we turned abruptly south to Leipzig. In a cunning ploy, nine Mosquitoes flew on to Berlin and dropped TIs to emphasise this deception. The Germans sent all their fighters to Berlin and none to Leipzig.

It was a dream operation with two accurate loads of markers being dropped by Pathfinder Lancaster Mark IIIs and H2S radar easily securing the pathway to target. Below us, 41 per cent of all housing was destroyed. This included a large pre-war exhibition hall and factories being used to assemble the dreaded Junkers aircraft. These buildings were smack bang in the middle of the supporting living quarters. Civilians were certainly a part of the mix of warfare whether we liked it or not. Could this be termed fitting retribution for these Junkers, the twin-engined night-fighters that were the scourge of Bomber Command, reeking untold and sustained casualties on our resolute bomber crews?

Philip's luck, or should I say skilled flying, held out on these two successive operations. We were to be tested right from the outset of my new partnership with this skilful crew of six. Crossing the Dutch coast, outbound near Zuyder Zee, a shallow bay with a cluster of small coastal fishing villages lying in the North Sea, we were jumped by a somewhat determined German fighter, hard to make out in the turmoil of the attack. It was almost on our own doorstep, as we had hardly crossed into enemy territory. Our two Jimmies put paid to this intruder. They pounded him with relentless crossfire as Philip dipped and weaved, cool at the controls. We managed to get away and proceeded on to target, somewhat shaken by our too early encounter.

After our earlier dice with the German fighter, there was more to come at Leipzig. They were ready for us. These big German cities were certainly not going down without a fight. We were hit by heavy bombardments trying to stop us as we ran up for the final drop. I had never experienced such concentrated flak before. The shredded metal rattled through the fuselage but somehow our Lancaster III 'G for George' remained intact, although with an increase in ventilation. We made it back to Oakington in one piece with no further episodes to quell our enthusiasm. My trusty flying log book recorded:

1 X 4000, 1 X 500, 4 X 1000. Combat near Zuyder Zee. Damaged by flak. Bombed on Y.

We had experienced 7 hours and 35 minutes of somewhat unhappy flying but had successfully dropped 8500 pounds of bombs at Leipzig, the home and breeding ground of our nemesis in the air, the Junkers fighter. Germany was not going to be a pushover.

On return from our first operation we had a couple of weeks before our next mission to Berlin, and were to hone our skills with cross-country air training and air tests using the ground-echoing radar H2S or 'Y'. We were given a welcome respite from combat with leave to Cambridge. It lay just 10 miles from Oakington base and was a veritable bonus to a man like me, who craved the very essence of education.

Cambridge in winter was like a mystical wonderland. A light dusting of snow adhered to bare elm branches and the pitched roofs of antiquated yellow-bricked colleges that lined the River Cam. Students, well rugged up against the cold, still plied this illustrious fast-flowing waterway in punts, wearing suits and addressing each other by initials and surnames. It had, however, transformed from an idyllic student enclave to a busy hub of activity with RAF training aircraft circling overhead, air-raid shelters gracing the front yards of student residences and ancient colleges alike, and ramparts of sandbags surrounding everything like the walls of old medieval castles. Petrol was in short supply and cycling students abounded, together with roaming servicemen on temporary leave. Evacuation drills were practised but student life carried on.

Lancaster 'G for George' had had a tricky beginning over Leipzig. Each individual aircraft of a squadron was allocated a letter, then referred to using the corresponding word from the phonetic alphabet. If lost in action, this designation would be passed on. It was impossible to resist a growing affection for our mighty Lanc, that it would get us through our second tour. I hoped we would guard carefully our assigned charge, like a jealous lover keeping all future suitors from the door.

15

THE MIGHTY LANC

Our mighty Lancaster gave me a feeling of confidence. In spite of its immense airframe, the Lancaster flew with the lightness of a bird, its huge wingspan making it float forever as you came in to land. It made you feel like you had joined a new generation of flying, that would change the very nature of air travel forever. The more you flew in this substantive craft, with its capacity and ability for sustained power and delivery, the more you experienced an endearing respect. Some said it was akin to love.

The Lancaster was purely and simply a flying bombing platform and it came to symbolise Britain's capacity to strike back at the enemy in all-out air warfare. The Lanc's wingspan was what made it extraordinary. Its 102 feet of sheer lift dwarfed my previous Wellington experience by nearly a third and gave the Lanc its immense bombing capacity. The size of its wings almost looked out of proportion to the rest of the plane and a view from the rear left you feeling that the fuselage needed to be bigger. This wartime heavy night bomber often appeared battered, beaten and slightly shabby in appearance, but this belied its undoubted air supremacy. It was a brutal monster that was rightly feared by the Germans.

The Lanc was an all-metal monoplane constructed in the mid-wing configuration with cantilevered struts for maximum strength. It was termed 'of monocoque design' where the aircraft chassis was integral with the body. It had a light alloy sheeted skin, affixed by countersunk-head rivets over a framework of transverse channel-section formers, and these were braced with longitudinal angle stringers. It was a much more powerful aircraft than the Wellington, with nearly twice the powerplant horsepower coming from its four robust in-line engines, fitted with three-bladed, variable-pitch, constant speed hydromatic propellers. It was a load-carrying workhorse with a cruising speed of 239 miles per hour and maximum take-off weight of 72,000 pounds when fully armed and equipped. It needed 1550 yards of runway to make it into the air and carried 1077 imperial gallons of gasoline in each wing, giving it a range of between 2700 and 3000 nautical miles.

Pilots were ecstatic. The Lanc was highly manoeuvrable and very sturdy, even able to fly well after considerable battle damage. It was, however, physically demanding to throw this heavy bomber with a full load around the sky when taking evasive action, as the flying controls were not power-assisted. In flight the mighty Lanc shook with massive vibrations and the noise was truly deafening, but became but a backdrop to the sounds of exploding flak and the rattle of machine guns, ours and theirs, in the heat of battle. Bullets penetrating the fuselage reverberated so you could almost hear the ear-splitting sound of metal alloy being stretched, before giving way to puncture.

The main colour of this magnificent machine was a muted sooty black to blend the massive shape into the night sky, denying any reflection to enemy searchlights and flares. This was topped with a dull green and brown camouflage to merge with the countryside below. Its massive hydraulic wheels had a reassuring bulk and substance as if they could withstand the intense impact of any difficult landing. The rear Dowty fixed castering tailwheel remained fully extended and was the last of the Lanc to lock you onto the runway and signal that you'd

made it home. The H2S radar pod in later Lancasters sat beneath the
central gun turret and gave the appearance of an aircraft bearing
a small progeny, like the warming pouch of a mother kangaroo
carrying her joey. This ventral radome, as it was called, added crucial
equipment to survey the land below to bring the plane to target.

Loaded up into the Lanc's 33-feet long unobstructed cavern of
destruction were the very largest of blockbuster bombs used by the
RAF, often supplemented by a suite of smaller bombs and incendiaries.
Lancaster bomb-loads were tailored to the task. If the raid was for
incendiary area-bombing then fourteen small bomb containers (SBCs)
would be used, each with 236 4-pound incendiary and explosive
incendiary bomblets. The codename was 'Arson'. Factories, railway
yards and dockyards were targeted with a load of fourteen 1000-pound
general purpose/high explosive (GP/HE) bombs using both impact
and long delay fuses. Codename 'Cookie' meant blast, demolition and
fire, with one 4000-pound impact-fused high capacity (HC) bomb
together with three 1000-pound GP/HE bombs and up to six SBCs
loaded into the gaping bomb bay of this mighty aircraft. 'Gardening'
involved the delivery to ports, canals, rivers and seaways of six 1850-
pound parachute mines to disrupt and destroy enemy shipping.

I'll never forget the mighty roar of the four American-built Packard
Merlin engines, driving the 'paddle blade' propellers, and readying
an Avro Lancaster Mark III bomber for battle. As we headed across
the tarmac, I could already smell the burnt-off gasoline even before
I put shape to the mottled green and brown fuselage looming out of
the chilled darkness. It was late into the night when these operations
began, and my second tour had started in the middle of a bitter English
winter. Not for the faint-hearted.

Before each operation, we were picked up with other crews in the
pitch black by a cheerful WAAF (Women's Auxiliary Air Force) driver,

who the Australians present warmly nicknamed 'Blue' as a sign of our affection. She drove a bulbous-roofed motor transport bus, maximum speed 30 miles per hour, that would take us to our Lanc. 'Hello, boys, off to the Fatherland again?' she'd quip, a twinkle in her eye.

Our skip would reply on cue with his wry yet reserved tone. 'We've got some early Christmas presents for those deserving haughty Huns.'

Johnny, our wireless operator, always chimed in with, 'Nothing like some nice Christmas crackers to cheer them up,' not wanting to miss out on the fun.

We had pleasant, happy banter with this chummy lady which put us more at ease as we were about to embark on another mission into the very heart of Germany. Blue was the last woman we'd see before we left British territory and she'd beguile us with a parting, 'Good luck, see you soon, lovies,' with just a hint of certainty that always raised a smile from us.

The red and blue of the RAF insignia, emblazoned on the fuselage with contrasting thin circles of yellow and white, signalled the small entry point towards the rear of our aircraft. We ascended the short ladder into the Lanc, in no particular order, between the mid-machine gun turret and the resplendent, elliptical right tail fin. We'd duly cast an amused deferential glance at the Elsan chemical toilet on the left, which was only used as an emergency, given the dangers of exposure at these temperatures. The skipper, navigator, flight engineer and bomb-aimer, supposedly shared the questionable source of warmth of the limited engine-generated heat from the meagre outlet next to the wireless operator. The two gunners only had plugged-in thermal suits to keep them warm. They often lingered until last, bidding farewell to our companions on the ground with a joking, 'Mustn't keep Adolf waiting,' knowing each trip could surely be their last. The ominous clunk of the rear door signalled our departure into the unknown.

We virtually climbed through the aircraft from aft to nose, working our way along the fuselage, stepping over the ammunition runways of the four synchronised .303 Brownings of the rear turret, then following the snaking hydraulic pipes dedicated to wing flap and rudder movement. We made our way down the shrouded interior of the fuselage with the help of the subdued internal globes and just the hint of transient moonlight coming through the dome of the top turret. There was a further nod of respect for the mid-upper gunner, as we noted the minimalist rectangle of canvas slung beneath his weapons. He would stay locked in this position for the entire flight, unless he received a calling from the Elsan.

It was a step up then, as the rest of us reached the superstructure for the vast 33 feet of bomb bay that now extended the full length of the aircraft and was responsible for the Lancaster's reputation as the most successful heavy bomber in World War II. We moved past the two substantive spars of metal tying the extensive wings to the fuselage and then through the doorway to our forward refuge behind armour-plating, protecting we five from rear assault. At this point each man just assumed his position, hooking up to oxygen and communication, and went into an automatic sequence of activities preparing for take-off. Our emotions now seemed calmed by the therapy of routine, as if we had somehow become merged, as one, with the machine.

For the bomb-aimer, primarily located in the clear perspex nose at the very front of the aircraft, it was like living in a goldfish bowl. Lying prone on the floor, the Mark XIV bombsight computer on his left and bomb-release selectors on the right, he alone looked directly down on the uprising flak as it burst all around. With searchlights seeking us out to lock on and take us from the sky, he had to keep his nerve until the target came into the bombsight, calmly giving directions to the pilot. He was of great value in assisting the navigator with map-reading and visual target identification out of the large transparent cupola.

Before crawling into his compartment the bomb-aimer manned the Frazer Nash FN5 nose-turret guns. He had to stand to place himself behind the triggers of the twin .303 Brownings, with an ammunition holding of 1000 rounds per gun, to fight off frontal enemy marauders. He also worked with the navigator to operate the H2S set and was responsible for dropping the Window. During take-offs and landings, the bomb-aimer sometimes stayed at the rest bed on the port side.

The pilot as skipper was ultimately responsible and had to be certain that the correct target was approached and the bombing run an accurate one. Bombs and flares were only dropped on his direct order, with the bomb-aimer being charged to carry out the attack.

The trick with the Mark XIV bombsight was for the bomb-aimer to release the bombs when the bombing marker and track marker intersected the target under the cross-lines called the graticule. It was a complex matter with six manual settings to be made. Fortunately, four of these could be made before take-off: sea-level pressure, target height above sea-level, terminal velocity of the bombs and their all-up weight. Wind speed and direction were fed into the computer just before the run-up to target. Wind velocity was absolutely critical as was steady flight for the last 8 to 10 seconds before the drop. The Mark XIV had a gyro fitted to cope with evasive action and could handle a 60-degree bank or 40-degree dive as long as the movement was regular. The course was fed in by the dead reckoning compass, with any changes in speed or direction being automatically conveyed to the bombsight. Shift controls were manipulated by the bomb-aimer to bring the target to the centre of the sight. It was like a screen image being projected onto the ground below. The aircraft's position was at the centre of a smaller circle on this screen, the radius of this circle being the distance the bombs would fall. The bombs were released when the circle perimeter touched the target graticule.

Moving back, the pilot and flight engineer sat side by side under the expansive, clear bulletproof canopy. The front paned windscreen, with a grey leathered dashboard, wrapped around to give the pilot maximum visibility. The pilot sat on the left on a raised portion of the floor, with a 4-millimetre thick armour-plated panel behind him to further protect his single seat from rear strafing. In front of him were dual cream steering yokes attached to a central steering column, like two car steering wheels minus the top arch. They were more u-shaped with three sturdy, supporting spokes riveted to a central plug, and each attached to the column crossbar. There was a detailed flight instrument panel, offset beneath by the gleaming throttle controls in the centre console.

The flight engineer sat at the right of the pilot, on the collapsible 'second dicky seat' that could fold away. The fuel selectors and gauges were located on a control panel to his right and behind him. He constantly checked the instruments and fuel supply, estimating consumption and range of the aircraft. A good engineer was a godsend to his skipper when things got a bit rough, lending a helping hand with course, altitude and airspeed, and anything else the skipper needed. With extensive knowledge of the workings of the flaps and undercarriage, he could also help with bomb-aimer or navigator duties having an understanding of bomb-aiming procedures and the Mark XIV bombsight. He could drop Window and was proficient in the use of a sextant and in star recognition.

The navigator sat in a cubicle behind the pilot and flight engineer, with his own mid-green map table illuminated by a small bell-shaped opalescent ceramic lamp, all tucked away from enemy view behind a solid curtain to allow his work to continue unimpeded. He was surrounded by dials and magic machinery to provide the information needed. This then had to be interpreted, charted and converted to action, the right pathway and timing to target, then out again. Reliability was the essential ingredient of this Pathfinder Force medley, success requiring each aircraft to be at a certain place at a definite time. Timing was the navigator's responsibility yet depended on the pilot maintaining a good course at a steady airspeed. It was a team effort, every crew member's role interwoven with the others to ensure results and survival.

It was always challenging, measuring angles and distances precisely on a chart to create a good air plot, while the aircraft was being constantly jostled by enemy flak. Space was cramped and the lighting poor. Headgear plus combined oxygen mask and microphone were worn most of the time as the fuselage was unpressurised, making it mandatory above 8000 feet. This was a further hindrance to the already gruelling work. Fixes needed to be taken to a regular time schedule, new courses and ETAs then calculated and accurate log kept, but you had to have the confidence and moral courage to change the rules. If you found a wind speed entirely different from that forecast, it would radically change the time to target and might require delaying manoeuvres, leaving you as prey for the German night-fighters. Precision was mandatory to get the bomb-aimer over target to drop the TIs in the right place at the right time, the build-up effect was crucial. Marking the target with the right concentration would create a strong homing beacon for the following main force.

There was an array of dials and equipment to help the navigator in his tasks. The initial plot and approach were helped by Gee, the signals appearing as blips on the frosted glass panel at the end of a cathode ray tube. Accuracy faded as you left the coastline and astrofixes and dead reckoning then played a role in reaching the target. H2S was also accessed, with the radar indicator unit sitting top right of the bile-green bench, neatly partnered beside the receiver/controller unit. This gave direct control of the aircraft onto the target but had to be intermittently turned on and off as it could be used by enemy fighters to home in on our aircraft. Oboe provided the best direction onto the target, with its reassuring pulse repeater, and certain access to the bomb delivery point.

Other devices on board to help in guiding our craft were the Air Position Indicator (API), which sat on the left of the bench and gave the exact position of the aircraft in conditions of no wind. It had a dull metallic blue glow from its primary dial and was connected by a multiplicity of pipes and wires to the Air Speed Indicator (ASI), the altimeter and the Dead Reckoning (DR) compass. The Group Position Indicator (GPI) was used for making DR runs to the aiming point, tracing the track of the aircraft with a known wind velocity. This was used to increase the accuracy of the drop.

If the headwind estimates supplied at the operational briefing were not correct and only a light air abeam from the north, the navigator had to detect this change to avoid reaching the target early. He would have to advise the pilot to 'dog-leg' up to four times to waste the necessary 30-odd minutes, so as to arrive over the target within the designated half-a-minute for bombing. Some less experienced navigators did not cope so well with this, resulting in a grossly extended bomber stream and early arrival at target, before it had been effectively marked. However, 'dog-legging' increased the risk of collision with fellow aircraft and could make conditions over the target chaotic.

The wireless operator (known as the 'wop') sat just in front of the dual wing spars and at the end of the navigator's chart table, hemmed in behind a wall of communications devices and gadgets. These included various airborne jamming devices designed to make life difficult for the German night-fighters. Later, a device called 'Fishpond' was added to warn the gunners of approaching fighters, giving a bearing and distance. Above the wop was the astrodome, used for visual signalling and celestial navigation. He also held the unlikely responsibility for a pair of homing pigeons taken on the flight, each with its own small rectangular hutch, pale brownish yellow in colour, with a tiny oval window for the birds to look out, bemused at the ensuing warfare. You could sometimes make out their bizarre warblings above the drone of the engines. They served as a means of communication in the event of a crash, ditching or radio failure.

The mid-upper gunner's bulging canopy was crisscrossed with curved, bolted metal struts encasing the perspex dome and added a threatening flavour to the whole machine, like the daunting, riveted shield of a Saxon warrior. He had a 360-degree view from his turret over the top of the aircraft, with a coaming track for the guns and interrupter device to prevent the gunner shooting the tail off his own aircraft. He was alone in his transparent shell, searching the heavens for the tiniest speck, a diving enemy fighter coming in out of the blackness. Gunners were always vigilant, taut and braced for the violence of surprise.

As with the Wellington, the rear gunner's primary role was that of lookout, on the ready to stave off attack. He entered his enclave through the rear turret doors from inside the fuselage proper. His space was so cramped that he often left his parachute hanging on a hook inside the aircraft, making his decision for departure a critical one, if flames declared the end of the journey. He would not give in easily as he never wanted to let his crew down. Ammunition for the tail turret was 2500 rounds per gun and, due to weight, was stored in tanks near the mid-upper turret and fed rearward in runways. Many rear gunners had their perspex window removed by choice to improve their sighting of the enemy fighters and to avoid any possible diverting reflection. This was called the Gransden Lodge modification, named after the base where it first originated. It added the price of tortured exposure to the rear gunner's committed watch, the concentration for survival. He was often the saviour, at the very extremity of the Lanc.

Escaping from a burning or disabled Lancaster was not easy. Only 15 per cent of crews facing this difficult task succeeded. The nose emergency hatch was in the floor of the bomb-aimer's section and only 22 inches by 26.5 inches, just two ruler lengths each way. This escape was hard to pull off when wearing a parachute, particularly as the aircraft was probably being tossed about the sky. In 'G for George', the bomb-aimer was nearest to this tricky exit into the slipstream, but the other four crew up the front end would also exit this way if time permitted. There was a removable panel in the side window above the flight engineer's seat, but this produced a dice with death over the wings and propellers. It was a last resort for the pilot, who would be trying to keep some control while his compatriots made good their uncertain departure.

The skipper's order of 'Abandon aircraft' was not given lightly and time was of the essence. The mid-upper gunner would leave through the rear entrance door, the largest exit point but still not a piece of cake. The tail gunner first had to grab his parachute from the hook inside the fuselage beside the turret doors. Once clipped on, he had to rotate his turret around and drop out backwards through the open doors of his familiar refuge into the void below, all while the aircraft was spinning out of control. If wounded, he could be helped out by another crew member through the operation of the 'Dead-man's Handle', located behind his station, which manually rotated his turret.

Escaping a damaged Lancaster was not something we thought about. It was extremely difficult for all crew members and probably a last resort, with the odds stacked against you. I hoped I would never have to face leaving the sanctuary of 'G for George'.

On the ground at any major operational station there were 2000 ground crew and WAAF staff, whose job was to fulfil the wartime slogan 'Keep 'em flying'. They worked against the clock to get the aircraft ready in time. Having the maximum number of serviceable bombers in the air was the key to Bomber Command's success. It was a team effort, with each section closely cooperating to ensure that they could all gain access to the congested areas of the aircraft to do their jobs. The work had to be done meticulously as there were no second chances in the heat of battle.

Faulty controls, unserviceable hydraulics or a sick engine could hamper a bomber's flyability and put the whole crew in jeopardy. The airframe-fitters and engineers often worked out in the open and were exposed to bitter weather, their eager hands having to remain pliant against the ice-cold metal as they sought to meet their deadlines. Electricians worked in very confined spaces, checking lights and power supplies, trying to avoid any carelessness that could cause the hang-up of a TI to ruin the attack.

A malfunctioning instrument or bombsights, compasses and the number of gauges and rev-counters not working correctly could bring about the destruction of a valuable bomber over enemy territory. Even countless small items only used in an emergency, such as fire extinguishers, had to be checked daily. Radar and radio mechanics specialised in each piece of equipment and constantly found themselves getting in each other's way to reach their particular boxes in the navigator's 'funk hole' and the wop's confined compartment. Cooperation was essential.

Armourers were the unsung heroes of the Pathfinder Force, with a 'chop rate' second only to aircrew. They reloaded the ammunition, cleaned and checked the guns and put their lives on the line in arming the bombs. There were grisly stories of Lancasters being debombed on return. In one unfortunate episode, a sudden explosion ignited the bomb trailer and killed seven of these valuable airmen, no trace ever being found of some of the bodies. Ground crew working nearby were also seriously injured.

Our ground crews were dedicated, with a devotion above and beyond the call of duty. One armourer with our squadron broke his wrist during the usual flap to get the aircraft bombed-up before an operation, but he continued with his duties for a stoic two hours until the worst of the rush was over. It was such stories as these that fired up 'Butch' Harris to demand a campaign medal for these worthy ground personnel, in recognition of their exceptional service. Unfortunately, his efforts fell on deaf ears, a further injustice of the war.

The WAAF were also ever present on the ground. They could be seen driving bulky khaki-green Fordson tractors with thunderous engines and huge saw-toothed rear-drive wheels, confidently taking custody over a bomb train of some sixteen SBCs, each packed with multiple incendiaries. They took in their stride such daunting tasks as the carriage, on a special trolley, of 4000-pound bombs from the bomb dumps out to the bombers. There was always a buoyant smile on their faces no matter what the job at hand. The WAAF motor transport drivers, we described as our 'lovely ladies', would sometimes wait up to eight hours for the return of their crews, lining the runway, waving and cheering madly at each Lanc as it touched down. It was as if they were willing us home.

The WAAF ladies of the parachute section were also filled with good humour. They were responsible for the packing of the chutes and wickedly contended that they never received any complaints. The only way to test them was to use them.

On arrival, you'd be greeted with, 'We've got a nice one here for you, duckie.'

'I hope it's an early opener,' you'd respond with the normal bravado. 'I like a drink.'

As you trundled off with your clothed canopy secured in its pack with harness, ripcord at the ready, you would be followed by mischievous parting words, 'If you have any problems, just bring it back and we'll issue a new one.'

We never doubted their packing skills but were certainly not keen to put them to the test.

The Lanc was undoubtedly a mechanical marvel, reminding me of the power of the steam-driven equipment at the Millaquin sugar mill in Bundaberg. I also vividly remembered another encounter, following my arrival in Scotland. I had marvelled as the *Flying Scotsman* steam engine arrived in all its glory at the Edinburgh train station, where I was waiting. Although painted in wartime black to disguise it from enemy fighters at night, there were still hints of its usual apple green on the four big driving wheels half hidden by 'the splashers'. At a loaded weight of 96.25 tons, this powerful locomotive could slice through the countryside at a record 100 miles per hour. I will never forget the taste, smell and mystical sounds coming from the smoky grey exhaust of both these machine-driven wonders of the 1930s, the Lancaster Bomber and the *Flying Scotsman*. These giants of the air and track simply took my breath away.

The Avro Lancaster Bomber was designed by Roy Chadwick in the late 1930s. Roy was the chief designer for the Avro Company which was located in Manchester. He was to become a doyen of British engineering and was responsible for the creation of my favoured Avro Anson, his designs showing an early capacity for ushering in light and visibility through a multitude of clear perspex canopies. I was intrigued to learn that, after the war, he died at age 54 in a crash during take-off of the prototype of the Avro Tudor 2, Britain's first pressurised airliner. He was taking off from the same Woodford airfield in Cheshire where the majority of Avro Lancasters had been test flown before being cleared for service. It was a bizarre accident, where there had been an error in overnight servicing with the aileron cables being inadvertently crossed. Chadwick had made a defining contribution to World War II.

An astounding 7300 of Chadwick's mighty Lancs were built. This intrepid plane and its many iterations flew 156,000 sorties and dropped 608,612 long tons of bombs between 1942 and 1945. Arthur 'Bomber' Harris rightly referred to the Lanc as the RAF Bomber Command's 'shining sword'.

16

BOMBING BERLIN

The first RAF air attack on Berlin was on 23 August 1943. At this time it was not only the first city of Germany, but the third largest metropolis in the world, with a pre-war population of more than 4 million. This was the administrative centre of the new German order, carved out of Europe by conquest and, more importantly, the communication hub for the Nazi offensive. Berlin was now the major home for Germany's war industry with factories packed in over its 900 square miles. Factories for self-propelled guns, field and heavy artillery, locomotives and rolling stock, small arms, mortars and ammunition manufacture, and supporting electrical equipment with Siemens plants dotted all over the city—these prizes lured the Allied air forces to the bombing of Berlin to win the war. However, the earlier devastation of Hamburg had given the German capital some time and the necessary stimulus to prepare for bombardment. They were waiting for us.

The Battle of Berlin was the longest and most sustained bombing offensive against one target in World War II. There were nineteen major raids between August 1943 and March 1944, with more than 10,000 aircraft dropping 30,000 tons of bombs. Bomber Command's Commander-in-Chief, Sir Arthur Harris, hoped to wreck this city from end to end and trigger the German surrender. This was not to be. Its sheer size and the tyranny of distance from England, the unforgiving darkness chosen for our missions that foiled the accurate pinpointing of targets, together with the sheer weight of the German night-fighter force launched for its defence, thwarted Harris's plan for a bombing-led capitulation.

While not achieving outright victory, he managed to weaken the resolve of Berlin's citizenry and draw vital German air defence forces away from other theatres of war. Night-fighter units were moved from France and Denmark to be concentrated around Berlin. The brave airmen of Bomber Command sacrificed 600 aircraft and their valiant crews to this daunting task. Bomber Harris was understandably very proud of them.

Philip was there for ten sorties to the capital, with myself and the rest of the crew facing nine of those challenges. It is hard to put into words our gut-wrenching experiences over Berlin, getting to and from the target in one piece. Our No. 7 Squadron at Oakington suffered more aircraft missing and more aircrew casualties on the Berlin raids than any other squadron in Bomber Command. The numbers from Martin Middlebrook's *The Berlin Raids: RAF Bomber Command, Winter 1943–44* tell the story of 7 Squadron Oakington:

Dispatched 353 Lancasters on 19 Berlin raids. Casualties: 26 aircraft missing (7.4%), 146 men killed and 39 prisoners-of-war.

The bombing raids on Berlin in November 1943 had been so devastating that many believed that the city was vulnerable and that it would not be able to withstand this continuing level of attack. German surrender would be inevitable. However, if Harris was to match the successful tonnage of bombs dropped in November, he needed to up the rate of Lancaster production to a point where it exceeded replacing losses. The realistic target date to achieve this increase was 1 April 1944, but he was no fool. He did not have the luxury of time. There could be no let-up and after a twelve-night gap, bombing resumed on Berlin. Our aircraft numbers were depleted and the recommencement of bombing possibly premature, but understandably, continue we must.

We left for Berlin in Lancaster III, 'G for George', on 16 December 1943 and it was one of my longest flights yet, at 8 hours and 15 minutes. This, our first trip as a crew to the capital, went down in history as 'Black Thursday', not just for our band of seven but for the whole of Bomber Command. It was unforgettable, a horrendous episode in a litany of threatening exploits. The description of this infamous day originated from the tally of Bomber Command Lancasters lost or wrecked in collisions and crashes, or abandoned by their crews over England. Again, Martin Middlebrook provides the statistics in his book:

25 Lancasters lost out of 483 dispatched (5.2%). Further 34 Lancs lost through collisions, crashes or abandonment (7.0%). Total aircraft lost 12.2%. Casualties: 294 killed, 14 prisoners of war, 7 interned in Sweden.

Looking back, this resumption was clearly ill-considered given the conditions. A daunting three-quarter moon was to appear later this night, and so take-off time was brought forward. We left Oakington at 1617 hours on the afternoon of 16 December, for a direct flight to Berlin over Holland and Germany. We had been heartened by a weather report forecasting that the German night-fighter bases would be closed in with fog and these defenders unable to take off. There was, however, a lingering fear that these suffocating mists might alternatively descend over our English airfields during the night. The operation went ahead in spite of the Met Officer at Bourne stating that he felt the raid should be cancelled.

Facing low cloud at take-off reinforced our doubts. We eventually broke through the milky haze to be rewarded by a glorious sky blue, vaulting above and tinged with the ruddy glow of the setting winter sun behind us. We flew out over the North Sea. It was these simple moments in flight that made you marvel at the sheer beauty of the elements in a world torn by the harsh metal of gunfire and endless bombing, the relentless human conflict below.

We hit the murk again at the Dutch coast and increased our use of H2S radar to keep us on track. The enemy used this to advantage to detect our approaching force and again predict our target as Berlin. They, however, remained sceptical. As it happened, there was a dense fog over the German airfields and so only the most experienced night-fighter crews were ordered into action. Those aircraft that made it through the ice and cloud were immediately directed onto our bomber stream and illuminated us out of the darkness, with long strings of fighter flares from the Dutch coast all the way to Hanover. These were intense phosphorus devices left in the air on parachutes to mark our path. The German attack was fortunately limited, but came early as some Messerschmitt 110s had been fitted with a new airborne interception radar, the SN-2, that jutted out like stag's antlers from the nose of the fighter and could see through our already deployed Window.

Funnily enough, conditions for our last leg into Germany were favourable. German fighters had not been sent to Berlin itself, as the controllers feared a repeat of the Leipzig raid with a suspected feint to Berlin before the sharp turn-off to the real target.

Nevertheless, flak batteries were brought into action at full bore but fortunately cloud levels prevented the searchlights from reaching our bombers' height to pick us out of the sky. The Pathfinders came in exactly on time with good marking runs made using parachute flares. It was an effective raid with bombs raining down for the first time on the eastern parts of the city and a number of industrial premises hit to slow their war effort.

There were two methods of marking a target, ground marking and sky marking. The latter was code-named 'Wanganui' by Air Commodore Bennett after the home town of one of his air staff officers, Squadron Leader Ashworth, a New Zealander. He then followed it up with further questions to those around him, dubbing ground marking using H2S radar as 'Parramatta', after the suburb in Sydney, Australia, and then, to maintain the balance of nations, he titled straight visual identification as 'Newhaven', the home in England of his confidential WAAF clerk.

Parachute flares were used for sky marking when the target was obscured by cloud and this was reminiscent of the land of 'the long white cloud' as New Zealand was called. These suspended marker beacons were followed by the main force, after they had been given a designated magnetic heading of travel. They would release their bombs when they had a flare lined up in their bombsight. It was called 'blind sky marking' and used when there was zero wind.

The main impact of this mission was on the railways with two passenger stations, a goods train, the Ostbahnhof marshalling yards and the state railway headquarters all being badly damaged. A thousand railway trucks, whose precious loads of weapons and munitions were desperately needed on the Eastern Front, were now blocked in the city.

Housing had now been hit the worst, with 175,000 apartments being destroyed and a further 70,000 to 80,000 seriously damaged. It was a crippling of one-quarter of Berlin's pre-war accommodation. This, my first raid to Berlin, produced heavy human casualties, with 720 people killed or missing. There was no discrimination in area-bombing. Those made to pay the ultimate price were 438 Germans including women and children but also forced workers and prisoners of war. Survival and the success of the operation was the solitary focus of our crew of seven. We had been hardened through too many operations and the havoc wrought by the Germans on the

British homeland. Maybe this bombing campaign would at last bring the enemy to his senses.

We started on our return trip to Oakington in full moonlight, not a German fighter in sight. Somehow they seemed unable to follow. We travelled in a loop north over the Baltic and Denmark and started across the North Sea homing in on our base, using our Direction Finding (D/F) radio receiver which was still functional and luckily not jammed. Our Wireless Telegraphy (W/T) and Gee radar had already packed it in. The D/F circuitry consisted of an ingenious twin-meter display unit, which was nicknamed by aircrew 'The Drunken Men', with two bright yellow needles that would prance around a central vertical line on the instrument. The trick was for the wop to tune the receiver to the appropriate beacon, set the master switch to 'visual' and rotate the external loop aerial to recentre the needles. The skip had his own visual indicator in the cockpit, set atop the dash at the base of the windscreen and left of the dead-reckoning compass repeater. His job was to maintain his course, keeping the dancing yellow needles touching the centre line. This was not an easy task when hounded by persistent enemy fighters.

As predicted by the Met Officer, extremely low cloud had descended over England and the only clear airfields were far away in Scotland, or in the west of England. None of the returning aircraft had the gas to get there, after the long round trip to Berlin. I could sense the building apprehension in our lumbering machine as the minds of our tight-knit crew started to focus on the challenge of simply landing. Now it was not the enemy that was our adversary, but the lethal dangers of unpredictable weather. We were flying blind with the final run to the strip being on Standard Beam Approach (SBA), a blind-landing navigation radio system only coming into operation about 20 miles out from the aerodrome.

SBA was made up of a single ultra-shortwave radio landing beacon placed at the end of the runway with three separate antennas in line.

It was first developed by the Lorenz company in 1932, in Berlin of all places. The central antenna remained fully powered, while its counterparts either side dispatched dots and dashes. The aircraft's radio was tuned to the broadcast frequency so the pilot could line up for landing. The steady tone, known as the equi-signal, was a reassuring indication to all in the forward compartment that we were indeed correctly aligned. Dots and dashes were a warning that you were off track.

We couldn't come in to land immediately. With well over 400 aircraft to get down that night in the dreaded pea-soup fog, crews would have to orbit above their home airfields and just wait their turn. Fifty aircraft circled over each airfield at 500 feet intervals, all watching their fuel gauges drop to the bare minimum. These brave men craved relief from the night's trauma. There were inevitable delays with numerous overshoots, as other pilots felt their way gingerly down through the thick cloud. Some aircraft crashed while attempting to land. Others ran out of fuel and their crews had to bail out or attempt crash-landings in the open country. It was indeed a bleak Thursday, not easily forgotten.

Conversation started to flow unusually over the intercom as we tried to find our way out of this debacle.

'You're on course, Skip,' our wop, Johnny, confirmed as we closed in through the thick fog on home base, still following the SBA beam.

'How much fuel, Wally?' Philip asked the critical question that would determine our destiny this night.

'I'm sure of another twenty minutes flying, Skip,' Wally quickly responded.

He stared into the murk below, 'Thick as pea-soup down there, Skip. No breaks in cloud cover.'

I heard Philip talking to the tower, 'Roger that, circling radio beacon at 18,000 feet. Confirmed turn thirty-six. We are low on fuel and damaged port side. Request earlier priority.'

'No can do. You'll have to divert to Marham,' came back dis-passionately over the airwaves. Philip's request cut no ice on this night of calamity. We had to wait our turn as 36 other aircraft circled Oakington home base, stacked up like pancakes and following a regulation ringed path with just the 500-foot intervals between them for clearance.

'Tower, "G for George" diverting to Marham,' Philip confirmed without hesitation. 'Course please, Gordon.'

I responded immediately with coordinates and track, having already worked out our alternatives.

'We should make Marham in fifteen minutes at current speed, Skip,' I added, knowing how tight the situation was.

'Wally, can you get me another ten minutes of gas?' Philip exhorted, needing some safety margin to allow for circling before warily setting our Lanc down through the fog. It would be a battle with the elements for our survival.

'See what I can do, Skip,' Wally responded. He was a miracle worker with the Lanc's engines; a master mechanic tuning his instrument for exceptional performance.

'Listen, chaps,' Philip counselled. 'I am going to land to save the aircraft. I'll take her up to 5000 feet over Marham and anyone who wants to bail out has my permission to do so.'

There were no takers.

'Let's get the bastard down,' the two Jimmies cried out as one with a cavalier laugh, like a pair of kookaburras celebrating the rising of the sun.

Marham was not equipped with FIDO, which was short for 'Fog, Intensive, Dispersal Of'. This was a network of pipes and petrol burners on the perimeter of the runway that could clear radiation fog up to a height of 200 feet. Petrol was burnt at a rate of 100,000 gallons per hour with the resulting heat doing the job. Too many aircraft needed to find a way out of the mists that night. Unfortunately, Downham

Market, our closest airfield with FIDO, was already spoken for with its own glut of Lancasters circling and desperate to get down. If we were to make an immediate landing, we would have to rely on Philip's deft skills to drop us through the fog and onto the strip.

'Five minutes to Marham,' I confirmed. Philip began his gradual descent through the thick cloud cover. The radio beam would bring us to the area, but we needed a visual to make it finally down.

'Flaps down, lowering landing gear. Keep your eyes peeled. We need those strip lights to get us in.'

'Nothing yet, Skip,' Alan acknowledged having moved to the bomb-aimer's position in the clear perspex nose. 'I'll stay here till we get down.' He knew Philip would need any last-minute guidance possible, if we were to make it.

'Five minutes of fuel left, Skip,' Wally warned.

'This is it, chaps. Hang on. Find me those circuit lights.' We were now committed to land and our nerves were stretched to breaking point.

'There they are,' chorused Alan and the two Jimmies in the back in unison, as a break in the cloud miraculously appeared. 'Circuit lights up ahead port beam,' Alan added, confirming our salvation. We were now at a mere 50 feet above the ground and dropping fast, with flaps and undercarriage fully extended. I peered round out of my navigational hidey-hole into the forward canopy, glimpsing the glow of the runway flares leaping out of the surrounding gloom. The rumble of the wind from the propellers on the runway signalled the looming ground close below. Philip lobbed her down smartly, the front wheels of our Lanc grabbing the tarmac in a firm yet assured landing. It was one of Philip's best landings.

'Nice one, Skip,' we all chorused.

'How did we do, Wally?' Philip asked in a relaxed tone that belied the sheer tension of the occasion.

'Barely enough juice left to fill a lighter, Skip.' Wally beamed.

I noticed another source of light, blistering out of the darkness. It was further up the runway, a forbidding glow that broadcast, to our dismay, the burning hulk of another Lanc that had not been so lucky. We were later to learn that some of our compatriots had been given the wrong 'Query Field Elevation', the setting given to adjust the altimeter so as to indicate the exact height of your aircraft above the aerodrome. At a zero reading you are on the strip. If the setting is wrong, you can easily hit the deck. Some Lancs, on blind approach out of the fog, had barely enough time to pull up to avoid crashing. Our skip had handled it, but there was still more to come.

'Christ!' Philip suddenly bellowed as we heard the deafening roar of another Lanc bursting out of the mists and travelling at breakneck speed down the tarmac, in the opposite direction. It missed us by mere feet. We had barely cleared the runway when it seemed to be on top of us. No time for evasive action, another crew desperately committed to a make-or-break landing. There were many collisions that fateful night both on the ground and in the air. We had been lucky.

My flying log book for my first journey to the capital read:

BERLIN – 5 X 2000. Flak opposition most intense to N.E. of TARGET. Sc 10/10. Diverted to Marham on return. (SUPPORTER).

There were some crews who preferred to remain at a distance from each other, as a means of coping, given the unpredictable nature of each mission, and the shock of losing a compatriot. Our first trip to Berlin had brought our crew closer together. We knew we had to rely on each other for mutual survival and now shared an unstated commitment to do our worst to the German capital. On each major raid, you teamed up in spirit with nearly 5000 other aircrew, all intent on the same destructive outcome, but each having his own way of getting through the ordeal. It was not really patriotism, just a hell-bent pragmatism to get the job done. We understood the tactics and the necessary brutality.

We had three nights of rest to cast from our minds the memories of accidents and to savour the relief of making it back home. Four days later we were off to Mannheim. This was a diversionary raid as part of a heavy operation to bomb Frankfurt on the night of 20–21 December 1943. This subterfuge now seemed to have minimal effect as we encountered little fighter action and the main force still copped it on their approach to the real target, losing 41 aircraft. The Germans were reading the tactics of Bomber Command more easily.

Christmas was upon us and the celebrations that morning were somewhat fractured by the early warning of operations that night. Just half an hour after this unwelcome alert the order was cancelled. Surely some sensitive souls up the command tree must have realised our crews needed rest and respite from their quest for survival. I suspect, though, it was the weather that was our salvation.

Aircrew fatigue increased noticeably in this gloomy so-called 'holiday period' of the winter of 1943/44. There was an increasing interest in sleep with limited mess parties, booze-ups and the like. Our squadron colleagues became quieter, more serious and introverted. There was some rollicking on Christmas day, but the crews needed a chance for some real fun and to let their hair down. They were crying out for a break from the constant thread of threat. Even our fabulous service crews needed a lift. They didn't have the luxury of holidays, but had to continue their relentless battle on the ground to keep the maximum number of Lancs in the air.

The next raid was ordered for the night of 29 December. This was raid number ten in the Battle of Berlin. Following on from this, we had two nights of rest with two further raids in rapid succession on 1 and 2 January 1944. Any joyous greeting of the New Year of 1944 was supplanted by the focus on battle. We took off at a bleak midnight for the first of these operations in the new year and our spirits were not high. All missions were to 'The Big City' with the pathway to target becoming increasingly dangerous. The weather was clear on departure from England but our good fortune was not to continue. While flying over the North Sea, a violent, multicoloured explosion erupted on the port beam. It was as if a giant fireworks display had been planned to announce the coming of another year. It was not welcome. The reds, greens and yellows of a Pathfinder's TI flares illuminated the sky after it had collided with another Lancaster. This further dampened morale.

To compound our woes, the Germans totally ignored the Mosquito diversion to Hamburg that night and their controllers had little difficulty in plotting our bomber stream to send in the fighters. We were fortunate not to be selected as a victim, although sixteen other bombers were not so blessed.

There was 18,000 feet of dense cloud over the target and a strong wind blowing. Our TIs disappeared into the foggy blanket and our sky-markers were scattered across the target by the breeze. We also had difficulties with our H2S radar that night. Bombing was scattered and relatively ineffective.

We then faced a long and wearing flight home battling headwinds, with some Lancs running out of fuel or experiencing icing and engine failure. On reaching England, our dedicated crews were very tired but still had to endure snow showers and fog, a grim reminder of Black Thursday. Our squadron lost another two highly prized Lancasters through bad landings. Philip's expertise kept us from these perils, somehow giving us immunity from crashing or ditching over enemy territory.

My flying log book for this first mission of the New Year 1944, on the night of 1–2 January, read:

BERLIN – 1 X 4000, 6 X 500, 6 X T.I. (BACKERS-UP).

The two Jimmies kept us going with their jocular banter. They were always up for a laugh with a ribald joke or two and talk of the odd prank to keep the members of the sergeants' mess on their toes. We needed their wicked spirit and willing temptation for the unorthodox to counteract the dark times of the winter. They spirited us through the remaining three months of European gloom where we were to be starved of our full complement of daylight.

Having just arrived back from Berlin on the morning of Sunday, 2 January, we soon received orders that Berlin was 'on again' that night. Our resolve was to be truly tested as many of us had celebrated heartily on New Year's Eve two nights earlier. We had been late to bed on return this day and now faced another eight-hour trip into hell, yet another midnight take-off through snow-cleared runways. To our dismay, it was to be direct in and out, with no diversionary tactics planned of any kind. By this stage, the German night-fighters were expertly engaging the bomber stream on this route much more often. Our skip, Philip Patrick, was now a wing commander in 7 Squadron at Oakington and I will never forget his vivid words describing this briefing, also reported by Middlebrook:

> That was the nearest thing I ever saw to mutiny in the R.A.F., when the guys walked in and saw the map showing Berlin again. There was a rumble of what I might call amazement, or horror, or disbelief. The Station Commander quietened the chaps down and there was no trouble, but you can imagine what it was like to be dead tired and then having to go again. Fatigue was the main problem. I always think that it was worst for the gunners, having to stay awake and keep a look-out for seven or eight hours at a time.

It was mainly a Lancaster raid and, because of the short turn-around, our squadrons could only muster 362 aircraft, 59 less than the previous night. A Canadian Pathfinder is said to have written in his diary on this occasion: 'Target—Big City via ye old tramlines', indicating his lack of favour for this proposed undeviating path.

That night, the weather was unconscionably foul over the North Sea, with thick cloud, icing and static electricity reaching right up to 28,000 feet. Not surprisingly, there was an unduly high rate of early returns. Sixty planes turned back, the greatest number in the whole of the Battle of Berlin, and it hit the much-needed Pathfinders of 8 Group hard.

Even though weather conditions improved in the last half an hour to Berlin, low cloud blanketed the city and completely obscured the targets. It was a fast run in from the north-west, taking advantage of the strong following wind. Only 36 of the original 50 Pathfinders had made it in, but all had great difficulty in concentrating their marking. The main force arrived late because of the bad weather. I suspect most of our bombing missed Berlin completely. The smooth low white cloud eerily silhouetted our bombers and they were lit up by the fighter flares and searchlights below. We were sitting ducks with six Pathfinders shot down in the target area. The remaining bomber force struggled back to England, our resolute pilots exhausted but yet determined. There were to be no crashes this night in spite of the necessary diversions for bad weather. My log book recorded:

BERLIN – 1 X 4000. 4 X 1000. 4 X T.I. (BACKERS-UP). Rockets etc over TARGET.

The return from Berlin on such dark winter nights was soul-destroying. Long and lonely mile after continuous mile in the tenebrous pitch black, with just the drone of the engines to mask long periods of total silence. You felt destitute, robbed of any rising sentiment that you had successfully bombed or 'pranged' the target. Even though you kept yourself busy to blank out dismal ponderings, you remained 'on edge', ready for the onslaught of the fighters, or the sudden sally of searchlights to wrench you from your seemingly short-lived reverie.

We were in desperate need of target triumph to pump up morale. Some even questioned the feasibility of the Bomber Command strategy to destroy Berlin.

The words of a Lancaster bomb-aimer from 156 Squadron Pathfinders, outlined by Middlebrook, describe the run in to target and demonstrate the sheer terror that the words 'Berlin is the target tonight' could conjure up.

> Lying in the nose of a Lancaster on a visual bombing run over Berlin was the most horrifying of experiences, the worst in a lifetime. As you came in slowly over the target, the city was ringed by blinding searchlights all seeking you out. The flak was fierce, its intensity buffeting you about the sky even though you were lucky enough to avoid a direct hit. The run-up seemed endless, with minutes of flying straight and level converting agonizingly into what seemed like hours. I sweated with fear, the perspiration freezing on my tormented body. I craved the release of the target below so I could set the bombs free and feel the jump of the Lanc. as it was relieved of its load. Every second I expected to be blown to pieces.

These were dark times indeed, and probably the lowest point in my own war. Sadly, four of the five raids carried out so far on Berlin had been designated as failures. Operating time and time again to this 'Big City' started everyone thinking. Our second tour chances had now moved to a mathematical zero. I ceased counting the missions completed in my flying log book and simply latched on to the determination to survive. As the non-moon period drew to a close, we had two nights of rest and then a last raid was ordered to the Baltic coastal port of Stettin. This ended the three-week period of bombing operations. We now got the break we all desperately needed.

17

A FRENZY OF FIGHTERS

No matter how many operations you had under your belt, no matter your experience, it didn't help to allay your apprehension. Philip and I would have a casual smoke and chat outside the briefing room before a mission and it helped to settle the nerves. You had to be on your mettle for each and every outing.

Tobacco was a welcome friend for young men facing battle. Although sporting a pipe earlier in my service, I now favoured Craven A cork-tipped cigarettes. A packet of ten sat snugly in my right chest pocket, the black cat trademark sitting neatly atop this small red box and hopefully rendering good luck to its bearer. Philip was more a pipe man, Flying Dutchman ribbon-cut tobacco filling his familiar briar adorned with woody nodules. He somehow always managed to secure a round tin or two in twin blue of this legendary aromatic mixture from Holland, two ounces deftly poking their shredded brown strands through the circular opening of the fanned, waxed paper lining. Sweet plumes of nutted smoke would waft from his pipe to divert the senses.

'Another trip to the Big City?' I asked, realising that Philip, as wing commander, was more in the know.

'I think we might be lucky this run, Gordon. Looks like Brunswick's our target with Mosquito diversions to Berlin and Magdeburg,' he responded with a bemused look of uncharacteristic relief. 'It's been a real grind for the men these past few months, and Berlin doesn't seem to be giving up the ghost just yet.'

We needed things to go our way a little more. The guys were tired and we needed a boost. Philip and I entered the briefing room hoping that morale could be lifted but nevertheless ready to parade renewed enthusiasm.

The new bombing period had opened promptly on the night of 14–15 January 1944. The target was indeed Brunswick, a medium-sized city in central Germany about 100 miles closer to England than Berlin. Unfortunately, the raid was a minor disaster. We were still unaware of the German breakthrough with SN-2, their airborne radar, and were becoming a bit perplexed by reports of many bombers being observed as shot down by 'predicted unseen flak'. Many aircraft appeared to be blown up without any evidence of conventional fighter attack. We were soon to learn, through our own peril, that there were an increasing number of long-range Junkers Ju 88s now equipped with upward firing cannons and shells that used only a dim tracer. The enemy had hatched a more furtive approach and changed tactics. The odds were moving against us.

The Germans also brought into play a new fighter tactic called Zahme Sau or 'Tame Boar', tenacious twin-engined night-fighters would attack us relentlessly along our bomber routes to and from the target. To this point, the German fighter defence had been concentrated at the anticipated target, as their radar sets had been blinded by the Window dropped from our Lancs. Now, Junkers Ju 88s, Messerschmitt Bf 109s and Focke-Wulf Fw 190s, fitted with a direction finder and landing lights, were on us from the very moment we crossed into enemy territory, coming at us from out of the night. The ante had been 'upped' another notch.

Brunswick contained two Messerschmitt factories but had never been the object of a major raid. On that night, the Tame Boar fighters were quickly into our bomber stream and simply followed us to target and then stalked us back to the North Sea coast. Bombing results were abysmal with the majority of the attack missing the city. We experienced our heaviest loss in six weeks, since Black Thursday, with 38 Lancasters lost, representing 7.6 per cent of the bomber force. Eleven of the lost aircraft were Pathfinders and this was a catastrophic toll of these most experienced of crews.

The gloom at this critical stage of the air war was summed up by an Australian pilot returning to his squadron after being on leave for a mere month. He felt himself to be a virtual stranger in the mess, given the appalling run of casualties since he had been away. Bomber Command was still having a devastating impact on German cities but at a much higher price.

Window no longer protected us. SN-2 radar had been produced in such numbers as to equip more than half of the German night-fighter force. With a working frequency of 90 megacycles, it could not be jammed by Window. Before this, we had been fortunate in having a pretty clear run to target, with only some of the more experienced German crews being able to pick out our moving bombers from the radar echoes emitted from the little clouds of Window falling below them. Now we were engulfed in a frenzy of fighters.

Compounding our newfound, but yet unrealised, 'visibility' to the enemy, German ground controllers could use ground and now also airborne radar devices to lock on to the H2S radar that Bomber Command employed during a major raid. They tracked the main bomber stream throughout its flight and reported our whereabouts on multiple radio channels in a running commentary to their circling night-fighters. When the time was right, the fighters were sluiced into our unsuspecting stream. Those equipped with SN-2 homed in on their individual bomber prey for attack. Those without were aided by the incandescent fighter flares dropped to dog us along our path. The fighters would then feel for our slipstream and look for our telltale vapour trails, eerily marking the night sky.

H2S was fitted to the less than 100 Pathfinder marker aircraft leading the nearly 5000 RAF aircrew that would take part in each major raid. Over Berlin few nights offered the opportunity for a visual identification of the aiming point, and so the decision was made to use blind marking by H2S exclusively for this tumultuous battle. We realised that our H2S radar set was like a honey pot to a number of very active and persistent bees, a malevolent maelstrom of German fighters.

Berlin was on again on 20 January 1944. It was a late afternoon departure and I remember feeling surprisingly heartened, and a sense of pride as I witnessed the sheer strength of our formation, stretched out across the reddening evening sky, off again to the Big City. There were 769 aircraft made up of 495 Lancasters, 264 Halifaxes and 10 Mosquitoes, all grinding their way in the dying daylight out over the North Sea, intent on wreaking as much havoc as we could on the Big City, courtesy of Butch Harris.

The recent success of the German night-fighters was forcing RAF Bomber Command to abandon straight-in routes to target. This meant taking more indirect pathways with longer and longer flying times, which took its inevitable toll on our tiring crews. The price paid was even greater flyer fatigue and a reduction in the bomb-loads we were able to carry.

As we hit the cloud of a cold front over Germany, temperatures plummeted. I commented to Philip over the intercom, in hope more than certainty, 'With a bit of luck this weather will keep the fighters off our back, Skip.'

'You can but hope, Gordon,' he responded. 'I fear the more experienced bastards will still put in an appearance. Keep your eyes peeled, chaps.'

As it turned out, this was the first occasion when the Germans could have mounted a full-scale Tame Boar operation, but only the twin-engined fighters and one-third of available crews were ordered up to lie in wait for us, orbiting the radio beacons along our supposed track. They got it wrong, fooled by the indirect route of our bomber stream. Eventually the controllers were able to zero in on our position, their fighters catching up with us near the Baltic coast. All hell broke loose. While not a perfect interception of our bombers, it was effective with 35 of our valued aircraft and crews lost, a telling 4.6 per cent of our force.

Philip steadied the ship with, 'They've found us now. Keep your focus. Let's get in and out fast.'

'Nothing behind yet, Skip,' Jimmy Brown chimed in reassuringly.

'Lanc under attack port beam, Skip,' Jim Smith reported from the mid-upper turret. A burst of fire could help our compatriot but also might divert the attack onto our own aircraft. 'Permission to engage.'

'Hold your fire, Jim,' Philip interceded. 'Let's drop our load first. We don't need any undue attention.'

'Roger that, Skip,' Jim conceded, knowing the marking of the targets had to be our priority. There would be time after the drop to engage the fighters. It was a long way home.

Our Pathfinder aircraft carrying H2S managed to work their magic through the murk, pinpointing the eastern parts of Berlin with consummate timing of blind markers and excellent concentration of sky markers throughout the attack. Area-bombing worked, knocking out important small segments vital to the German war industry and keeping their workforce in disarray. Industrial buildings were also destroyed, railways damaged and the Lichtenberg power station was put out of action. Power was cut to several eastern districts of the city. A direct hit by one of our squadron's 4000-pounders rendered the small firm of Roland Brandt defunct. This was indeed a welcome blow of destruction as it had been making the SN-2 radar components for the Luftwaffe that were causing our recent diabolical troubles. Ten thousand people were rendered homeless with damage to residential property and 243 civilians were killed. My flying log book read:

> BERLIN: 1 X 4000 – 4 X 1000me; 4 X TI – 1 SBC. Wanganui.
> BLIND MARKER.

We were ordered out again the following night to Magdeburg on 21–22 January 1944. The favourable weather demanded our return to action. We had less than 24 hours to recover as we had returned from Berlin just after midnight the previous night.

We were joined by Alan Coleman for the trip to Magdeburg. He replaced Alan Drew as bomb-aimer. Our second Alan was to be our set operator and his addition to our crew would ensure the successful delivery of our TIs. Bomber Command had made the decision that the workload entailed in operating the H2S set and also providing the necessary calculations was too much for one navigator. The emphasis in Pathfinders was on accurate navigation to effectively mark the target.

The post of navigator II, known as set operator, was created to follow the position of the Pathfinder aircraft continuously by plotting from the H2S screen every three minutes a fix by bearing and distance from the nearest built-up area. Although H2S lacked definition over many types of terrain, towns and villages gave the best return on the screen. As navigator I, I would take from Alan's log such fixes as needed for my calculations and then the two of us would combine our efforts for the run in to target and the timing for the actual release of the TIs. When radar was not in use, the set operator would act as the visual bomb-aimer. However, during a radar attack the flight engineer now moved to the bomb-aimer's position to drop the bombs when instructed to do so by the H2S operator.

Alan was a charming and well-educated character. He was born at Salford in Lancaster and trained as a teacher. After a period in the

Swansea University Air Squadron, he had completed his instruction to be an air observer in South Africa, and was then commissioned before he was selected for Pathfinders at No. 7 Squadron. He was one of only six from his course to be selected for Pathfinders.

He had an amazing RAF career, surviving three tours of bomber operations, numbering more than 100 sorties which included 37 raids on Berlin in Lancasters and Mosquitoes. Thirteen of these were as master bomber. He had a strong religious conviction but was never seeking to pass on any worldly wisdom to the unsuspecting. His belief system possibly carried us all on a hallowed cloud, floating us through the dark and trying days of Berlin. He was later recognised with the Distinguished Flying Cross followed by the notable addition of a bar. At the end of his war he helped out a Radnorshire vicar as a lay reader but was unable to afford to study for ordination. He returned to the RAF in 1951 and in the 1960s carried out intelligence work in West Germany, as he spoke fluent Russian. He was finally ordained in 1967 and fulfilled his destiny with a long and varied career in the Anglican Church. While not sharing his faith, his survival of such an unbelievable time unscathed over enemy territory does start you thinking.

Back to operations. Our crew of seven was briefed for Magdeburg, a late target switch and the first raid on this city about 80 miles west of Berlin. A substantial decoy raid was ordered on Berlin with 22 Lancasters and 12 Mosquitoes of 8 Group. The German fighters ignored this diversion. Our H2S radar, or 'Y' as mentioned in my log book, became unserviceable but we managed to line up to drop our indicator flares. Many of our compatriots were in difficulty that night from the fighter onslaught.

We were just over the target when rear gunner Jimmy Brown warned, 'Junkers at 600 yards, Skip.' The grey monster loomed in out of the dark to get us, a touch of yellow on each tip emphasising the might of its winged expanse. The glazing of its forward nose canopy gave it a beetle's eye appearance, glinting menacingly in the muted light of the trailing fighter flares. The sound of its twin engines growled and whined and I could hear the cartridges rattling out of the sturdy breaches of its twin cannons, as it roared remorselessly towards us, intent on our demise. This was not a novice out for his first spin.

'See to him, Jimmy,' Philip encouraged, knowing we were committed to our bombing run.

The Junkers made its first pass and Jimmy saw it off with a determined barrage of bullets.

'He's coming again,' Jim Smith joined in from the mid-upper turret. Both gunners fired and tracer was seen to enter the German fighter which throttled back out of range.

We completed our run and, just after we had dropped our markers on the button, I heard Jimmy Brown, up back, muttering in a determined tone, 'You won't catch us napping, my German friend. He's 500 yards behind us, Skip, and closing. Leave him to me.'

The Junkers had hoped our gunners would be fire-watching after the drop. On its last run at us, with nerves of steel, Jimmy Brown held his fire until the range was very close. He opened up on this reviled Ju 88 at the very last moment and we saw bullets ripping into its fuselage, a blaze of flame and the fighter careening down out of control.

'You bagged him, Jimmy, no doubt,' Jim Smith confirmed. 'Probably someone famous.'

We later learnt that the Magdeburg raid cost the enemy two of its most renowned German night-fighter pilots that night, Wittgenstein and Meurer. The former had 83 kills to his name in the west and in Russia, and the latter German ace was the commander of the premier unit of the Luftwaffe night-fighter arm and the third highest-scoring night-fighter pilot. Maybe this was a sign that the tide of war was now to turn against the much-feared German fighter frenzy. The best could be beaten.

There was a further glimmer of good fortune as we returned from this raid when we were some miles off the English coast high over the icy North Sea.

'I think that's one of ours, Skip,' Alan suggested, still in position as bomb-aimer, always vigilant from his prominent position in the nose to any possibilities, even when we were close to home. None of us ever took for granted for a moment that we could yet be free of strife—not until our feet were actually touching tarmac.

Philip responded immediately, easing the steering column over. I looked out from my station and sighted the languishing Lanc through the dim night light, off to our right. There was dense black smoke pouring from its two port engines. It was in trouble and having difficulty maintaining height.

'She's going in,' Philip simply concluded as he smoothly brought our Lanc down low over the restless ocean. Our miserable compatriot was now in easy view beneath us, skimming the water before coming to a shuddering halt, caught up in the wake of its own bow waves.

I replayed the nightmare of sea rescue in my head before snapping myself out of it. 'Ready for a Gee fix, Skip.'

Philip gratefully responded, 'Roger that, Gordon. Let's get those poor sods out of there.' I took my quick Gee fix and Philip immediately radioed off the coordinates to base, as a dinghy seemed to miraculously pop out of the rapidly submerging Lanc, like a beautiful yellow butterfly emerging from its metallic chrysalis. We were informed the next day that two of the crew had been picked up from their life-raft by a rescue boat, immediately dispatched from the homeland. They were lucky that a Gee fix in this area was probably accurate to within half a mile. Alan's presence may have worked a miracle, at least for some of the poor unfortunates. My flying log book for this expedition with our new man of religion read:

MAGDEBURG – 1 X 4000 – 2 X 1000MC; 3 X 500 G.P.; 3 X
T.I. – 4 bundles flares. 'Y' U/S. Bombed. BACKERS-UP (+T.I.'s).
(BLIND MARKER). (1) J.U. 88 shot down by R/G over Target.
J.U. 88 seen to crash (confirmed). (2) Aircraft seen ditching off
English coast. W/T message resulted in dinghy being picked up
(2 survivors).

We had two more trips to Berlin on 27 and 28 January that were
highly successful. Two days later we were again briefed for Berlin and
the game changed. This trip of 30 January was to test us the most
and demonstrate the undisputed worth of our two gunners.

It was the end of the dark night bombing period with the
unwelcome appearance of a quarter to half moon, illuminating our
camouflaged shape on our outward flight. It was our third Berlin raid
in four nights and none of the crews were happy, particularly with the
prospect of moonlight. On approach to target, there was a surprising
lack of heavy flak compared to the previous raids. Another ominous
sign was the large number of fighter flares dropped over the target to
light us up like sitting ducks for the marauding fighters. This certainly
set us on alert for a German aerial onslaught and we were not to be
disappointed, if that is the right word to use.

The first attack came from a Junkers Ju 88 while we were flying
straight and level, coming in, at our most vulnerable, on the bombing
run. The Junkers was powered by twin engines that jutted menacingly
forward from the bulk of its wings and were complemented by an array
of radar antennas and dual gun emplacements. It was like a ferocious
beast, its bulbous three-bladed propellers driving it at a frightening
pace at us, out of the night sky. I never lost the chill of despair as the
clamour of its guns opened up, choking my senses.

'Junkers 400 yards astern. Engaging now,' rear gunner Jimmy
Brown shouted, as he matched the fighter's furore with his own deadly
mix of bullets.

'Dive to starboard,' Jimmy yelled above the deafening clatter as he seemed to hit the fighter amidships with at least one burst. But the Junkers was resolute, unstoppable, and it throttled back to follow us, as if attached by some unbreakable strand of chewing gum commandeered from our American allies.

'He's still with us,' Jim Smith confirmed from the mid-upper turret as the fighter reappeared on the starboard quarter, rattling in again towards us at breakneck speed.

'Dive to port,' was Jimmy's follow-up order. Philip responded immediately with a suitable deft orbit that allowed the tracer spitting from the fighter to pass underneath our port wing. Philip was the master of evasion and we were to remain untouched. Both gunners opened up as we fell away, their long continuous bursts being rewarded by the eerie vision of their yellow-tinged tracers ripping into the nose and cockpit area of the fighter. It dived away steeply into the cloud, brindle flames confirming the end of its efforts for this night.

'Take that, you bastard,' roared the two Jimmies.

'Back to business,' Philip confirmed as we levelled out to continue our bombing run. We confirmed our track to target and opened the bomb bay doors, oblivious to the glow of the fighter flares still lighting us up like a Christmas tree. Our ordeal was not to be over yet.

'Fw 190 on low port beam,' Jim Smith exclaimed as he opened up with his twin Brownings. Jimmy immediately joined in from the rear. The noise through our aircraft was deafening as the .303 cartridges jounced wildly out of the gun breeches of our two valiant defenders. The forward lights from the fighter added to the terror, picking us out of the night sky. It came in fast.

'Bank left, Skip, give me a last crack,' Jimmy roared, catching his breath. As Philip put the Lanc neatly into a deft slide to the left, both Jimmies now opened up in a relentless dual fusillade from rear- and mid-gunner positions.

'He's hit, he's not coming back,' Philip cool-headedly confirmed, the puff of black smoke from the German's right wing registering forever in his mind. This grew to a dark glow of fire, signalling the fate of this sleek killing machine. The Fw 190 disappeared from sight below us.

'Great job, you two.' Philip was a man of simple words, but you could read in his tone the knowledge that good gunners had just got us through the war. Their vigilance and immediate reaction made the difference between a damaged or exploding Lanc, and the enemy being dealt out of the action. These life and death moments came and went in but an instant.

The formidable Focke-Wulf Fw 190 fighters had a cruising speed of 351 miles per hour at sea level (407 miles per hour at 20,000 feet) and were powered by a single, twin-row BMW 801 radial engine with a yellow-pointed three-bladed propeller that seemed to hum like the crushing machine at the sugar mill ratcheted up to full bore. The airflow was accelerated to the cylinder heads through the use of an internal spinner inside the front dome of the propeller. Designed for speed with a small wing platform, it was armed with two 20-millimetre MG 151 cannons hugged close either side of the plane's body. With a bubble canopy supporting a three-paned front window and an imposing blackened eagle emblazoned either side of its fuselage, it was intimidating, to say the least.

The Fw 190 became the backbone of the Luftwaffe's 'Jagdwaffe' or Fighter Force, along with its better-known counterpart the Messerschmitt Bf 109. With increased firepower and manoeuvrability at low to medium altitudes, the Fw 190 was unfortunately well suited for the attack on our Lancasters coming in for their bombing run.

A fighter attack always brought for me a sense of helplessness. I focused on my navigating but couldn't help feeling like a top-order batsman watching from the sidelines as the tail-enders struggled to make the last ten runs needed for victory. I gripped the bench as the twists and turns for our Lanc's survival ensued. Glimpses came of the tracer glow of battle and the noise left me with ears ringing. My fate was to be determined in mere seconds and I was powerless to intervene, trusting in my mates to get us through. No one could deny the value of the gunners in a Lanc. The two Jimmies were worth their weight in gold.

We had our bomb doors open as the Fw 190 attacked. This second onslaught totally disrupted our bombing run and we were now beyond our allotted marking time. We could not drop our TIs and were forced to return home with our load intact. This was the first time that our bombs had been withheld. Bombing had given way to survival. My flight log for this, our first double dose of German fighters, read:

BERLIN – 1 X 4000 – 4 X 1000 M.C. 4 X T.I. – 1 S.B.C. Wanganui flares. 2 Combats – (One on bombing run.) JU 88 – R/G – strikes observed – FW 190 when bomb doors open. T.I.s and flares withheld. Large numbers fighter flares. (BLIND MARKER).

Since the start of the Battle of Berlin, the men of Bomber Command had undertaken seventeen heavy raids, fourteen of these in less than three months. Wreckage, rubble, death and destruction came from our every expedition, but Berlin no longer contained sufficient close building structure to support the cataclysm of fire that had destroyed Cologne and Hamburg. Our last trip to the Big City was 15 February 1944, completing my lucky nine, and Bomber Command's last foray was on 24–25 March.

It was time for lightheartedness and a lift from the torment of never-ending trips to destroy Berlin, plagued by a frenzy of fighters. The two Jimmies would join me in this quest. We were still young and in our twenties. Something had to give.

18

A LITTLE LEVITY, LEIPZIG AND WIND SPEED

The war was ruthless, wearing and with no clear sign of resolution. Berlin was proving difficult to conquer from the air. It was February 1944 and the invasion of Europe by the Allies was still months away and kept top secret. Morale was being sapped by unfriendly weather patterns, lost friends and comrades. Things were far too serious and an antidote was needed.

Guns and explosives had been an integral part of my life growing up. My pyrotechnical skills and knowledge had been well refined alongside my cousins Jack and Guy as we used small explosive devices to maximise our catch during our early fishing expeditions in the flattie on the long reaches of the Burnett River. Guy was studying industrial chemistry at university in Brisbane and was our theory man and Jack was an engineering apprentice in the mill workshop and could easily put our contrivances together. With a couple of years of sugar chemistry under my belt, I was an able co-conspirator in the formulation of devices of detonation. So I was well schooled and ready for my pioneering exploits with explosives and humour. It was time for a little fun.

When I had finished my first tour of operations and been sent to Lichfield as navigation instructor, I was still a country boy at heart, even though I had reached the lofty rank of squadron leader. At 26 years of age I was no longer young by aircrew standards, but held on to a bit of the bumpkin, remaining a little naive and open to persuasion.

The navigation section at Lichfield Officer Training Unit was responsible for navigation training and mastery of all the necessary equipment, including calibration of sextants and chronometers. At the end of each course every trainee was provided with a detailed assessment of his work, both in the air and on the ground. The survival of a navigator's crew depended on being at the right place at the right time. A serious business, one might say, and consequently the atmosphere of the place was austere. Nicknamed Kelly's Brickyard, it occupied a single-storey building standing in a hollow, echoing square, just opposite the headquarters for the station and squadron commanders and their staff. It was like an auditorium and ancient Roman amphitheatre rolled into one. It was ripe for performance.

I was in desperate need of diversion from the brutality of warfare and so had embarked with others on harnessing the hidden properties and magic ingredients for propulsion of the Verey pistol.

The Verey pistol was an integral part of aircraft equipment and was used when you were in distress or for signalling. Its singularly simple mechanism, thick butted handle and 1-inch bore, and snub-nosed muzzle with intriguing stepped barrel, held an aura of antique mystery, reminiscent of the pirate's blunderbuss of old. Its cartridges were about 3 inches long and 1.5 inches in diameter and ejected long-burning stars of selected colours, launching them a couple of hundred feet into the air. These stars could be extracted and used for questionable purposes.

A few reprobates and myself discovered the propulsive power of magnesium powder contained in a Verey pistol cartridge. It was called 'white smoke puff' and could be harnessed with devastating effect. The powder could be easily ignited by a relatively small electric current supplied from a furtively hidden 12-volt battery. The detonation circuit was created using a short length of fine steel wire embedded in the volatile powder. When the current was applied, the wire would glow and fuse, and do its work with the explosive magnesium, confined and compressed against the wire by tightly wound heavy-duty insulation tape. The firmness of the packing and the amount of insulation tape used proved to be critical factors in the delivery characteristics of propulsion.

After considerable periodic test flights, the 'standard bucket ascent' came into being. There would be a muffled explosion from our launches ringing out in the vacant square opposite the centre of authority, the bang on ignition broadcasting a booming thud reminiscent of a thousand corks of finest French champagne being popped in unison. A battered red fire bucket could be observed rising 30 or 40 feet in the air, leaving behind a magnificent burnished trail of wispy white smoke. This unusual phenomenon would occur in the central quadrangle of Kelly's Brickyard around 11.00 a.m., only twice weekly to avoid predictability. While it became an anticipated part of the routine, it was never wholly accepted by the ruling authority. They, however, never sought to unearth the perpetrators. Maybe they didn't really want to.

Now, after our sixth harrowing mission to Berlin, we were celebrating the start of a welcome short rest from operations at Oakington during the full moon period. The two Jimmies had been meticulously trained in the opportunities of the Verey pistol cartridge, the potential uses of the white magnesium powder and the stars mixed in with these volatile particles. They were excellent students, highly motivated and creative. Eventually things got slightly out of hand.

We first slyly inserted the stars into the mess open fire when, unsuspectingly, our victims would bare their nether regions. These poor folk had just survived another trip of certain death over Germany and were shamelessly seeking some much missed bodily warmth after being chilled by too many hours in a shuddering flying machine encased in a cocoon of icy metal. The stars each had their own dazzling hue and the subsequent mild explosion with a coinciding flash of red, blue or green fire would appropriately sear their revealed and vulnerable buttocks. Alarm and surprise were our reward and we watched as they spontaneously leapt into the air, releasing their bound-up tension. It was as if we were ministering to the needy; after all, our intention had purely been to raise the spirits of our compatriots.

We soon moved our pastoral care to an even better venue for rest and solitude, the airmen's private quarters. Several long huts stretched alongside dark green moody hedgerows, bleak and dismal save for the compact coke fires glowing through the small glazed porthole of the individual braziers in each of the six rooms. Six inviting chimney openings lay in ordered array across the roof, irresistible for a man on a mission of mischief with borrowed ladder and six Verey pistol stars in his pocket. One star dropped down the top of each smoking chimney into the fire below produced a syncopated furore for each of the unsuspecting inhabitants, like starting an orchestral piece from Rachmaninoff when only a quiet sonata is expected.

We had now created a state of wariness in the mess. No member of our hallowed group would ever remain near the mess fire if another approached. It was time to move to a higher plane and begin the construction of bombs, not with lethal intentions but merely to continue our mission of relieving surprise, leaving a lasting impression with just a tinge of embarrassment. We now shifted gear to fully utilise the known power of 'white smoke puff' powder, developing a new-generation fragmentation bomb, based on the 'bucket ascent' principle. We filled the central core of an extra-large air force issue toilet roll, complete with all its voluminous tissue, with the magic white smoke ingredient, the fuse wire delicately placed in the powder and the cylinder plugged at either end and then tightly bound with insulation tape. These external leads were then attached to a 40-foot long electric lead which snaked back to the operators in another room. Ignition was stupendous, a total diversion of gaseous smoke, like a puffy cumulonimbus cloud encased in a room, the fragments of toilet paper creating a huge contained snowstorm so no one could ever discern the source of combustion.

We mad bombers remained unidentified for a long period of time but we eventually went too far. We secured the use of a flight van with a 12-volt battery in the back. We only chose mornings with heavy fog, of which there were many in winter, when aircrew reported to their flight rooms dotted around the airdrome, ready for their day's task, either test flying, training or operations. Visibility was probably down to 50 feet outside, so no one would notice a flight van driving slowly through the fog along the perimeter track. We would stop outside the flight room and lower our pride and joy, the Fragmentation Mark III, through a previously unlatched window. We were never seen on approach, and following detonation of the Mark III the flight van would accelerate instantly into the fog, dragging the lead and effecting full recovery on the move. The flight room was left with visibility down to a few feet and so our escape was guaranteed.

Perhaps we became a little cocky. One day our bomb technicians overdid things. They developed the Mark IV with added tight windings of insulation tape designed meticulously to allow for the larger airspace of our ultimate target, the three-storey control tower. This was inhabited one foggy day by worthy types doing nothing but sitting around drinking tea. While no harm was done to anyone or anything in the building, unfortunately the air pressure generated by the blast neatly took out all the windows in the tower itself. The CO, a ribald man with a well-tried sense of humour, spread the word that, provided an envelope with the necessary cash for window replacement was on his desk the next morning, he would not seek to publicly identify the perpetrators. No more would be said about it. Philip was never directly involved in our enterprises but encouraged each of us to come up with the necessary £12, a not inconsiderable sum in those days. This was to be the end of our bombing runs.

We now reverted to other simple pleasures. After this somewhat expensive last escapade, our excursions to the Cambridge pubs had to be restricted for lack of ready spending money. We were forced to favour the Oakington mess with drinks charged to the monthly mess bill. The scene for these quiet nights between operations was an unassuming two-storey red-brick and tile building with wide expanses of window gazing out over the close-cut green of the airfield. While not gracious, it was charged with luxury and opulence, typical of the high society reserved for permanent RAF stations in peacetime. The furnishings were stylish, with well-worn studded leather chairs and deep piled carpets in scarlet red and emerald green filling the room.

There were usually three choices presented. A night in a secluded corner with a convenient bell-push for the ordering of drinks all evening; joining in with the hilarious crowd at the bar with the diversion of good humour; or lastly, full-blooded raucous song-making around the piano. Traditional, relatively clean songs, like the fairly innocuous children's ditty 'The Muffin Man' were sung until around 9.30 p.m., when the customary 'Goodnight, Ladies' would ring out and all WAAF officers were expected to depart. As the air thickened with cigarette smoke like a London fog descending, the songs degenerated and drinking prowess was tested.

The night usually ended with the song 'I Drink to the Health of Cardinal Puff' with unrepeatable words and a test of manual coordination and dexterity. The test involved taking three separate big gulps to empty a pint pot of beer. The first drink involved a following one tap of the tabletop with one index finger, one tap underneath, stomp right foot, stomp left foot, then stand up, stand down, place both hands back on the table. For the second drink, the cardinal, as the player was designated, had to do his routine with two fingers extended and two of all the other sequence requirements.

It was not easy. When the further three fingers episode was completed, the cardinal would drain his glass with his last guzzle, making sure he got every last drop by licking the rim and even rubbing it on his face. Stiff penalties were enforced if the sequence of this strict ritual was broken somewhere along the line, and usually by 11.00 p.m. there were very few who could achieve the feat of completing the routine and 'drinking to the health of Cardinal Puff, Puff, Puff for the third and last time'.

The mad bombers were not alone in their pursuit of the unusual. There were other artistes and teams of humorists. It became almost as traditional as the furniture for our splendid mess room to be emblazoned about halfway along with a trail of large black oily footprints. They started at floor level on one side and travelled vertically up the wall, across the high ceiling and down the other side. They had been placed by the ingenious piling up of available chairs and tables for a platform and a compliant officer with blackened bare feet being pressed against the ceiling by his compatriots. All this while perched high up on the pile of furniture which would then be moved and re-stacked as necessary. You were left in awe and wonder as to how they managed it.

A further refinement was added later, which may seem to the layman as a little unrefined but nevertheless a sign of the thirst for levity and good humour by young men away from home and facing their mortality. A gap in the trail of footprints, halfway across, was filled by two etched ovals, sooty and perfectly adjacent, like a large kidney bean cut in half. It reminded me of our earlier fireside exploits with the rear ends of our fellow revellers; an amazing feat of balance and teamwork by the ceiling-walkers to deliver this quintessential impression.

I reveal to you a last example of foolishness, merely to reinforce that we were not alone in our efforts of apparent madness. Imagine an aircrew member making his unsteady way to his hut through the surrounding total darkness, picking out landmarks warily through thick fog, such as a hedge, large oak tree or dry irrigation ditch. This poor soul must have felt great relief and a certain triumph in finding his own compact quarters in the stretch of uniform grey housing. His relief was to be short-lived. Three small holes had been drilled into each of the fibreboard dividing walls of his sanctuary and now were cunningly loaded with 'at-the-ready' nozzles of foam fire extinguishers. Once the man had undressed, the full contents of the extinguishers were fired simultaneously, filling the compact space nearly to shoulder height with dense foam. The airman was temporarily disoriented, taking a little time to wrench from his addled brain the expected terse words of indignation.

While the rank of squadron leader brought responsibility in the air, on the ground it was different. We needed to lift our spirits, especially because things were about to take a further turn for the worse.

It was close to midnight on Saturday, 19 February 1944. With improving weather conditions, a planned raid was to go ahead for what would be one of the most significant operations of the Battle of Berlin, but Berlin was not to be the target. Bomber Harris had switched destinations to Leipzig, home to three Erla Maschinenwerk aircraft factories that produced the reviled Messerschmitt Bf 109 fighter planes. On this fateful night, our take-off was dampened by the white-flecked remains of waning snow showers. Harris had ordered maximum effort with 832 bombers braving the sleeted conditions. This desperate offensive unleashed all our worst nightmares rolled into one.

The wind totally fooled us. The briefed forecast was for a steady headwind that would slow our travel, but in reality this proved to be only a light air abeam from the north. The more experienced navigators picked up the discrepancy in wind speed and advised their pilots to dog-leg a total of four times in order to lose the 30 minutes required for arrival over target at the designated marking time. The less experienced crews arrived early and started to orbit the area, waiting for the markers to go down. Some decided to bomb before Zero Hour using their H2S radar. When the Pathfinder flares did find their mark, there was a wild scramble as several hundred heavy bombers lumbered in from all directions to drop their bombs and get out fast. The noise was thunderous and collisions and confusion erupted, filling the night sky with fireballs of calamity, our own rending destruction on one another. Then the flak batteries opened up, scoring multiple successes in this arena of illumination.

Along with astrofixes, dog-legging was abhorred by pilots. I remember telling Philip to alter our heading on one of our dog-legs to an angle at 60 degrees to the main bomber force, a no-choice option for marking the target at the right time. I will never get out of my mind the terrifying and immediate unremitting roar of another bomber's engines, suddenly on us before we knew it. My mind quickly calculated and awaited the signals of collision or reprieve. The friendly Lanc must have passed over the top of us, nothing more than a few feet between our rigid metal frames. Philip was heard to utter a profane remark under his staid Scottish breath.

We were like fish in a barrel at feeding time, racing in all directions to complete our task, hoping somehow to survive. The German controllers carried out their best Tame Boar operation to date with ample time to direct their fighters into the slow-moving, well spread out bomber force. The elusive winds had grossly extended the bomber stream to and from Leipzig, making it vulnerable to easy attack. On this shocking evening of destruction, Bomber Command lost 78 aircraft with an overall rate of 9.6 per cent of heavy bombers, its highest loss in the war so far. It was gruesome and must have started Harris thinking.

As we limped home, chastened by the fright of mass confusion in the air, I recall fondly the first sight of snow-covered fields crisscrossing the earth, leading in to Oakington. The serenity of the snowscape, with a dramatic backdrop of orange-tinged clouds stretching out before us, soothed my psyche. We lowered landing gear, locking the Lanc's big, bulbous and black tyres into position ready to engage the runway. Philip put her down neatly as always and we prepared for a better day, free from the turmoil of night warfare, the deadly blow of weather and wind speed.

My flying log book for the trip to Leipzig revealed for the first time the inescapable price of battle over the industrial cities of northern Germany:

LEIPZIG – 1 X 4000; 2 X 1000 M.C.; 8 X T.I. SPECIAL BLIND MARKER (B/U) Markers withheld – Y U/S. 78 aircraft lost.

Leipzig was a turning point for my life as well as the priorities of Bomber Command. I was now determined to grab hold of what had meaning while I could.

Wind speed again played a major role in the demise of Bomber Command's last mission to Berlin on 24 March 1944, its nineteenth raid on the Big City. Air Chief Marshal Harris was committed to making one last dying attempt to render irreparable damage to a frustrating section of this expansive metropolis that remained intact, in spite of our repeated efforts. As always, he took the decision on his own. It was to become known as 'The Night of the Big Winds'. Jet streams were discovered that portentous night. Our crew had been spared from this last desperate foray to Berlin and this further battle with the elements.

It was again the weather and unbelievable wind speeds that tipped the delicate balance. Our gallant bombers were to fight against incredible unseen forces that greatly slowed them, pushing them off track. Wind speeds forecast before take-off for the leg over the North Sea were shown in the navigators' logs as '340/21' and '358/44', that is 21 miles per hour from 340 degrees for the first part of the flight increasing to 44 miles per hour approaching the coast of Denmark. Unfortunately Gee signals for the route over the North Sea were jammed by the Germans, limiting wind estimates for about an hour. By the time the bombers hit landfall they were 30 miles south of track and the wind speed was probably closer to 100 miles per hour. For the first time the expression 'jet stream' was used.

Pathfinder navigators reported headwind speeds of up to 130 miles per hour to their experienced Lancaster pilots and were just not believed. They were considerably watered down in reports back to base, and in turn to the following main force. The bomber stream arrived at the Danish coast well scattered, some aircraft turning north to regain their track, others continuing on, south of track, over Germany rather than Denmark. The saving grace was that the extreme winds hampered the Germans' full-scale Tame Boar operation but only on the inward journey. A great gaggle of more than 700 of our aircraft was now spread over a front of at least 70 miles, well to the west of the identified target. Pathfinders did their best under difficult conditions with no effective concentration of marking and only half the bombs falling on Berlin itself.

The return home brought the heaviest casualties, the slaughter of young men in aircraft. The bombers were now scattered on a frontage of more than 50 miles and with a length of up to 150 miles. Fuel reserves had become depleted in the fight against the wind. The conditions were ideal for the Tame Boar night-fighters and the carnage began. They waited like a pack of wolves south of Berlin, catching the bombers as they emerged from the target area, SN-2 radar guiding them into their prey. Fighter attacks continued from Berlin all the way back to the coast. Nineteen bombers were shot down in the first 60 miles of the return route and 72 aircraft were lost in total on the mission, only six less than our devastation in the air at Leipzig, a month earlier. Fifty-six bombers alone were sacrificed on that appalling return flight to the Dutch coast. This was to be another ravaging loss, at 9.1 per cent of the total force.

Wind speeds, mere forces of nature beyond our control and effective measurement, had again been the undoing of our powerful war machines of the air. The impact of weather had extended the bomber stream and made it vulnerable to the now highly effective Tame Boar clusters. It was to be the last dark night of the air chief marshal's mission, his 'main offensive' to break Germany. Harris realised that little more could be done against the targets of northern and central Germany and that he would have to content himself with costing Hitler the war. He had not been able to effect the hoped for surrender through bombing from the air, the model of complete devastation gleaned from Cologne, Hamburg and Coventry, but he had forced this petulant despot to throw too many resources at the defence of the capital and his hardware-producing northern industrial cities. Bomber Command now turned south, taking new routes in to avoid detection and attack from the Tame Boar night-fighters based in the north. To this point, the cities of southern Germany were comparatively undamaged. Again, Harris took the decision on his own, knowing he could not afford to sacrifice further the morale of his men.

Perhaps jet streams were nature's way of simply reminding us that we humans were but transitory occupants of the universe, in spite of our powerful machines of destruction.

19

LOSING THE TWO JIMMIES

It came out of nowhere. You could feel the cannon shells rattling up through the plane, the sound of sheared, tearing metal and ricocheting projectiles intent on finding mortal targets. Even with the incessant noise of the Lancaster's motors, the howling wind and the dulling from helmet and earphones, I could clearly hear the very loud barking of a fighter's cannons. I sensed a jolting muffled thump under my seat and lost count of the shots coming upwards at us but knew we must be fatally hit. An acrid smell launched itself immediately through our vulnerable shelter. It was all so quick, with no warning over the intercom from the two Jimmies.

It was 25 February and we were on our way to our target Augsburg, not far from Munich and a key part of the Reich's industrial system in southern Germany. It was probably not too heavily defended compared with Berlin.

It was on the outbound journey about halfway to target that we were attacked by the fighter. We were passing abeam of Saarbrucken and it was a crystal-clear moonless night. Neither of the gunners saw the fighter. On his second run to finish us off we identified a looming Junkers Ju 88, finally putting a face to our brutal attacker.

Philip came alive over the intercom. 'Damage report. Corkscrewing starboard.'

Engineer Wally lunged out of his seat, screaming through the canopy, 'Skip, we're hit amidships. Large fire just aft of the main spar.'

I could hear their talk through the cabin, but nothing came over the intercom. No words from the two Jimmies. Intercom must be out, I thought. The plane lurched immediately to the right and started to rotate wildly clockwise, diving at the same time. It was a desperate, turbulent ride to evade our enemy. I was hurled against my compartment ceiling and then rammed down hard, right shoulder to the floor, as we levelled out.

Wally howled again in a throaty choking tone, 'Fierce flames, Skip. Fire's not out!' Visibility in the cockpit was now down to about 3 feet, with gagging fumes and smoke making it impossible to breathe.

'Abandon aircraft. Get ready to jump,' Philip ordered, as we pulled up from our first rotation of the corkscrew. If the wing petrol tanks were on fire we knew we had less than 60 seconds to clear the aircraft before our flying careers ended with an exploding fireball. The flames were now streaking aft down the fuselage in a blue shimmering haze of destruction. I suspected both the gunners would have already gone, faced with this inferno and no coms with the skip. Jimmy Brown would have bailed out through the rear turret and Jim Smith would have quickly followed him using the rear exit.

'Get us out, Wally!' Philip yelled before we dived again, this time the other way, reversing the spin of our craft.

The corkscrew was an amazing flying manoeuvre that saved many a crew of Bomber Command, throwing off the hell-bent attack of countless German night-fighters. This steep spiral-like downward curve into the darkness was developed to counteract the increasingly effective Lichtenstein radar beam that could now single out our bombers.

If a fighter came in on the port side, you would corkscrew to port. This was very much the call of the rear gunner. If he called 'Corkscrew port, go!' then the skipper responded immediately. He would put the aircraft immediately into a steep diving turn to port, until he lost some 600 to 1000 feet. He would then pull out of the dive and convert to a steep climbing turn still to port, regaining some 700 feet of the height lost in the initial dive. Then he converted to a climbing turn to starboard and at the top of this climb he would have regained all the height lost. This all happened in the space of half a minute, with a range of airspeeds between 140 and 250 knots. The reverse movement applied if the attack came in from the starboard.

The appearance from top and side of this hair-raising gambit would be like the arc of a curving wave with the aircraft rotating through two separate planes. The effect on craft and crew was a violent shuddering action, giving the alarming impression of a pilot intent on tearing the very fabric of flying from the fuselage of his aeroplane. The gunners were ready, knowing the opportunity they would be given to train their ready guns on the marauding fighter as the relative position of the two combatants changed, that is, if the fighter didn't give up for easier prey after the first dive.

The Lancaster was light on the controls and a dream to handle for the corkscrew manoeuvre by the experienced pilot, although a little more challenging with a full bomb-load. It was pure aerobatics and Philip proved himself to be a maestro at it.

Wally now turned his attention to the escape hatch located at the bottom of the forward cabin. Alan and I grabbed our parachutes from their stowage and moved forward a little, ready to take our turn through the front escape hatch. I was on edge yet surprisingly calm, knowing the need for an ordered approach, if we all were to make it out. We were in this together. I could dimly see Wally toiling down under the pilot's feet, hurling bundles of Window up from the nose of the aircraft. These had been stacked either side of the hatch ready for use, but now threatened our departure rather than protecting us from the enemy.

'Hatch is jammed with Window, Skip. I can't budge it,' Wally confirmed. Suddenly the fighter reappeared, coming in to finish us off.

'Hang on, chaps. Fighter on port beam. Taking evasive action.' Philip coolly warned as once more he threw the aircraft around the sky, his deft hands at the controls. We lost the Junkers in the clouds and levelled out. The nominal 60 seconds to oblivion had passed and the gas tanks hadn't blown. Most of the Window had fallen back on top of the hatch.

Philip spoke calmly. 'Wally check for damage rear. Looks like we're staying put.'

We grabbed the fire extinguishers and threaded our way back up the fuselage to help Wally. Philip had already jettisoned our bombs after our first attack from the fighter. There would be no comfort in having an explosive load of bombs and flares sitting just below a blazing inferno. We discovered that the aircraft hydraulic system had been shattered and set on fire, not the tanks in the wings. The oil burnt fiercely along the port side of the fuselage and was mustered into a kind of blowtorch effect by the gale of wind roaring through the gaping shell holes. The heat was so intense that the aluminium forming the skin of the fuselage melded in red-hot with the raging oil. It was an unnerving sight to witness the very fabric of our metal home ablaze.

Wally reported back immediately. 'Skip, hydraulics are lit up and we have a gash in the fuselage. Both Jimmies have bailed. Getting the fire out.'

Philip steadied the ship on full flaps just to keep her airborne and muttered quietly, 'Gordon, get us home.'

I drew the most direct track I could on my chart, avoiding defended areas and any possible encounter with heavy flak, which in our sorry condition would have spelt our end. I made sure that the heading for home base was well away from our bomber streams and their telltale streaks of grey–white across the night sky. It was doubtful that any night-fighters would bother with a lone aircraft well away from target, when there were such rich pickings to be had on the fringes of our bomber formations.

Most of the blind-flying instruments on the pilot's panel were no longer functioning, leaving Philip to fly virtually on airspeed and altitude. Only a skipper of his calibre would be able to maintain the headings I gave him, let alone land the aircraft safely back at base aerodrome. He was a master, leaving no doubt as to why his rating certificate was endorsed as 'exceptional heavy bomber pilot'.

'It'll be a slow trip home, chaps,' Philip quietly reassured our remaining crew of five as if he was flying a fully functioning Lanc, not a badly wounded bomber. We had no gunners up back for protection. Wally remained there to monitor the damage and keep an eye out.

Eventually, we made it safely back, a mission leaving lasting memories that would drift up from the subconscious even years later, a recurring nightmare of life almost lost. We never did catch sight of Augsburg and didn't return to Berlin.

My flying log book summarised the trauma we endured on that fateful night:

AUGSBURG: 1 X 4000 – 3 X 1000 MC – 4 X T.I. – 5 SBC. flares.
SPECIAL BLIND MARKER
Attacked twice by fighter on outward journey.
Aircraft hydraulics on fire. Ordered to abandon aircraft.
M/U & R/G bailed out.
Escape hatch jammed – fire died down (with help).
Returned to base.

Wally Lee, our intrepid flight engineer had played a major role in our survival on the trip to Augsburg. He was still titled sergeant in rank but held an expertise and ability that would take him far.

He helped Philip to coax our wounded Lanc home and was always there when needed. Philip was to insist on Wally's presence for all his tours until he was finally seconded as personal flight engineer to Sir Arthur Harris, the Commander-in-Chief of Bomber Command, in his Dakota. He was then promoted rightly to the rank of flight lieutenant and flew on a tour of honour with Sir Arthur at the end of the war. There were certain inconsistencies in the system of recognition for war heroes, but Wally was finally awarded the Distinguished Flying Cross and MBE (Member of the British Empire) at the behest of his leader. When asked by his wife, Drusilla, why he received these awards, he replied with tongue firmly inserted in jowl 'for merely doing what was expected of me'. That was Wally, a man with a quiet but well-developed sense of humour, not prone to getting too carried away with himself. He went on after the war to qualify as a pilot with the RAF, undoubtedly inspired and energised by the skill of his wartime skipper.

Wally was a great deal of fun off-duty in our relaxing sessions at the pubs of Cambridge, ready for a laugh and a pint of beer. One of his many jobs on those long operational flights was to throw down the chute bundles of the renowned Window, the diabolical metal strip designed to confuse the German radar. On one of our stand-down nights touring the university town's usual watering holes, I remember him saying, 'If I had a pint of beer for every bundle of Window I have handled, I would be a permanent drunkard.' Young men on a break from warfare were certainly inclined to bend the elbow, not out of boredom, but because they felt they were on an exciting adventure and entitled to a good time. Wally was no exception.

I had been at Oakington for an intense four-month period. Joy was now working almost permanently in London and this thankfully allowed her to come to Cambridge by train on the weekends that

I had leave. These weekends were a godsend, treasured moments of normality where we could share the harrowing experiences of warfare as well as the good times. On the night of the operation to Augsburg it was Joy's twenty-fourth birthday and we had planned to celebrate it together the following day after the mission. We were to meet as always at the Royal Oak Hotel, Cambridge, have a few drinks with the crew and then savour the environs of Cambridge, its historic university culture and haunts for dance and a bit of fun. It was usual for me to meet her at the station, then we would walk back slowly to the hotel, enjoying each other's company and the chance to just chat and be together.

I was not at the station that evening when Joy got off the train. She decided to go to the hotel in the expectation that I would make my way there directly if I had been held up. She told me that, even then, she felt decidedly unsettled as she had no way to find out if anything had happened to me. Uncertainty seemed a constant companion in these troubled times. I had impressed upon her that she must never ring the squadron to make inquiries about me. This was the way things were done to keep order and sense in a chaotic world. I had told her that if anything did happen to me, I had organised that a telegram would be sent to her at her parents' home in Wimbledon Park.

Unfortunately, there was no way she was going to be any the wiser while she was waiting for me in Cambridge. She endured two long hours of endless torment, with no immediate means of resolution, hoping for the best but knowing the odds favoured the worst.

You can imagine her elation when I found my way to the room and just knocked on the door. In her arms I felt the consoling proof that I was truly alive and in one piece. I can still see the intensity in Joy's questioning eyes as she opened that door. These memories stay with you for an eternity.

We quickly put all gloomy thoughts aside. There was no talk of Augsburg or the mission, just about the future, our impending marriage and children. There was no celebratory drinking with the crew that evening. Joy and I were together and that was all that mattered. We had a simple pub meal tucked away in a corner next to the Rock-Ola jukebox. Joy played her favourite, the lilting strains of Vera Lynn 'A Nightingale Sang in Berkeley Square', time and again and then we strolled around Cambridge, the spires of King's College guiding us home. She said it was the best birthday present a girl could ever have. After a long and lazy breakfast, I took Joy to the station to catch one of the few available trains to London and then returned to Oakington for further operations.

We found out months later that our gunners, Jimmy Brown and Jim Smith, both made it down safely in their parachutes, were captured and made prisoners of war. They returned home safely to England after hostilities ended. Still, Philip had to perform the unenviable task of writing to Jimmy's wife in Perth, Scotland, to advise of his loss over Germany. Thoughts passed through my head again about the risks of marrying at a time of war but were quickly discounted by the exultation at finding a companion for life, no matter how long that may be.

Our ever-faithful ground crew took great delight in extracting the splayed 30-millimetre cannon shell that had neatly lodged beneath my seat, slowed in its trajectory by the watchful superstructure below. They happily presented it to me as a memento of my close call of the nether regions. I never did tell Joy.

Our crew was given replacement gunners and a new G3 Lanc and we were next sent to Stuttgart on 1 March. This target was again in the south of Germany and just east of our near fatal altercation point. On the evening following this operation, we were all in Cambridge at the Royal Oak Hotel, the regular crew hang-out, and I found myself chatting to our new gunners, rear gunner 'Taffy' Jacobs and mid-upper gunner Eric 'Hoppy' Dawson. It was less than a week after Augsburg and I was still trying to come to terms with how the two Jimmies, our resolute protectors, could have missed the approach of the German fighter and allowed it to get so close to do such damage. Taffy and Eric confirmed rumours of a new radar-driven German fighter strategy that was giving our bomber forces curry.

I had also heard stories of our aircraft flying into a field of fighter flares ahead of their track, picking them mercilessly out of the darkness. This was followed by a stream of very dim tracer bullets coming from below. The reports came in of Lancasters erupting in flames as their wing tanks were hit. These strikes seemed to come from underneath and astern of the aircraft, giving the rear and mid-upper gunners no chance to spot the assailants.

We were later to learn that we had fallen victim to a new German Luftwaffe technique called 'Schrage Musik' that allowed the fighters to avoid the Lancaster's turret guns and take advantage of its blind spot underneath. It was the worst quarter for visibility compared to looking up into the night sky. Equipped with upward firing guns and guided in by radar in the darkness to a distance of about 1500 feet below our bombers, it was the German radio operator who directed this final approach with the fighter pilot taking over when visual contact was made. Firing would start when the nose of the bomber appeared in the fighter's gunsight and then the Junkers would slow down to let its victim pass over them, while continuing the lethal fusillade.

The Junkers 88G-6 night-fighter was both fast and manoeuvrable and fitted with a special gunsight with a reflective mirror above the pilot's head. This was like a periscope and allowed him to sight the upward-firing guns raked backwards at a 70-degree angle. Special ammunition was used with a faint glowing trail replacing the standard tracer and combined with a lethal mixture of armour-piercing explosive and incendiary cannon shell. Two 30-millimetre Mark 108 upward-pointing cannons dispensed 600 rounds per minute, that's a devastating 10 rounds per second to rip through a Lanc's aluminium and magnesium fuselage, starting an immediate blaze, as if it were no more than paper. The intent was to hit either one of the petrol tanks in the Lanc's wings with a spray of deadly cannon fire. Arguments were later put by the Germans that this means of attack had the honourable intent of starting a fire and forcing the crew to immediately parachute out.

Schrage Musik was the German term for jazz music and derives from the colloquialism for shaky, off-tune music. It literally translates as 'slanted' or 'oblique'. The technique was the brainchild of a Luftwaffe night-fighter ace Oberleutnant Rudolf Schoenert, who first started an experiment with upward-firing guns in 1941. He overcame great scepticism from his superiors and fellow pilots and, working with an armourer Paul Mahle, initially mounted a pair of MG FF/M 20-millimetre cannon in the rear compartment of the upper fuselage of a Messerschmitt Bf 110. He was the first to use it to shoot down a bomber in May 1943. From June 1943 an official conversion kit was produced for the Junkers Ju 88. Schoenert was to become Germany's seventh-highest scoring flying ace and the recipient of the Knight's Cross of the Iron Cross with Oak Leaves, recognising his extreme battlefield bravery and successful military leadership.

Bomber Command was slow to react to this new threat. Rumours of the reasons for the violent flaming explosions lighting up the night sky in the vicinity of the bomber streams persisted. Had the Germans invented 'Scarecrow' flares to demoralise us and simulate erupting aircraft? In fact, there were no such shells, only exploding bombers. Most Lancasters lacked any effective ventral armament, leaving them easy prey to attacks from below. Towards the end of the war they were fitted with a ventral machine-gun turret under the mid-upper gunner station.

Schrage Musik was possibly somewhat over-lyrically described by Max Hastings in his book on Bomber Command as 'the sky was lit by exploding aircraft as frozen gunners, numbed in their turrets, missed the shadow slipping below the fuselage that a few seconds later consigned them to oblivion'.

The Junkers' attack on us finally made sense. Our two gunners had proven themselves too good in the past for them both to have missed the approach of a fighter from any normal quarter. It was our good fortune that the first burst of its 30-millimetre cannon fire was slightly off target, hitting us about 3 feet aft of the wing fuel tanks. Philip had not allowed them any second chances. Our immediate corkscrew had made it difficult for the attacking fighter to gather speed and follow us down in the initial dive. There was also the severe risk of collision, falling debris or an exploding bomb-load to also take the fighter down. He was unable to keep us in his deadly sights.

I had been agonising over the image of the two Jimmies, our brave protectors and compatriots at the rear, ejecting themselves from the safety of our Lanc. Plummeting through the void towards the uninviting earth below, the cold air tearing at their exposed bodies, had they tormented themselves with thoughts of failure, anguishing over their forced desertion of a stricken plane and their fellow crew members? Even if they survived, they faced certain captivity, an end to their flying exploits. Would they come to understand that they had not failed to repel an enemy fighter's onslaught, that there were new tactics afoot to blight the record of the experienced gunner?

There is an intense feeling of emptiness when you lose two close companions in the one hit. Their familiar faces kept popping back into my head at the most unexpected times. Their absence became a constant reminder of the known casualties of war, friends lost from the mess, like a school roll being called at assembly with a punctuated silence for each of those missing.

20

A HAPPY GATHERING

My last operation with 7 Squadron was a goodwill gesture. Group Captain Kenneth Rampling had 'borrowed' me for this auspicious trip, my twentieth with the squadron. He said his navigator was sick but, looking back, he must have known something was in the wind for me. I think he was keeping a watchful eye, wanting to ensure my survival. He was the squadron commander, flying with his men when the situation prescribed it. The destination was Frankfurt and the mission relatively uneventful, with the briefest of mentions in my flying log book. This final foray over Germany lasted a mere 5 hours and 25 minutes. My entry indicated our special role in marking a target obscured by cloud, with zero wind:

FRANKFURT: SPECIAL BLIND MARKER

It was not the recording that was significant but the memorable, striking signature, 'KJ Rampling', signing off my log on the completion of my tour on 19 March 1944. The final underlining stroke beneath his name seemed to emphasise the importance of his intervention in my life. Two days later, he chose to go on another bombing run to

Frankfurt as skipper of Lancaster ND523 for 7 Squadron, replacing one Flight Lieutenant Ferguson. He had got me through to my next posting but was not so lucky himself.

He took off at 19.02 on 22 March 1944 from Oakington but a night-fighter attacked his Lanc at 17,600 feet while he was approaching the target. The Lanc was on fire but Rampling managed to clear the target area before ordering his crew to abandon the aircraft. A few seconds later the Lanc went into a spin and exploded, finally crashing at Sprendlingen. The Commonwealth War Graves Commission records simply state: 'G/C K.J. Rampling DSO DFC 34248 R.A.F. (Pilot) killed.'

Rampling had given his life on his very next operation, to the same destination. This appalling loss was uncanny.

Rampling was a great commander, concerned for all and much admired by his men. With a relaxed temperate manner, he got the job done with a minimum of fuss. A good-looking gentleman of classic Anglo-Saxon cut and complexion, he hailed from Middlesex, was happily married to Kathleen and had a beautiful daughter, Madeleine. With much to live for, he was 31 when he died and was buried with his crew at Durnbach War Cemetery, just south of Munich. It's to men like Kenneth and their families that we all owe a significant debt.

After Augsburg, I had had one last mission with Philip and our recast crew, 'Taffy' and 'Hoppy', to Stuttgart on 1 March 1944. We made it there and back without incident. These last two destinations of my second tour brought 7 Squadron less than half the losses experienced in our recent testing raids on Berlin.

Following our providential return from Augsburg, I was once more in serious contact with the legendary Air Vice Marshal Donald Bennett, leader of the Pathfinders. While I had had several casual meetings with Bennett during my second tour, some at Group Headquarters and others at the PFF Squadrons, none had been for a job. He was a very direct man, some even saying he lacked tact, and he welcomed first-hand feedback on our battle experiences, how marking and navigational techniques could be improved. I relished contact with him.

This time the gist of my demanding interview was the position of group navigation officer, working for Bennett. His present group navigation officer, 'Wingco' Cousins, was to be appointed as squadron commander for a new PFF squadron, No. 635 at Downham Market. This was a break with RAF tradition as previously the squadron commander had always been a pilot. It was a significant development in the force, reflecting Bennett's insistence that every priority be given to navigation.

Our exchange did not last long.

He went straight onto the subject of radar, electronic theory and the radar aids then being developed. I was completely out of my depth on these subjects. I levelled with him that my forte was the practical use of these aids, not the theory behind them. I didn't get the posting but I must have left my mark, because it was this contact that probably was to secure me the position of navigation leader, working with Cousins at the newly formed No. 635 Squadron. On my return from Frankfurt, I had been advised of my new posting to Downham Market.

In contrast to Group Captain Rampling, Bennett could be a bit insensitive. It may have been his Australian origins steering him to call 'a spade a spade'. One night at Downham, all of the squadron's senior officers were in the operations room, listening as usual to the scrambler phone briefing by Bennett for that night's operation. The majority of the squadron were British RAF with their families, wives and babies, located in or near London, as they were not allowed to live at the station at Downham. It was well known that both Harris and Bennett deplored the use of Bomber Command for targeting the German 'Crossbow' sites that were launching 30,000 or more V-weapons at London and the south of England towards the end of the war. These sites were difficult to bomb effectively, with most of their weapon storage deep underground. The frameworks for launch could also easily be replaced if our bombers did manage to hit them. On this particular night, Bennett's briefing went something like this:

'Well, gentlemen, I see that tonight we are to risk our aircraft and waste our resources bombing a buzz-bomb [V-weapon] site in France, just because the limeys can't take it. However, orders are orders and we will do our best.'

I had mixed feelings as I knew what Joy was facing in London, but respected Bennett's realistic assessment of the use of our depleted resources in the air as the war reached a critical point.

I was sad to leave Philip Patrick and the rest of the crew, who were the vanguard in forming the new No. 582 PFF Squadron at Little Staughton. Philip was made flight commander in charge of the squadron's training. He also had to assist the other flight commanders in looking after the welfare of their men and keeping up squadron morale. Training became critical to Pathfinders' ongoing success, with Philip organising the specific training for his squadron; cross-country, low flying, night flying, fighter affiliation, landings (standard beam approach or SBA flights), practice bombing, air-firing, and 'Y' training (ground radar H2S). His experience and ability to teach the art and tactics of battle flying to raw recruits made an enormous difference to their success rates.

My resolute skipper went on to make a further significant impact on the war. With the invasion of Europe only weeks away, he joined a new concentrated attack on targets that would prevent the enemy from rushing troops to the front. These strikes were focused on destroying the vast communications networks that crisscrossed Europe, allowing the Germans to move men and munitions great distances at will. Attacking railway marshalling yards became key with multiple smaller raids, many with less than 100 aircraft, becoming the norm. Target-marking aircraft and master bombers were required for every operation and Pathfinders' resources became stretched to breaking point. It gave you some sympathy for Bennett's position on bombing the Crossbow sites.

Philip continued to fly with the same crew on operations, with my good self being replaced by Alan Drew as navigator I, returning loyally to the crew. Johnny Sage and Wally Lee had been with Philip from the very beginning and the rest of the crew stayed with him, Alan Coleman (navigator II, the H2S set operator), 'Taffy' Jacobs in the rear turret and 'Hoppy' Dawson mid-upper gunner. Jimmy Humphrey, his new bomb-aimer, stayed with him for a time. It was hard to put behind me a group of men with whom I had engineered survival. These characters buoyed you up in the subtlest of ways with a ribbing or a joke or two, nothing serious even though the stakes were grievous. Nineteen missions over Germany, including nine to Berlin, gave us a lifelong bond.

I took up my new position as navigation leader at Downham Market. It was a navigator's dream come true with accurate target marking becoming Pathfinders' absolute priority. I made use of all the extensive resources put at my disposal, setting up equipment for H2S ground- and air-training, as well as training and practice in the Mark XIV bombsight, and more importantly a full realistic mock-up of a navigator's station, suitably darkened. It included an automatic dead reckoning assembly that put increasing pressure on the navigator to work at speed to keep up with this ingenious apparatus. They would replot their chart work from every operation, discovering mistakes made when under stress. I never checked their replots, only ensuring that they were done. I left it to them to learn from their own mistakes, to optimise their own proficiency. The object was to short-cut the navigators' learning process—operational trips being lethal places to use as a training ground.

The first five trips of any tour were statistically the ones carrying the greatest risk. The source of destruction was usually the simple lack of technical know-how and its application in the heat of battle. At

635 Squadron, I flew once a month with crews identified as inexperienced and needing support to get through these first five missions. My thoughts often strayed to Group Captain Rampling and the dangers of protecting the potentially vulnerable and inexperienced, and I had to push thoughts of my impending marriage to the back of my mind.

My first operation was to the marshalling yards at Malines, France, on 1 May 1944, where our aircraft was to act as deputy master bomber, marking the target and circling to assess the results. Our task was to re-mark the target or back up the existing markers as necessary. Then the main force of 132 bombers was directed in to bomb on the flares, left or right of them, and undershoot or overshoot depending on the accuracy of the markers. Only nine Pathfinders Lancasters from 635 Squadron went on this trip, supported by a force of eight Mosquitoes, dropping Window ahead of the attack. I needed to get through this mission and make it to our wedding day. Still, I vowed not to let my conscious hopes for survival impede my performance in the air. Aerial battle was known to take a heavy toll on those who acted cautiously. That night all aircraft from 635 Squadron returned home safely.

It was the afternoon before the happy ceremony and Joy was to face an unexpected challenge to her determination. A simple suitcase was to be her last hurdle to reach our happy day. She had meticulously planned our wedding day for 20 May 1944 and persistently cadged enough clothing coupons from family and friends to fund her wedding dress and going-away outfit. Material was in scarce supply and so mid-length dresses were now the order of the day. While modest, the outfit was smart, yet glorious in pale blue, reflecting Joy's delight in dressing up for an occasion.

She had gone 'up-town' to secure this important purchase, choosing a refined clothing store in Regent Street, London, called Dickins and Jones. This was a department store of the finest standards, and one in which Joy had the greatest confidence. Dickins and Jones had underground cellars where clothes could be kept safely until needed, secure from the onslaught of the V-1 buzz-bombs. Joy wanted no doubt that her clothing would make it to her wedding day. There was already enough uncertainty around the attendance of the bride and groom. A suitcase was required for storage and Joy had especially bought one brand new, duly providing it to the store. As well as her wedding dress and hat, she included her going-away outfit, two pairs of shoes, her night attire and dressing-gown of the finest quality. The suitcase was quite heavy.

Joy left from work the afternoon before the wedding and went straight to collect her clothes. She took the bus home that stopped at the bottom of Stuart Road, Wimbledon Park. It was a bad decision. The double-decker buses were always crowded, with any bags having to be left in a small alcove under the stairs. Having dropped her case, she was reluctantly propelled by the crowd to the front of the bus. She arrived at her stop and was horrified to find her case missing. A very scruffy alternative stood pathetically in its place. With great presence of mind and, in the split second before her stop would pass her by, she took hold of the frayed and faded interloper.

On searching the bag, she miraculously found a name and address murkily presented on a stained square of paper among some rather disreputable clothes. It was twenty minutes away, back on the same bus route. She launched into action, crossing the road to catch the return bus. On arriving, she knocked firmly on the door of the run-down residence.

'Is this George Dainty's house?' Joy inquired, as a woman of timid appearance initially opened the door a tiny crack.

'Yes, dearie,' she replied, 'but he's not here. He's down the pub.' As the woman opened the door further to talk, Joy glimpsed her pristine suitcase in the drab hallway.

'That's my suitcase, right there!' Joy blurted out.

'Sorry, love, you'll have to talk to George. The Pig and Whistle's at the end of the road,' the woman responded, closing the door sharply in Joy's face.

Joy was angry now. Clearly, it was no unintended slip by this George. He knew exactly what he was doing when he grabbed her suitcase. Joy approached the pub, entering through the doorway of the public bar, a territory reserved for English males in the 1940s. The women were only permitted to partake of their delicate drinks in the lounge.

'Where's George Dainty?' Joy demanded of the barman, ignoring the wolf-whistles as she pushed her way forward through the crowded bar.

'George, your young lady's here to see you,' the barman called out in a more than insulting tone. Joy waited patiently for George to appear, not wanting to give any hint of the anxiety she was feeling. A man of slight build edged nervously forward.

Undaunted, Joy went in for the kill, like a prosecuting barrister. 'Is this your suitcase?' Her direct tone reinforced the fact that nothing short of full confession would be acceptable.

George paused. The jig was up. 'Yes, that's mine,' he admitted, 'but listen, love, why don't you come back tomorrow. I'm not ready to go home yet.' His manly bravado was now buoyed by the company of his fellow male revellers.

'Not bloody likely,' Joy retorted. 'I'm getting married tomorrow and you've got my bloody wedding dress.' The words leaving her delicate lips were curt and sharp.

The whole pub seemed to erupt. A swell of cheers from his friends pushed George out the door. He returned with Joy to his house and handed over her case, now apologetic with questionable excuses. Joy made it back home in time for the dinner her parents were holding for all the members of my two crews from 460 and 7 squadrons who could make it to the wedding. Rooms had been booked for them at the Dog and Fox, a quaint little hotel at the edge of Wimbledon village, where our reception was to take place the next day. We men were to take the opportunity for a bit of a stag party that night after the meal. Joy made no mention of the 'suitcase incident' until days later, when we were relaxed and on our honeymoon in the Lake District. She was both amused and slightly chuffed by her triumph.

We were married the next day in a lovely old flint-stone church called St Mary's, on the very crest of Wimbledon Hill. It was a ten-minute walk from the Dog and Fox and I remember enjoying the relaxed stroll, chatting amiably to my wartime compatriots, all in dress uniform and full of the fun of the previous night. It was a sublime morning in spite of being a little overcast.

Joy had asked me to turn and smile at her as she started her journey down the long aisle of St Mary's. She was supposedly nervous, but as I turned all I could see was my glorious girl on the arm of her good-looking father. She was the picture of English confidence and self-assuredness.

Joy's father, William Turner, was a man of imposing stature, clean-cut in his striped double-breasted suit with an upright stance from his days of infantry service in World War I. You could sense his pride and strong support for Joy's decision. I could hardly believe that I was here on the other side of the world about to marry this woman. Joy arrived at my side and my heart skipped a beat at seeing her. I managed a wink of reassurance as she released herself from the button of her father's suit-sleeve, which had become entangled in Joy's headdress. My Australian nod of things being 'right as rain' assured her all would be well, now and forever more.

Our words of lifetime commitment were easily said. The service over, Joy and I walked with confidence down the long aisle, heads held high and brimming with the pleasure of what had just taken place. We rolled happily through the beautiful church nave before reaching the tower exit, where we were greeted by bells ringing out from high in the church tower, defiant in their optimism. We were lucky. Since June 1940, church bells in the British Isles could only be rung to announce air raids or the invasion of the country. With this threat now diminished, restrictions had been lifted on Easter Sunday 1943.

Joy's parents, William and Ada, my best man, Arthur Doubleday, and Joy's matron of honour, Phyll, stood side by side with Joy and me for the photos, captured forever in black and white.

Arthur and Phyll were always our great supports. Having tied the knot the previous year, Phyll had prevailed on her husband to waste no time—they weren't getting any younger and couldn't wait until after the war to have a family. Arthur and I had gone full circle, hesitant about the perils of commitment at the start of our flying service, but now throwing caution to the wind. Life had to go on. Phyll was now pregnant with twins and Joy had chosen their wedding outfits so that her bump would not be too noticeable in these still conservative times.

Both my skippers were there for this happy gathering. Arthur was still in the thick of it as squadron leader, now flying with 467 Squadron, with many shorter but risky missions to France softening up the enemy before D-Day. Philip and Olive had left their son, Ian, in the care of Olive's mother so that they could attend the wedding and stay on to enjoy the reception. Three other members of Philip's crew also came to support me: Wally Lee, our engineering magician always in fine form, 'Sagey' working the wireless with his sardonic sense of humour, and lastly Alan Coleman, who was like my second pair of hands. We had become quite close at 7 Squadron through our navigational partnership in the air.

The wedding ceremony had been a simple affair with limited attendance of Joy's family in these austere times. I had satisfied my requirements of duty to my own family by sending a telegram to my father informing him of our wedding day.

The reception at the Dog and Fox was held in the scullery, the cosiest space for a sit-down function and close to the restaurant. Joy's mother, Ada, seemed to lift her spirits for the occasion, putting aside her grief for her son to make me feel wanted and welcome to the family. Speeches were simple and kept to a minimum. We had a great lunch of special sandwiches and cakes, which were not often part of our diet at this time.

By early afternoon, it was time to change and depart. Phyll had tipped me off that the crew members had been active in dressing our wedding car, a handsome gleaming silver Sunbeam-Talbot 10 saloon, with a bevy of matching shiny tin cans, the deafening noise from behind the vehicle leaving no doubt that we had tied the knot. Once out of sight, the driver pulled up and got rid of them. We made our way more quietly to the Hyde Park Hotel, near Kensington Gardens, for the night. We took a relaxing walk along the River Thames to Westminster and Big Ben, unwinding after the day's proceedings and enjoying seeing these famed sights still standing.

We left by train the next morning for the Lake District. It was as far away as we could get from the war in Europe, four hours north at a relaxing steam train pace. Arriving at Oxenholme, we took a bus to Keswick, our place of refuge. We spent a week at a little pub, the Queens Head, savouring steak pies packed full of tender pieces of real meat and the splendid local ales on tap.

We walked for miles into the verdant green of the magnificent countryside, calm lakes lapping with tranquillity at lush sloping hill-sides. We indulged ourselves with rowing boat trips gliding effortlessly on mirrored lakes, and afternoon teas soaking up the cosy atmosphere of village life. Time was suspended, our war put on hold for seven glorious sun-filled days, where darkened night skies were but a brief visitor after we were long in bed. It was all over too soon and we were forced to go our separate ways, Joy to London to continue her work with ICI, living again with her parents, and myself back to Downham Market to continue my war in the air.

21

THE BUZZ-BOMBS STRIKE

On the very first day of July 1944 I received an urgent phone call from Joy, asking me to ring her at work.

Her phone message was out of the ordinary as we usually made designated times to call and to meet, to avoid any distractions at my end. She understood the dangers the newly married faced.

'It was always such a safe place for us, Gordon,' she burst out at the sound of my voice, somehow needing to reassure herself of her disbelief. 'Arthur was doing a course in London, run by the BBC, to teach master bombers to speak clearly and concisely in the chaos over the target. He had a day to spare at the end of the course, and so he and Phyll arranged to meet at the Regent Palace Hotel, as they always do. Just after twelve noon the next day a V-1 hit and blew the side out of the building. The blast knocked Arthur and Phyll down a flight of stairs, as they were going to lunch.'

I had prepared myself for the worst and simply asked, 'Joy, are they all right?' Two tours had hardened me to the loss of someone close but the uncertainty of not knowing caused the greatest heartache. This had been brought home to me by the loss of the two Jimmies.

They were okay but the blast and Phyll's heavy fall down the stairs would not have done the twins any good.

I later learnt that a V-1 flying bomb had struck the north-eastern corner of the annexe's roof on 30 June 1944. It had taken its toll on the Regent Palace, badly damaging the internal courtyard and much of the surrounding area. A fleet of ambulances and heavy and light rescue team vehicles raced to the scene. By 3 p.m. 38 casualties had been found, including our friends. It took another hour to fully clear the site and the final tally confirmed 168 injured, with 58 of these having to be hospitalised. The reports recorded the death of a poor chambermaid, who was blown out of an upper floor window. Phyll and Arthur were all right.

These German flying bombs created apprehension in the hearts of both civilians and servicemen on leave, supposedly away from the dangers of battle. The sound of the V-1 was most disturbing. It emitted a rasping noise like a two-stroke motorcycle, a distinctive, spluttering 'duv-duv-duv' heralding its arrival. It was the stopping of its buzzing that was the most sinister. It signalled the direct descent of this deadly killer, dropping like a dart to explode in a fireball. It was 21 feet long, made of sheet metal and plywood, with a tapered rocket mounted above the tailplane. Its pulse-jet engine fired at 50 times a second, with a threatening flamed vapour driving its course. It was called Vergeltungswaffe 1, V-1 for short, by the Germans. The word meant 'revenge weapon'.

V-1s were more affectionately called 'doodlebugs' by the civilian population under their assault. This sentiment, I suspect, was more like the fondness one feels for a colourful Queensland diamond python when caged and unable to strike. Mirth and bravado put paid to the odds of sustaining a direct hit. Some say it got this name from the buzzing sound of an English dragonfly, others from the appearance of the terrifying antlion, a menacing insect mistaken for the dragonfly at dusk. In their larval state these insects look prehistoric, setting up traps to guide unsuspecting ants to their sickle-like jaws. They then inject venom and suck out the bodily fluids of their victims. It is a voracious predator.

I clearly remember my parting words to Joy, as I clung to the phone trying to process the news. 'You take care of yourself. Give my love to Phyll and Arthur.' I was quietly confident that Arthur would soon resume flying. My old skip had a country matter-of-factness about him that defied disaster. The harshness of the Australian outback had bred into him the resilience that would overcome yet another near-death experience, this time on the ground.

On returning to Downham, I had focused on my training responsibilities as navigation leader for 635 Squadron. A fully professional orientation was Bennett's catch-cry and the key to a new crew's survival. When Joy phoned me I had been preparing for my own return to the air and my second operation with the squadron. Our target was to be Wizernes in the south of France, one of the rocket launch sites for the V-1s. I had put myself down as navigator II set operator and teamed up with Warrant Officer Shirley, a gallant young pilot fresh to Pathfinders who needed the steady hand of experience on board. We faced Wizernes together on 5 July in clear weather and our TI concentration was well placed. In a trip lasting 2 hours and 45 minutes, we successfully did damage to those extensive German Crossbow flying rocket sites.

We teamed up again on 7 July in a mission to Caen. Visibility was good and marking was 'on the money', with main force bombing in three stages, between the red TIs, directly at the yellow TIs and the third run targeted at the centre of these two TI markers. The purpose was to help the British 2nd armies and the Canadian 1st push forward with force. The Germans were set up in the open lands of the Normandy battle zones, north of Caen, and were blocking

Allied progress. We hit them hard, freeing up the advance for our compatriots on the ground.

Wedged in between these two operations with enthusiastic young Shirley was a mission to Coquereaux on 6 July to mangle beyond repair its German Crossbow sites. I was called upon at the last minute as navigator II set operator to provide navigational and battle support to this young, inexperienced crew. We were also to be accompanied by Wing Commander Brooks, the CO of 635 Squadron. He had replaced Cousins who had been unfortunately killed in battle after just one month of service over Germany. Rank provided no advantages in the quest for survival. Three missions in three days certainly got my adrenalin running, tuning up my skills in the heat of battle.

By August 1944, I was halfway through my third tour at Downham Market. Joy was still living at home as she was not permitted to live with me at the aerodrome. She would come to visit as often as she could, but it was difficult with her job at ICI. The war seemed to be drawing to an end and we decided it would be better for her to live close by in Downham as we would see more of each other. Having already given one month's notice to her work, she was getting ready to go to ICI on one of her last few remaining days of employment. She was filled with the excitement of leaving London, when she heard her father desperately calling from downstairs.

'Joy, get down here now. Get into the shelter.' He was firm. There was no time to spare. He was an experienced air-raid protection warden and knew what he was talking about. That morning, like many others, was heralded by the distant hum from the engines of one of the first generation of V-1 buzz-bombs. He knew from experience that too many poor souls had been caught on their way to protection, assuming the odds would remain in their favour.

'Coming, Dad,' Joy answered as she hesitated to put on her lipstick and grab her handbag for the day. She later admitted to being a little careless, assuming that the bomb would continue on overhead as they had so many times before. As she left the upstairs room, heading for the stairs, she heard the bomb's engine cut out. Terror gripped her.

'Joy!' her father urged, as if to somehow propel her faster to safety. She bolted the treads of the short flight of stairs three at a time and shot into the lounge room at the back of the house. Arriving at the table shelter, the angry arms of her father propelled her into the refuge and he quickly followed. Throwing himself on top of her, there was no time to raise the metal grating for protection at the side.

The Morrison shelter, named after the Minister of Home Security, was a cage-like indoor structure, 6 feet 6 inches long, 4 feet wide and a confining 2 feet 6 inches high. Used as a dining table in the daytime, the family could sleep on the mattress-type floor under the shelter at night, its one-eighth of an inch steel plate tabletop designed to withstand the force of the upper floor of a typical two-storey house falling. It could not withstand a direct hit and only had the supports to hold up the weight of the upper floor, not the whole house.

A deafening sound preceded the bright flash of destruction. The bomb exploded with an almighty blast and Joy and her family plummeted downwards, the floorboards giving way. They plunged into the damp foundations deep under the terrace house. The shelter followed, containing them, still covering their heads. When Joy regained consciousness, darkness was everywhere and the air was laden with the dust from the pulverised bricks and mortar, which had been reduced to rubble. The fine particles made it difficult to breathe.

'Who's that?' Joy remembered asking as she felt a gentle patting on her back. She was confused, disoriented and trying to make sense of the situation.

It was her adored maternal grandmother. Ruth was a very upright, true Victorian lady, never relaxed even when seated. She nearly always

Gordon with his father Ralph and two sisters, Rina, nicknamed Nug, and Rua Jean, at the family home in Montville, Queensland. *Goodwin family collection*

Leaving Bundaberg (*second from left*) in 1939 for the 8th Division, Australian Imperial Force, Redbank training camp outside Brisbane. *Goodwin family collection*

Bombing and gunnery school with Course 70H at Mossbank, Saskatchewan, Canada, after graduating training (*middle row, fifth from right*), with the mighty Avro Anson Mk I in the background. *Goodwin family collection*

Training airmen's 'A' barrack room, Mossbank. *Goodwin family collection*

Flight Sergeant Gordon Goodwin with pipe, now qualified on his flying log book as observer/navigator. *Goodwin family collection*

460 Squadron crew with (*top row*) Gordon as observer/navigator; Flight Sergeant Geoff Carter as wireless operator/air gunner; Flight Sergeant 'Chappie' Chapman as front gunner; (*bottom row*) Pilot Officer Bert Walker as rear gunner; Pilot Officer Arthur Doubleday as skipper; and Officer Commanding A Flight, Flight Lieutenant Oakley. *Goodwin family collection*

460 Squadron provided eighteen aircraft in Bomber Command's first 1000-bomber raid on Cologne at the end of May 1942. Skipper Arthur Doubleday said, 'it was the most successful raid they had carried out'. Six hundred acres were laid to waste, 45,000 people lost their homes with 12,000 fires burning out of control. The cathedral and collapsed bridge over the River Rhine are in the background. *Author's collection*

Gordon (*left*) at the ceremony at Buckingham Palace in August 1942 to receive the Distinguished Flying Medal from King George VI. Although now a Pilot Officer, at the time being with the first crew in 460 Squadron to survive a tour of duty, he had yet to be commissioned. *Goodwin family collection*

Acclaimed RAF pilot Squadron Leader Philip Patrick at the helm of a Short Stirling four-engined heavy bomber on his first tour of duty. *Philip Patrick photographic records courtesy of Ian Patrick*

(*Top row*) Squadron Leader Philip Patrick, Squadron Leader Gordon Goodwin, Flight Lieutenant Wally Lee, Warrant Officer Johnny Sage formed the crew of 'G for George', 7 Squadron Pathfinders, together with (*bottom row*) Warrant Officer Jim 'Smithy' Smith, Flying Officer Jimmy Brown and Flying Officer Alan Coleman who joined them for the trip to Magdeburg on 21–22 January 1944. All the photos of Patrick's 7 Squadron crew, apart from Coleman, are 'escape photographs' to be used for false identity documents if shot down.

Philip Patrick photographic records courtesy of Ian Patrick

Left: Joy and Gordon's wedding at St Mary's Church, Wimbledon, on 20 May 1944, with Arthur and Phyll Doubleday and Joy's parents Ada and William Turner.

Goodwin family collection

Right: Joy waiting at the window for Gordon's return from another mission over enemy territory.

Goodwin family collection

Top: Joy's parents' house at Stuart Road, Wimbledon Park, after it was hit by a V-1 'buzz-bomb' on 15 August 1944.
Author's collection

Middle: A Junkers Ju 88 fitted with upward-firing guns like the one to the right nearly shot down 'G for George' on its way to Augsburg. The weaponry was called 'Schrage Musik' by the Germans.
Author's collection

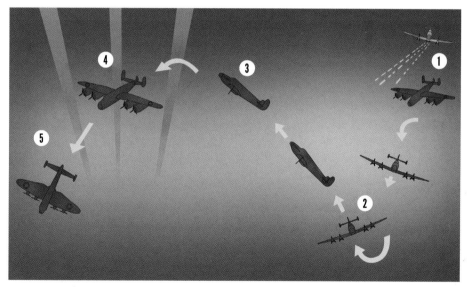

'Corkscrew' manoeuvre by RAF bombers to thwart the attack of a night fighter:
1. Steep diving turn into the direction of the attack at an angle of bank of 45 degrees. Bomber descends through 1000 feet reaching a speed of 300 miles per hour.
2. Maintaining the turn, the bomber pulls up and climbs for four seconds.
3. Rolling in the opposite direction, the bomber continues climbing for four seconds gaining 200 feet in altitude, dropping speed.
4. Bomber then rolls into a climbing turn, again slowing the aircraft.
5. At the top of the climb the nose is pushed down again and, after descending 1000 feet, the turn is reversed and a further 1000-foot descent completed.

Ground crew prepare to load ordinance into a Lancaster prior to a mission. *Author's collection*

635 Squadron Pathfinders air and ground crew. *Goodwin family collection*

Flight Sergeant Vines (*third from left*) and crew, 635 Squadron. He was later promoted to Pilot Officer. *Courtesy of Christopher Coverdale*

WAAFs and ground crew welcoming a Lanc home after a mission. *Author's collection*

Gordon (*fourth from left*) at the delivery flight of a Qantas Super Constellation 1049C, VH-EAH, from Lockheed in Burbank, California, to Sydney on 26 April 1954. *Goodwin family collection*

Gordon (*fourth from left*) at the first trans-Pacific jet passenger service and first Qantas service from Sydney to San Francisco on 29 July 1959, with Boeing 707 VH-EBC, 'City of Canberra'. *Qantas Airways Limited*

Qantas 'Fiesta' route proving flight, Sydney to London via Mexico, Boeing 707 VH-EBM, November 1964. Gordon, seated centre, was Chief Navigator from 1958 to 1971.
Goodwin family collection

Paul Goodwin with father Gordon together in 2009.
Goodwin family collection

The memorial to Bomber Command, finally unveiled in Green Park, central London, by Her Majesty Queen Elizabeth II on 28 June 2012, in the year of her Diamond Jubilee.
Goodwin family collection

dressed in black with skirts down to her shoes. Unperturbed, she was just letting Joy know they were both alive in the compressed cocoon of debris.

'Stay still, no talking,' Joy's father hissed. He began tapping very gently on the edge of the shelter. It took time but they soon heard muffled voices above.

'Keep still, we're digging for you.' The instruction now came from above. A small portal appeared on the side of the shelter where the guard had not been raised, as if they knew where to get Joy and her family out.

'Come on, love, you're first.' Joy hoisted herself with difficulty, as she was lying at the top of the pile, resting on her family. To gain leverage she unwittingly placed her feet firmly into the stomach of her grandmother. Not a sound was uttered.

Joy's mother was next, hauled out and given the fireman's carry by her not-so-experienced rescuer. He had mistimed the move and launched her beyond his supporting shoulder, resulting in an uncomfortable landing on piles of debris strewn across this now desolate place she had called home. More than her dignity had been wounded.

'The house is gone, Dad,' Joy declared as the family stood outside, a new eerie light now pouring into their street. The houses on either side had been destroyed. They were literally gone. It was a scene of total devastation. Only a skeleton of a staircase remained, leading to the bare bones of the upstairs bedrooms. It looked like a doll's house with rooms exposed, the residue of living hanging precariously from the edges. Her father, mother and grandmother had all made it out with Joy. Only her grandmother would need hospital care for her shallow dust-laden breathing. The bomb had landed in the middle of Stuart Road just opposite their house.

'We were so lucky, Joy,' her father reported. The fireman had told him that the heavy metal sheet forming the top of the shelter had buckled with the weight of the rubble. Had it moved any more it would have lost the support of the uprights and they would all have been crushed. If the side guard had been raised it would surely have prevented their immediate escape, adding the danger of time to their extraction.

'It's a miracle,' Joy's mother, Ada, shrieked as she headed towards the rubble. 'He's watching over us.' She pointed towards the wreckage of their house. Lying there for all to see was the air force scarf of Joy's dead brother, Derek, together with a picture of him as a choir boy.

Unbelievably no one in the street was injured. Joy's parents' ginger and white cat, Miffy, was perhaps the only casualty. She had a special spot in the morning sun, snugly perched on the back of a chair by the window in the front parlour. She was never seen again.

It was quickly resolved that they would stay with Bill's sister Gertie who lived only a mile away. She had heard the blast and took them in without hesitation.

On that fateful day, I had been feeling optimistic as we took the upper hand in the skies. Leaving at 10.07 a.m., I was not to forget the day of my first fully daytime mission in years, 15 August 1944. The target was the German night-fighter base at Tirlemont in Belgium. I was acting as navigator, with Flight Sergeant Bobby Vines as skipper. It was a crystal-clear morning and I can distinctly remember the excitement at being able to actually see all the action from 12,000 feet. We were able to report effective marking and resulting success, with the runway severely cratered by the raid and the second run of bombs aimed at the hangars finding their mark. Our fighter nemeses, while still a force to be reckoned with even at this late stage of the war, were stalled on the ground, like angry bees locked away in their hive.

I had been on a previous night mission with Vinesy in July to hit the oil refinery at Wesseling on the Rhine. We experienced an easy run with minimal flak to contend with. All was quiet and, while you can never afford to relax until rubber touches tarmac, we felt the worst must be over. We had reached the Dutch coast and were about to cross the Channel for home. All hell broke loose as an 88-millimetre-gunned flak tower opened up on us from out of the darkness below. On my later reckoning it was from Fort Kijkduin, north of Amsterdam, which we found out was being used as a training fortress for German naval artillery. Vinesy confirmed that it was not his first encounter with this very annoying and unexpected irritant.

So, before we set off for Tirlemont, I had double-checked my calculations as, on our return track, we would again be passing close by Fort Kijkduin. We would hold back one 4000-pound HC cookie blast bomb from our raid to Tirlemont and deliver it as a parting gift to the German folk at the fort. There was good cloud cover on the coast and we were able to come in low and unobserved to make the drop. The bricked rectangular walls of the fortress came into clear view in the daylight as we dispatched our offering, a direct hit on the added top layer of reinforced concrete holding the artillery. The Germans' training would now have to be put on hold and our crews would not have to suffer any further disquiet from this fort at the Dutch coast.

My amusement was to be short-lived. On returning at 3.10 p.m. in the afternoon from this escapade and, after debriefing, I received the unwelcome message that Joy had been hit in an air raid. There was no further information and I had no idea how she was. I phoned her work and was told where she was. I rushed to Wimbledon.

Joy must have seen me coming down the road at full tilt. Who was this very grey, ash-covered person running towards me? I swept her into my arms. She was a ghost of her normally well presented self, but she had made it through.

'Thank god you're okay. The family?'

'We're all fine. Grandma is still in hospital till she gets her breathing right,' she replied. Messages received in wartime were often very finite and life-altering. You just took the good days and wrapped them up forever for safe-keeping. 'Mum's very distraught,' she continued. 'It's the loss of Derek and now the house. She's at breaking point.'

The next morning Auntie Gertie's husband, Fred, went with Joy's father to the bombed house to see if they could find anything. This was a risky venture given the instability of the teetering structure. Joy's father should have known better but he always liked a bit of a gamble. They climbed up the broken staircase and rescued much memorabilia, including all our wedding presents from Joy's bedroom, which had been stored in a cupboard against an inner wall, as well as quite a few clothes and Ada's jewellery. The rescued clothes survived one winter and then displayed an interesting phenomenon. They became riddled with holes, as if the very fabric for living can be shattered by the machinations of war. It was unsettling.

Having endured the mixed feelings of fear and then relief in finding Joy safe, I was once more thrown into action. It was probably a good thing as it released me from preoccupation with what might have been. Only three days after my previous raid to Tirlemont, I was asked to act as navigator II set operator for a crew whose navigator was shaky and suffering 'the twitch', a known indicator of paralysing fear in the heat of battle, and a condition that was a danger to the rest of the crew. I was always happy to stand in when one of my navigators felt he couldn't make the trip.

The skipper of this crew, a wing commander, had also endured this dicey experience on the previous raid to Stettin, a port and industrial area. The pressure had been on them from the outset, as Bennett had chosen 635 Squadron to lead the raid. Their aircraft had difficulties in climbing to bombing altitude. Still they kept going, running in to target on H2S, releasing six clusters of hooded flares at ten-second intervals, then their TIs and finally bombs. Immediately after the drop they were coned by twenty searchlights, followed by a big flash at the port wing. The flak took out the port outer engine with a serious oil leak in the port inner engine. It, too, was failing fast. The Lanc's accumulators ran flat meaning the radio was out of action and there would be no assistance if they were forced to ditch. Their fuel tanks were holed and the rear turret, powered by the port outer engine, was now non-functional. They had to fly four long hours home, lower and more slowly, making them easy prey for flak and fighters. Still they decided to press on, rather than bailing out over neutral Sweden. They thrashed the two starboard motors mercilessly and miraculously made it to the Downham runway. On landing they suffered the last barb of this 'shaky do', swinging perilously off the tarmac with a puncture in their port wheel.

I had hoped our trip to Ghent-Terneuzen in Belgium would be an easier one as the pilot needed a good run to settle himself again into the questionable routine of battle.

We were to attack an oil storage unit, acting as blind marker illuminator. This meant laying a trail of parachute flares in the cloud to lead the main force to target. We went in at an edgy 12,000 feet to drop our illuminating flares and then went back for a second pass, unloading our bombs as directed by the master bomber. It was a perfect run and a massive conflagration ensued from our bombers' efforts with a grey and orange blaze sending thick black smoke to a height of 4000 feet. No opposition of any kind was encountered over the target. It was good therapy for the wing commander and his valiant crew. This success would recharge them and counter the inevitable fright of war.

It was early September 1944 and I had just returned from Lumbres in France with yet another crew on a daylight operation to bomb a V-2 rocket-launching site. The abandon mission call sign 'Fruit Juice'

was given on this one, as the target was completely covered by cloud. Two backers up, there to drop further markers after the lead planes, had swooped down below 12,000 feet to attempt a run over the target, under the cloud. No go—defences were too well primed with heavy and very accurate flak. This was to be the last of my Crossbow duties as Bomber Command had done its job, now moving to other targets.

After Joy's lucky escape, these flying bombs fascinated me. My research revealed that towards the end of November 1943, a number of 'ski sites' for launching them began to appear in reconnaissance photos over northern France. They were large concrete and steel structures, shaped like a snow ski with a hook at the end to catapult these sleek projectiles. Massive storage bunkers were located behind the start to the flat track and this was the target for our bombing.

Hitler had hoped to launch his V-1 flying bomb campaign at a rate of 6000 of these diabolical devices per day, commencing in early 1944. This was to be his twisted New Year's present for the people of London and a warped expression of this despot's sick sense of humour. It was also a desperate counter-measure for his failing fortunes of war. The bombs could reach the south of England, with the majority directed mainly at London.

Bomber Command combined operations with the Allied Expeditionary Air Force (AEAF), which included both the US Ninth Air Force and the recently created RAF 2nd Tactical Air Force, to destroy the camouflaged ski sites. Small forces of bombers, using master bombers to pinpoint the targets, launched concentrated attacks on Crossbow sites. By the end of May 1944, this beautiful blend of American and British forces in the air laid waste to 103 of the 140 ski sites. These offensives were so effective that they caused the enemy to abandon their construction.

It forced the Germans to start building smaller structures for launch, called 'modified sites'. These were much easier to conceal from the rain of our Allied bombs, but the Germans struggled with reliable and accurate mass production and rushed final preparations with the imminent landing of the Allies in France. The introduction of these modified V-1 sites was delayed until the night of 12–13 June 1944 when only ten flying bombs were launched from the now 55 remaining sites. Only three of these rockets ever reached England.

By mid-June 1944, it was well and truly on. The Germans launched 144 bombs across the Kentish coast with 73 of them reaching London. The British authorities were stung into vigorous action. From mid-June to mid-August 1944, Crossbow operations ranked only second in priority to the urgent needs of the battlefield. V-weapon objectives now absorbed 40 per cent of our efforts and reduced significantly our ability to bomb German cities.

Bomber Command was now operating day and night, virtually every day, against flying bomb targets in France. Over 16,000 sorties had dropped some 59,000 tons of bombs against V-weapon targets, concentrating on the larger assembly and storage depots, including the massive quarry site at Wizernes. Britain had also significantly improved its defences against this attack with such anti-aircraft weaponry as shells with proximity fuses, designed to blow the rockets up in mid-flight, cutting the number of these bombs making the capital down to 20 per cent. The last V-1 launched from France reached England on 2 September 1944.

This was not to be the end of it. The V-2, called the Aggregate A-4, was the world's first long-range guided ballistic missile and was meant to be used in an all-out strike to wrest the initiative from the Allies. Earlier Bomber Command attacks on the Peenemunde Army Research Center in 1943 had done much to delay the development of this demonic 46 feet and 2200 pounds of warhead. Lancaster raids in June 1944 against the massive concrete storage bunkers, built into the hillside at Watten, near Calais, also drastically reduced the V-2 infrastructure.

From September 1944, however, they were used in large numbers, with 3000 launched against London, Antwerp and Liege. Fired from mobile sites, using trucks with launch trailers, they were effectively hidden on roads running through dense forestry. With a liquid-propellant rocket engine, they were vertically launched with a single stage. The V-2 propelled itself skywards for up to 65 seconds to a height of 50 miles and then the engine shut down, the rocket continuing on a ballistic freefall trajectory. Given its speed and track, it could not be brought down by anti-aircraft guns or Allied fighters. Unlike the V-1, you couldn't hear it coming. I would be pleased to have Joy out of London.

Although it had the potential to be a lethal weapon for Hitler, the last V-2s to explode targeted Kent in England on 27 March 1945, too late to turn the tide of battle. The earlier delaying efforts of Bomber Command and the later Allied liberation of launching areas relegated these flying machines of civilian destruction to the scrapheap. They were to become the foundation for the future of sophisticated rocketry for intercontinental warfare and space exploration.

Some civilians under the strike of the buzz-bombs remembered them as a constant threat throughout the war, however their onslaught had only lasted a mere nine months.

I had again received bad news from Joy. Arthur and Phyll's beautiful twin boys had been born early and had not survived. It seemed this terrible misfortune would deprive Arthur of his future plans and dreams, denying him the offspring needed to follow him onto the land. When there's trouble, being there is all that's required.

Arthur was now a wing commander of considerable note, in command of 61 Squadron and stationed not far from me, to the north at Skellingthorpe. We had agreed to meet roughly halfway at the Blue Bell Inn, Tattershall Thorpe, one of Lincolnshire's oldest pubs and a renowned haunt of the 617 Dambusters and 627 Pathfinders squadrons. Arthur had done a great job with 61 Squadron, building back morale after great losses over Berlin.

He told me Phyll had taken some time to come to terms with their loss. They both still wanted kids but maybe would wait till the end of the war. Arthur was staying positive. There would be more Doubledays to enjoy the burnishing Australian sunlight of Coolamon.

For me, it was now clear that Joy's mother, Ada, could not remain in London. Joy's father needed to stay for his job with the Electricity Company, so it was decided that he would board with Gertie and that Joy and her mother would come with me to Downham and find lodgings close to the base. After leaving hospital, grandmother Ruth had gone to live with another of her children in London. On the passing of grandfather Edward, before the war, it had been agreed that Ruth would spend three months in turn with each of them.

Joy had left her job and could now happily be not far from me. She would be clear of danger and would only have to contend with my mortality and the counting of planes as they returned from Germany. She had been nearly lost to me on a number of occasions, confirming my belief that civilians were constantly in danger and certainly endured many hardships of war.

Joy, her friend Phyll and my resilient adopted English family had clearly disproved the Bennett drift that 'limeys can't take it'.

22

DUISBURG AND THE DENOUEMENT

Little did I realise that my war was drawing to a close. Joy was safely established in Downham with her mother and it was now up to me to make it through. It was only to be a matter of months, if I kept my focus on the mission at hand. By the autumn of 1944, the war in Europe was at a turning point. Although the Allied armies were sweeping through France and Belgium, the Germans were still holding out in Calais, protected by strong gun positions, particularly at Cap Gris-Nez.

Unfavourable weather conditions, including fog and thunderstorms during September and into the last quarter of 1944, hampered Bomber Command's operations. At this time, I again teamed up with Flight Sergeant Bobby Vines. We had already had two earlier missions together. Bobby was small in stature, almost weedy thin, with a delightful boyish grin that defied fear and ill-fortune in the air. He was masterful at the controls of his Lanc in spite of his apparent lack of torso muscle. I always enjoyed flying with him. 'Vinesy' had yet to be recognised with the rank of officer but in the rush of war it was not unusual for these formalities to be missed, the deserving going unrewarded. He simply took it in his stride.

On return from every mission, Bobby and Flight Engineer Herrick would give their chocolate rations, which were dished out after every raid, to 635 Squadron's Signals WAAF Daphne Pointer. She was their talisman and this ritual bestowing of simple gifts upon Daphne, not only recognised the importance they placed on the supporting staff back at base, but also somehow verified the denial of their mortality each time. It was a nice touch.

I remember having a drink and a smoke in the sergeants' mess after a particularly gruelling trip of his to Kiel, an industrial port on the Baltic, north of Hamburg. He had been part of a determined campaign to again wear down the enemy's oil supplies. This trip in Lancaster PB 435 completed his 30 operations with 635 Squadron. It had been in difficult weather, with more than a hint of haze. They couldn't see the target until a break in the clouds on the run in. Flak had been heavy and the coning by searchlights formidable. Their attack was preceded and complemented by a light night striking force of Mosquitoes from 608 Squadron, also based at Downham Market.

The key to halting German resistance now lay with the oil supply to run their war machine. Ten large synthetic oil plants in the Ruhr Valley were capable of producing one-third of Germany's output. While the shortage of fighting men was limiting Nazi incursion, damaging the morale of industrial workers still lay at the very core of Bomber Command attacks. The destruction of their homes, workplaces and neighbourhood amenities would undoubtedly impact on the output for refineries and fuel stocks. Area-bombing was non-negotiable.

Blanket bombardment seemed to be our only course, but still I pitied the poor German bastards crammed into their shelters below. Nearly losing Joy had perhaps tempered my resolute commitment to total enemy obliteration, civilian or soldier. The message emblazoned in bold print on the exterior fuselage of the Halifax bomber, 'Friday the Thirteenth', said it all: 'AS YE SOW . . . SO SHALL YE REAP'.

This was also reminiscent of the thinking of Bomber Harris as he watched Coventry burn at the start of the war. The enemy must not be allowed to replenish their equipment losses through the Normandy invasion and the wastage of men and hardware inflicted by the Russians on the Eastern Front. The essence of warfare was violence, maintaining the momentum of destruction. The Reich couldn't be allowed a chance to get out from under, to get their weapons and munitions production going again, or to give their refineries a chance to recover. The mantra of winning at all costs had no room for morality or moderation if Allied victory was to be ensured and Nazi domination avoided.

On 28 September 1944, I was off to join the attack on Cap Gris-Nez and the coastal batteries off the French coast of Calais. It was the last of six concentrated attacks in September to break the German hold on Calais and we were to act as deputy master bomber—tactical. The entries in my flying log book were now curt and to the point, as if my war was on the fast track to conclusion. I was ever mindful to remain alert and take nothing for granted. In nine days in September, Bomber Command flew over 3000 sorties and dropped some 8000 tons of bombs against these gun positions. By the end of September 1944, we had cleared the Germans from Calais and the Channel ports. Turning away from Crossbow activity, Harris now used Bomber Command's powerful resources to hit gun positions and support our ground forces. The momentum of war was about to swing in the Allies' favour.

I had reached my ninth operation with 635 Squadron and was now to join in one of the most significant operations of Bomber Command history. On 14 and 15 October 1944, as part of the Second Battle of the Ruhr, Commander Harris had detailed two separate 1000-bomber raids in the space of 24 hours, to virtually finish off the mighty city of Duisburg. It was appropriately called Operation Hurricane. Duisburg, an industrial metropolis with rolling mills and heavy industry, was a great wartime producer of coal and steel, and one of the most important industrial and communications targets in all of Germany. As the Reich's largest inland port, it was located at the junction of the Ruhr Valley and the Rhine.

I chose to accompany Vinesy on the second of the assaults on Duisburg, as he had just returned to action with his crew for a second tour after a month's break. His navigator was still on special leave to get married and I knew Bobby would appreciate a familiar face in the navigator's chair. He had at last been promoted to flight lieutenant, a recognition of his great proficiency as a pilot, always rising to the challenges that fell his way. It was to be the third last raid of my war in Europe.

We were to join up in this all-out venture with the 8th United States Air Force, and Bomber Command was to muster 1013 heavy bombers from all groups, with the added support of a sizeable fighter escort. It was the culmination of Harris's demonstration of the Allies' wartime dominance, through maximum-strength aerial bombardment.

We assembled outside our Lanc in the early hours of the morning of 15 October, awaiting final orders to board for the second run. We talked of our illustrious squadron commander, 'Tubby' Baker, who was held in high esteem by his men. He had certainly got 635 Squadron on the map. The AOC (air officer commanding) Pathfinders Force had chosen our squadron to lead these double raids on Duisburg, with responsibility as both master bomber and deputy master bomber. Tubby had prevailed upon the ever-willing ground crew to ready our available strength, eighteen lusty Lancasters, for the two successive journeys to this industrial powerhouse in the Ruhr Valley. Ground and aircrew alike would do anything for him.

Tubby was of humble origins, born in Bristol. The railways were in his blood with three years spent as a clerk with the London, Midland and Scottish Railway, before joining the RAF in March 1940 to train as a pilot. He was stocky in build, hence his nickname, and of good humour. In contrast, he was ruthless in his pursuit of the enemy. He relished seeking out Hitler's lifeblood of industrial might. He believed that when the squadron was stood down, it really stood down. There was no time for unnecessary parades or 'make work' projects to give the appearance of being busy. There was a meticulous emphasis on detail, every crew member understanding the plan and their role in it. With no room for complacency, Tubby Baker's simple focus was on success. He got the best out of his men.

All eighteen aircraft from 635 Squadron had made it back safely from the first early morning raid to Duisburg. Our normal full complement was twenty Lancs, a mix of Mark I and Mark IIIs. Tubby had detailed himself for the first operation and, having made it back, was now standing aside so another crew could go. By 1215 hours, our crews headed from debriefing to their billets to freshen up, grab a shower and shave, resting up before the next briefing which was to be at 1800 hours. Take-off time was scheduled for 2000 hours.

The ground crews had been ready for the squadron's return from the first attack on Duisburg. The moment our aircraft had touched down, they were waiting to assess any damage and get the maximum number of planes back into the air for the second operation. They had worked tirelessly to repair the damage and service the engines. It had been bloody cold with lousy weather. 'F for Freddie' and 'J for Jeg' were in need of some bigger repairs and were withdrawn before take-off. Another aircraft had problems with correct start-up and, because of the danger of breakdown during taxi, was scrubbed. Thus only fifteen of our aircraft were to make the second trip to Duisburg, ten of these being manned by the same gallant crews as the first trip; an outstanding effort.

Several other squadrons struggled to prepare their returning aircraft for the evening operation due to high levels of flak damage. Bomber Command had no choice but to delay take-off until early the next morning, 15 October, at 0100 hours. We had been ready, but now had a further five-hour wait before departure.

The prize of Duisburg lay at the end of a wide, snaking river that wound its way through the low-lying hills to target. On the first mission all aircrews were able to clearly identify the target in spite of 6/10 strata cloud in the area and very few clear breaks in the puffy mantle over the aiming point. Bombing was accurate and intense, overcoming the enemy smokescreen put up to hamper our efforts. Fires erupted like small active volcanoes, with black billowing smoke remarkably rising from the target to 7500 feet. Flak was heavy but no enemy fighters were seen.

The weather was better for us on the second run, with no cloud and good visibility. There was still some smoke and haze over the target, but Duisburg was easily identified by the glow of fires blazing into the night, guiding us in to wreak more havoc. On our second assault, 635 Squadron brought a further devastating payload to finish the job. Christopher Coverdale's book *Pathfinders 635 Squadron: Definitive History March 1944–September 1945* records the tally:

32 × 250lb TI's green.
9 × 4000lb AC Minol cookie blast bombs.
16 × 1000lb MC bombs.
73 × 500lb GP bombs.

We bombed in a concentrated eight-minute period from 0321 hours, our Lancs delivering their assault from a range of 19,000 feet down to 15,000 feet. Main force bombing was extremely well concentrated. There was slight to moderate flak with approximately 50 searchlights coning our aircraft, intent on stopping the onslaught. Again no German fighters were to be seen on this second devastating raid.

This double attack on Duisburg was to be Bomber Command's peak effort for any 24-hour period and delivered a far greater weight of bombs than had been dropped on the enemy in the infamous ten-day Hamburg ordeal of July–August 1943. Duisburg surpassed Hamburg, which had been nominated by Bennett at the time as our greatest victory. Tonnage of explosives and incendiaries carried by Harris's bombers, again from the statistics in Coverdale's book, tell the story:

No. of Bombers	High Explosives	Incendiaries
First Daytime Attack 957*	3574 tons	820 tons
Second Night Attack# 1005	4040 tons	500 tons
(*1015 dispatched # 2 waves, 2 hours apart)		

In spite of the city's wide-open spaces between built-up industrial zones, the whole town of Duisburg was seemingly ignited, with widespread damage and large areas completely devastated. Thyssen's steel plant, warehouses round the docks, marshalling yards, the main railway station, boatyards and building barges were all burnt out. This key producer of coal and steel was brought to its knees, cutting the rate of production of replacement war machinery and operating fuels.

Destruction on an unparalleled scale was our signal of intent, city by city, to prove the futility of continued resistance and end the war sooner.

I faced two more long missions of six hours apiece, the first ten days before Christmas and the second just after New Year 1945. These last two, the duo of my denouement, were to be the longest trips I was to have with 635 Squadron as navigation leader. I joined with 341 aircraft of Bomber Command to bomb Ludwigshafen, doing great damage to the chemicals manufacture of industrial giant IG Farben, including synthetic oil production. These oil plants had been closely involved in the improvement of German gasoline quality by dehydrogenation.

I was then with 500 bombers to hit my last target, Nuremberg, destroying this extensive Nazi industrial headquarters. It was symbolically located in the centre of Germany and had been the site of the original Nazi Party rallies. Flak was heavy but our luck held with no physical damage to our craft or crews. My resolve was certainly being doubly and sorely tested before I would be allowed to complete my nine months' service and final mission.

I vividly remember touching down from Nuremberg, for the last time at 2206 hours on 2 January 1945. It was pitch black, a moonless dark night. Snow had been cleared from the tarmac and I can still see and feel in my bones the surreal effect of the mounds of white beside the strip, welcoming me back like ghostly rows of belated Yuletide snowmen. The ground crew were there to see their charge home, our muted landing lights picking up their smiling faces, the dedicated men and women lining the track in the bitter cold. For my last three missions I had started recording the actual aircraft numbers in my flying log book. This is hard to explain, something I had never done before. I think I simply wanted to memorise, etch into my brain and history, the brilliance of the Lancaster and all my superb flying war machines. Those last three representatives were ND 877, PB 435 and PB 555.

Vinesy had finished up a month or so before I did. He had had a good run and the crew and he felt they didn't need to tempt fate. They had done ten more operations with 635 Squadron after Duisburg. Their last raid was early December 1944 to the synthetic oil plants at Merseburg and it wasn't an easy one. Bad weather made it impossible and one of his good mates and crew copped it. They all decided to call it a day at 41 ops.

Tubby Baker had also made it through. He was amazing. Apparently he attacked Wuppertal in daylight on 13 March 1945 and on landing was told by the CO that he had been grounded. He had completed his 100th operation. The story had it that he almost had to be dragged from his Lanc on touchdown. He was not one to go quietly. Every one of Tubby's bombing operations was completed during the height of the strategic bombing war, when enemy defences were at their most effective. The average life expectancy of a bomber pilot was some ten sorties.

Bomber Command finally got the German battleship *Tirpitz*, which Bennett had earlier attempted to bomb. For me the sinking of this German naval juggernaut was a premonition of the end of World War II, in Europe. Even though she had only once fired her guns in earnest off Spitsbergen in September 1943, it had become a symbol, a quarry that could not be forgotten.

On 12 November 1944, Operation Catechism was the final operation by a force of 32 Lancasters from two squadrons who dropped 29 Tallboy bombs on the ship with two direct hits and one near-miss. The coup de grâce for the *Tirpitz* was a hit amidships, fittingly between the aircraft catapult and the funnel, Bennett's favoured spot, blowing a very large hole into the ship's side and bottom. There was significant flooding and within ten minutes a severe list to port caused the captain to issue the order to 'abandon ship'. Half of her crew was sadly lost as this mighty battleship tipped slowly onto her side in the shallow fjord, the red paint on her suppliant keel signalling surrender. Several other bombs had landed within the anti-torpedo net barrier and caused significant cratering of the seabed and, with the removal of the sandbank, the ship capsized. The *Tirpitz* rolled over and buried her superstructure into the sea floor, with the wreck remaining in place until well after the end of the war. It heralded the end to German tyranny, even the most powerful eventually facing vulnerability and defeat. Bomber Command had done their job. And I am pleased to say that it was the mighty Lancaster that dealt the final blow from the air.

Kiel was the target for the very last RAF bomb of the war dropped on Germany. The city and date of delivery were inscribed in chalk, 'Kiel. May 2nd 1945', on the side of the resplendent 4000-pound

'Cookie' blast bomb. This final attack was to prevent a last stand by German troops, who were planning to make a break for Norway. It was secured into a Mosquito bomber, the powerful twin-engined bandit, and was from Pathfinders 608 Squadron, Downham Market.

I had completed a total of twelve operations with 635 Squadron. The squadron's motto was *Nos ducimus ceteri secunter*, 'We lead, others follow', reflecting our success, and the value of a skilled leader with an egalitarian approach. Skippers like Vinesy gave it their all.

At the heart of the squadron's badge was a dexter gauntlet holding three flashes of lightning. This powerful mailed fist symbolised our heavy striking force to Winston's 1940 formula and the flashes of lightning, arcing outwards, demonstrated our valued provision of light for target indication. The background of nebuly represented the clouds in the sky, with deeply interlocking curves of white on a backdrop of royal blue. These ever-stretching blue heavens with their glorious puffs of iridescent white were often our protectors, shielding our unified formation of mighty Lancs as it ground relentlessly onwards to the next key target. We had felt impervious.

I was filled with mixed emotions as the final chocks engaged our wheels at standstill. I reflected on my questionable crossing of the Atlantic in a smaller-scale Hudson, with the grim possibilities of sea rescue. I remembered the intensity of my second mission with Arthur in a Wellington bomber, the murderous flak and coning searchlights. I revelled in the miraculous contortions of flight pulled off by Philip, to disengage us from the enemy. The superb flying of my skippers, the skills of the tail gunners and the rest of my crews had got us through. My total flying time was logged at 795 hours, with 65 total operations flown. Tubby Baker duly signed off at the bottom of my flying log book, authorising the end of my war in the air.

I was going to miss the roar of the four thunderous Packard Merlin engines and their burning machinery smell, as sparking gasoline puffed white–grey plumes of ignition into the cold night air.

Most of all, even as my years rolled by into their nineties, I could never forget the camaraderie of young men, hell-bent on marking targets and making questionable missions of survival. The dreams and nightmares of warfare would always stay with me.

In late January 1945, I was appointed to the Pathfinder Training Unit at Warboys in Huntingdonshire as Chief Ground Instructor for Pathfinders. Life was to be idyllic, three months of normality with Joy by my side. I found accommodation for us and her mother at a charming inn nearby, called The Old Ferry Boat. This historic pub was ideally located on the banks of the River Great Ouse, in the tiny hamlet of Holywell.

The Old Ferry Boat had a mere seven bedrooms and a homely snug atmosphere with well-padded, enveloping armchairs near the bar which made us feel welcome. I had a living-out pass and would happily cycle the 8 miles to work from this haven each day, through the glorious Huntingdon countryside. It is hard to put into words the release of not having to face being shot down, the delight in just sharing a bed with Joy and knowing that she and her mother were safe. I got to know Ada and she became more relaxed.

The wife of the inn's manager had unfortunately just lost a child through miscarriage and so Joy and Ada pitched in, happy to cook meals and help behind the bar. Joy even learnt to pull a good beer. She loved to talk to the patrons and we found the pub to be full of men of all nationalities, some of whom had been dropped behind enemy lines on intelligence work. She said they would chat away quite openly to her about their experiences as they breasted the bar, seemingly keen to join in the celebration of survival.

We delighted in taking a punt out during the warming days of spring, revelling in the extending daylight hours. It reminded me of my misspent youth and expeditions with my cousins Jack and Guy on the Burnett River at Bundaberg. The simple things brought delight, the enjoyment of living taking on a new meaning. Three months of absolute pleasure gave us time to ease back with no responsibility and yet endless possibilities as the war drew to an end.

Quite suddenly and unexpectedly I received a call from RAAF headquarters at Kodak House in London. I was informed that Scotty Allan of Qantas fame was in London from Australia recruiting flight staff for Qantas operations after the war. I talked it over with Joy that night and we had no doubt that it was our best prospect. The war had brought me a skill and a standing beyond sugar boiling. At the interview with Scotty I asked a lot of questions about the future of the Qantas operation. I was excited about their plans to become a round-the-world airline. I would be in on the ground floor. My proven skills at the highest levels for navigation as squadron leader had given me my ticket out of the science of sugar into the new profession of civil aviation.

I met up with my old skip Arthur Doubleday. It was hard to comprehend that my war was over and that I would now be starting a new life with Joy back in Australia. She had survived her own life-threatening struggles.

Arthur and I met at the Strand Palace Hotel where Arthur was staying, the Regent Palace no longer a happy place for us. The Strand Palace was an art deco showpiece, a stately hotel. With the blackout lifted, it was the ideal spot to see floodlit Fleet Street, Trafalgar Square and the glorious dome of St Paul's, searchlights now weaving their shafts across the sky in celebration. Arthur had joined many of his Australian RAAF compatriots on the fifth floor as they prepared to celebrate the conclusion in this theatre of war. This was a most unusual time, as some young men let their inhibitions unleash, concentrating their lost innocence into wild uninhibited revelry and drunkenness. Others just escaped to their quarters or went to the pictures for a quieter evening.

Arthur and I had forsaken the livelier bars at the Strand Palace, agreeing on a quieter locale to catch up. We had opted for The Coal Hole, a quaint little pub just a couple of minutes' walk down The Strand, neatly tucked in to the right of the Savoy Hotel.

Arthur was planning to head off to America to fight in the Pacific War. Phyll didn't want him to leave, but he felt he had to keep going until it was all over. As it turned out, Arthur never made it to the war in the Pacific. Events overtook him and perhaps he earned a justified reprieve, having given so much dedicated service already to his country. He had earned a return to the family property at Coolamon.

I explained to my good friend that I had actually found myself with this lousy war. I could not see myself returning to my life in Bundaberg. I was to leave the next week on a Qantas Lancastrian, the name for a Lancaster bomber converted for civilian use. Bound for Sydney, I would be acting as relief navigator so they could check me out. I was then to transfer to the RAAF in Sydney where I would be demobbed, so I could join Qantas.

I had spent the best part of four years at war and was now to leave from Hurn Aerodrome near Bournemouth, a place close to where I had first been inducted into British life at the reception unit for overseas crews. Here I had faced the bitter cold of this land's surrounding ocean, before taking to the air in a Wellington bomber. My time in England had come full circle.

The next day I had a short training run with Qantas, before flying out the following day for Lydda, then Karachi with the final destination after Learmonth in Western Australia being Mascot, Sydney. It would take us a total of six days to get there. Little did I realise that I would not see Joy again for ten months, abandoning her to pack up and cross the seas on her own, leaving her home and family behind.

I was now released from the searchlights, the fear of flak and the frenzy of fighters coming at us. My only danger now was the weather, the robustness of our machine of the air and the great oceans of the world that I would be flying over. By now, it had been confirmed that the two Jimmies had been released from capture and were already on their way back home. Joy was free from the buzz-bombs and I now had to depend on the memory of our three months drifting together on the Great Ouse.

By February 1945, the end of the war in Europe had been clearly in sight, with the Russians in strength across the Oder River and the Western Allies likewise across the Rhine. Still no one would venture to surmise that it would all be over within less than three months. The end of March had delivered to Churchill the clearer picture that Germany was on the point of collapse, probably hastened by the unrelenting area attacks continued by Bomber Command with undiminished force. There was no room for complacency among those still flying, with a raid against the south German town of Nuremberg in March 1945 producing a staggering 8.7 per cent of planes missing.

Bomber Harris had got his wish, building up Bomber Command to nearly 100 operational squadrons by the end of the war, compared to the paltry 23 in 1939. It was the British area offensive on Germany's major towns that was the predominant cause of the limitation of Hitler's war machinery output, at the necessary cost of the whole-sale slaughter of 300,000 civilians and another 700,000 injured. The effectiveness was unquestionable, but the morality remains still open to controversy.

Many years later, when I was living in Sydney, a new German neighbour arrived on the block next door. He was an accomplished builder and was to build his house from the ground up. Dieter related his first-hand experience of an RAF bomber attack. He was on leave from training and walking to his parents' home in Essen. After more than twenty years, he could still vividly describe sighting, through partial cloud above, two of our Lancasters. He recalled the forbidding drone as our aircraft came in and out of view menacingly through the misty haze of the night sky. He reported the devastating results of area-bombing, the whistling of bombs, the wilful demolition of buildings and whole blocks of flats, as the crushing impact of detonation and a hurricane of wind spread the firestorm. His parents had survived, his father putting out the fire in their third-storey roof, domestic property being of secondary importance to the German fire services. Dieter had vividly brought to life for me the human toll resulting from our bombing.

My thoughts strayed to Joy's encounters with the V-1 rocket bomb in London. The Germans were also keen to evoke terror, fear and apprehension, the full psychological effect of the unpredictable, in civilians. The V-2 was then sent by the Germans later in the war as a 'vengeance weapon' to flatten our Allied cities. The 1358 V-2 attacks on London from September 1944, although failing in their execution, still killed an estimated 2754 civilians, with another 6523 injured.

The stats on the Lanc tell the story from the Allies' point of view: 7377 were built for war and 3922 were lost in action. Of the total of 125,000 men in Bomber Command, 55,573 were killed. Seven per cent were Aussies. It must be remembered that it was the men of Bomber Command who paid the highest price with a total casualty roll, including the wounded, of more than one in two.

Churchill, as early as September 1940, recognised that the bombers alone provided the means of victory. In his words:

We must therefore develop the power to carry an ever-increasing volume of explosives to Germany, so as to pulverise the entire industry and scientific structure on which the war effort and economic life of the enemy depend . . .

Bombing and warfare were indiscriminate, with both sides trying to win at all costs, civilians and armed forces caught up in the carnage. The pundits may ponder, but for me Bomber Command and Pathfinders should not come into question over area-bombing. It was warfare. Maybe, at the end of the war, the moral questioning was just the propriety of politics at play.

23

QANTAS AND A NEW LIFE

Out over the Arabian Sea, on my third full day of flying between Pakistan and Ceylon (now Sri Lanka), the penny finally dropped. I no longer felt the apprehension and tightening of the stomach as the trip unfolded, the anticipation of arrival at target, facing the lethal lottery of enemy ground resistance, and the dreaded fighters on the return journey.

I was second navigator flying with the consummate Captain Thomas. He was of calm demeanour, his face prematurely lined through his long years of aviation with Qantas, before and during the war. He was a man of mettle, much needed for his civilian service, which had included troop transportation and recovery, not to mention the vital postal links to England. He had had to endure such things as a 30-hour journey in a Catalina flying boat fitted with a large (eight-sectioned) auxiliary fuel tank in the fuselage to enable the crossing of the Indian Ocean. It had involved the tricky unsticking of a supremely overloaded flying machine from the water to allow the delivery of diplomatic mail and microfilm for the armed forces. Operating in radio silence, using only celestial navigation and dead reckoning for the 5652-kilometre hop between Perth and Koggala Lake, the largest natural lake in Ceylon, it had been a tense and lonely flight over the vast and unforgiving ocean.

He had my complete confidence. We flew for roughly nine hours each day with an early start at around 0400 hours. Our crew were the stewards of transport to Australia for Qantas's second Lanc, one of only five that were to be on hire from British Overseas Airways Corporation (BOAC), to commence the Qantas round-the-world service. I was quietly elated.

We were in a very different breed of Lancaster from the ones I'd been flying in. This one had added fuel tanks instead of bombs to get us the distance. This did make for a smell of gasoline as the vapour had an uncanny ability to find its way into the main cabin as the flight proceeded and was particularly exacerbated with the switch between tanks in the bomb bay.

Passenger comfort was far from indulged on this basic machine of war. Three couches were positioned along the left side of the aircraft, giving seating for nine passengers by day. Three bunks could be lowered from above these couches, only allowing six to sleep in relative comfort at night. There were no windows on the port side and the starboard windows were badly positioned, making it impossible for the travellers to see the ground, as they stared interminably across the fuselage. The same substantive spars of metal, tethering the Lanc's wings, now acted as an unwelcome barrier for the lone steward dispensing food and drink in flight. Five crew were needed and only six passengers could be reasonably carried on the long journey.

The Qantas Lancastrians helped establish a fast Sydney to London service. Travelling at a remarkable 230 miles per hour, they could make the journey in 67 hours compared to the nine and a half days it used to take in 1939. Initially, this express excursion was flown weekly. It was so different from my European and Canadian exploits. I felt like a true citizen of the world, civil aviation now releasing me from the narrow country experience of my childhood.

When our aircraft arrived in Sydney on 30 April 1945 I returned to Bradfield Park, where I had completed my initial RAAF training some four years earlier. I duly checked into the officers' mess, mindful of all that I had been through, and how only Scrubber Scott had ever prepared me for the real rigours of war, with his mantra of focus and casting aside of hope. The bar was fairly well populated with a number of senior officers round my own rank, so I found it hard to understand the chilly atmosphere there. No one offered to buy me a drink, no one came over to have a yarn or to ask me to join their group. They were pointedly unfriendly. I got to talking to an aged squadron leader pilot, who was on the staff at Bradfield when I passed through on training. He was truly ancient, having flown such things as the Sopwith Camel over the Western Front in World War I.

He was able to provide the much-needed insight for my frosty reception. I had thought that these disdaining officers would want to know a bit more about the war in Europe and the experiences of Bomber Command. He explained that while I had trained and done my time here at Bradfield, I had then gone off to another theatre of war. With the ensuing war against Japan, they somehow misguidedly thought I had deserted my country.

I countered that when we had all left for final training in Canada, we were surely on our way to do our country's bidding to help repel the attack on the empire. Australia was far away from battle and Japan hadn't even entered the equation. He agreed but went on to outline their evident resentment. These guys lacked my first-hand war experience and were perhaps a little bit apprehensive. My decorations and exposure to battle were probably daunting for them as they faced their own moment of truth in the Pacific.

The squadron leader had had a similar experience after World War I. No one could really understand what warfare was like. It was no picnic, but when he came home the world had changed and it was almost impossible to share it with someone who hadn't been there.

In the end, he just chose not to talk about it. I was really surprised at the attitude of these RAAF personnel at Bradfield. In England, we were united in our efforts—British, Australians, Canadians and even the Americans—all working as one just to get through. It was a bit rich coming home to find yourself resented, with no appreciation of what you'd been through. I let my wise confidant know how much I appreciated his counsel, his friendly face. Qantas would have to be my reward.

I spent six long weeks at Bradfield Park, trying desperately to be demobbed from the RAAF. This included one abortive trip down to the air board at RAAF headquarters in Melbourne, where I was told surprisingly that things would have to take their course. Again, there was no real recognition and appreciation by the Australian authorities of my service in Europe and over Germany. I contented myself in seeking a bit of a diversion in the small library at the camp, where I came across an annual publication called the *RAAF Log*, which sought to informally document the service's activities in 1943. I passed some time perusing the stories of the Pacific Front, the Battle of the Bismarck Sea, Milne Bay, Timor, the Solomons and North Africa but was surprised to find that less than a fifth of the stories covered the war in Europe, at the very height of Bomber Command's activities.

The first article of the log recorded the detail of the first member of the RAAF to win the Victoria Cross. Flight Sergeant Rawdon Hume Middleton was serving with No. 149 Squadron RAF in England and received this much-admired award posthumously for sacrificing his life so that those of his comrades might be saved. He was a country boy from Yarrabandai in New South Wales, not too far from Arthur's property. There was something about the spirit of Australian country boys. His award recognised a devotion to duty, in the face of overwhelming odds, that is said to have been unsurpassed.

In spite of a substantive wound—a shell splinter that tore into the side of his face, destroying his right eye and exposing the bone—and severe injuries to his body and legs causing major blood loss, he continued to fly. He experienced momentary loss of consciousness but, on coming to, insisted on making for the English coast. He experienced diminishing strength from his wounds but still fought off enemy fighters many times on this perilous journey. With five minutes of fuel left, Sergeant Middleton ordered the crew to abandon the aircraft, while he flew parallel with the coast for a few miles. Two remained in the aircraft to help him, but it crashed into the sea killing these brave men. They typified the sacrifice made routinely in Bomber Command.

On 4 July 1945, I eventually became officially ex-RAAF, finally able to join the Qantas staff but it was not until 20 August, after the conclusion of the war in the Pacific, that I became airborne again. I flew a trip a month until just before Christmas 1945, in one of the Qantas Lancasters, the pride of the airline's new international fleet. It was essentially from Mascot to Mauripur in India or Negombo in Ceylon, where we would stay at Speedbird House before the return flight. A BOAC crew would then take the passengers on to England and we would await the arrival of another flight from the motherland and take these passengers back with us to Sydney. Each time I would be away for between two and three weeks, with eight to ten days off between trips. I flew in Lancaster G-AGLX on four occasions in this period. This was later to haunt me.

Even with the end of the war in the Pacific, there was still no indication when Joy might be coming out. In this early stage of my Qantas career, I had not been able to fly back to see her so letters and limited phone calls were all we had. It was a lot to ask of Joy, but she remained stoic and committed.

Joy and Phyll had been talking about coming out together on the same ship but Phyll got organised more quickly than expected and left before Joy.

Joy's parents were able to rent the upper floor of a very old house in Wimbledon while waiting for their house to be rebuilt. Joy was always one to show initiative and she secured a job with a local engineering firm as secretary to the general manager. She stayed with her parents before she received notice from Australia House of a berth on a ship leaving on Christmas Eve 1945. With due confidence she advised them she could not leave her parents then, as it would be their last Christmas together for a long time. She secured a place on a troopship, the *Rangitiki*, leaving on 2 January 1946 for Australia and New Zealand. The trip would take five weeks.

Joy was to join one of the many 'bride ships', there being 110 in all, making 177 voyages to Australia with servicemen's wives, fiancées and children granted free passage under the auspices of the Repatriation Commission. I took some leave in January and February 1946 to prepare for her arrival in Melbourne.

It had been hard for Joy leaving her family, but her father had been rock solid in his support. Her mother made things as easy as she could, telling Joy to go quickly. Her best friend from school Joan Woods, 'Joey', was waiting in the taxi to go to Wimbledon station. She somehow spirited Joy away with a positive enthusiasm, travelling with her on the train to Kings Cross station. Joy's boss in the engineering firm, Waggie Oura, took a personal interest in all those who worked for his company and with the staunch support of these two, Joy boarded the boat train for Tilbury. I have felt forever indebted to them.

Life on board ship was fairly tranquil for Joy. Passengers on a troopship were not allowed to disembark, as the war had only finished four months before. Early in the voyage she faced a tumultuous storm in the Bay of Biscay. It had been extremely hot and humid as she travelled down the Suez Canal and she languished for several weeks in the Indian Ocean before the *Rangitiki* eventually arrived in Fremantle. She had felt far from home.

Joy made no secret of the fact that the wives on the ship were certainly in demand for dancing, deck tennis and table tennis, there being only 40 girls to the 400 Fleet Air Arm officers, returning home to New Zealand. She felt herself fortunate to be sharing a deck cabin, made possible by my rank. Most of the other wives were consigned to travelling below deck, which was difficult when there were stormy seas.

Joy never let me forget her arrival in Melbourne. She talked of looking longingly at the lights of Melbourne, as the ship lay out in Port Phillip Bay ready to dock the next morning, trying to imagine my face after nine months of separation. She had talked to me of the unnerving story of her cabin mate, Sheila, who had boasted to her that she had been drunk at her marriage ceremony and could hardly remember what her husband looked like. It did not help matters that I was sporting a felt hat with a wide brim, such as country people wear in Australia, as well as a dark grey baggy striped suit, the only one I possessed and given to me when I was demobbed. I looked nothing like the man she had known, resplendent in RAAF officer's uniform. I was waiting on the dock when the ship came in and spied Joy standing at the rail of the top deck, watching for me. She was a glorious sight, petite, familiar and sublimely pretty.

On boarding the ship, I found Joy waiting in the queue to go through customs. I sidled up beside her removing my hat. 'You're here at last,' I blurted out to announce my arrival.

'It's you,' she responded, I think amazed that she had been fooled by my attire. 'The hat's got to go,' she confirmed with a smile.

We embraced as if the months hadn't mattered. Disembarking, we took a taxi back to the Menzies Hotel, booked for the night. Unfortunately the Fleet Air Arm boys had got wind of our destination and were quick to join us that evening for a night on the town. We could not disappoint our New Zealand compatriots, but slipped away early to be together. My broad-brimmed fedora had been deserted earlier in the back seat of the taxi and, other than for work, I was never to wear a hat again.

24

LANCASTER LOST AND FLYING BOATS

Our new Australian life had begun. We'd reverted to an easy normality, exploring Melbourne's museums, parks and the zoo with its unique Australian creatures to further confound Joy: kangaroos, emus and wild dingoes. My saviour and mentor, Uncle Stan Moore, was also in Melbourne on sugar business and he joined us for dinner the next evening at the Menzies Hotel. We talked of the war and life in Queensland.

After my less than easy start to life, Uncle Stan expressed his admiration that I'd made it to squadron leader in the RAAF with Bomber Command and Pathfinders, in four short and action-packed years. He was proud of me and understood that I would not be returning to the mill in Bundaberg. He was truly pleased I'd found a new career in civil aviation. He talked easily to Joy, wanting to appreciate her wartime experiences. We both had been lucky to survive.

I put into words my eternal gratitude for what he had done for me. I just wanted to hug him, but my well-learnt wartime reserve had kicked in. I explained that we planned to settle in Sydney, but first I had to take Joy home to meet my parents. He gave me a quizzical look, then warned me that my father and mother were lost souls, people who had missed out on a meaningful life and were now filled with rancour and venom. We should not seek their company for long. Sydney would be the best place for us.

We left Uncle Stan in good spirits, then flew to Sydney for a few more days, which we spent at the Australia Hotel. The trip was Joy's first plane flight and, although nervous at the beginning, she began to enjoy it and now understood what it felt like to soar above the clouds and reach a destination in next to no time, secure back on the ground, wondering if it all had really happened.

In Sydney, I wanted to give Joy the best and she was impressed, but tried to temper my unneeded extravagance, always having a watchful eye on the pennies, and also the longer term. We then flew to Brisbane to meet my younger sister, Nug, her husband and two children. She was to be our saving grace in these early times in Queensland. Nug was vivacious, pretty in a natural country-girl way and my only remaining sibling, after the dreadful loss of my elder sister, Rua, to pneumonia while I was training in Canada. They both had played an important part in my life.

My last gesture of improvidence was a stay at Lennons, the best hotel in Brisbane. I was then on the straight and narrow, with the train replacing plane for the trip to Bundaberg. This was as much of a mistake as the visit itself to my parents. Running on narrow gauge, these locomotives of antiquity rattled along noisily, carriages swaying from side to side. We travelled all night, the sounds and motion depriving us of any possibility of sleep. This mix of discomfort was compounded by seats of black vinyl that seemed to unnecessarily store the 108-degree Fahrenheit heat of the day, in Queensland's hottest month. There was no such thing as air conditioning.

Joy had been further tested as the only female in the compartment. Our companions for this gruelling ride were a bunch of male cane-cutters, returning to work with the able assistance of crates of beer in the carriage, the stocks of which had been rapidly depleted.

Sporting tattered navy blue singlets, they had perspired heavily and this combined with the added insult of their ale-laden breath was oppressive. Each finished bottle had been dropped on the floor as the train rocked from side to side, the empties rolling with each lurch to add a rhythmic clanking to our progress.

Dressed in her finest blue linen suit with white hat, bought for the occasion in Melbourne to impress the in-laws, Joy was less than responsive to the increasingly friendly offers of beer. We were pleased to arrive at Bundaberg station to be met by my mother, my father having to remain at his work at the sugar mill. While I was away they had finally lost the orange orchard when the banks made them bankrupt. Struggling to make ends meet, my father had grudgingly gone out to work. Uncle Stan had got him a job in despatch at the mill.

This visit was to be a bitter experience, one that should not have come Joy's way when she was far from her family and support. Uncle Stan was quickly proven right. On our arrival at my parents' home, devoid of any insect screens and only serviced by an outside drop dunny, Joy was faced with the well-intentioned treat of a large bloody steak. In England during the war meat was in short supply, with a chop a week at best, and toast being the only offering for breakfast. Sweet mangoes came next but were overpowering to an English girl who had been sugar-deprived by the war. Sticky flies invaded the house by day and large moths circled lower and lower by night, becoming entangled in Joy's long hair. Cane toads sat puffed up on the pathway to the toilet hut, which had no sewerage just an ominous drop into the void. I had foolishly advised Joy the toads were poisonous, but had not explained that they were only to be avoided and would not attack. Night excursions became a source of terror for her and my hardened parents immediately considered her to be a weakling.

I received an urgent telegram from Qantas asking me to return early to work. I would be away a little over two weeks and had to leave immediately. I felt severe misgivings at leaving Joy at the mercy of my parents. However, she insisted I must go, that she would cope until my return to Sydney, where she would join me. My less than friendly father and mother had also reassured me it would be good for Joy to join them for this time on their annual holiday to Tin Can Bay.

It was a mistake, reputedly the worst period of Joy's life, harder to endure for her even than the bombing. The fishing shack at Tin Can Bay was primitive and tiny with only a fuel stove for cooking. A walk along the shoreline was not for the faint-hearted. Large crab claws poked out from the slimy grey mud, the main body hidden yet ready for combat. My mother was down in a flash, wrenching the huge claw to reveal a gigantic mud crab, which was secured by string and handed to my father. Joy was soon expected to take charge of one of these monsters. Further weakness was revealed . . . yes, confirmed.

After a week of this mindless ill-treatment, Joy was finally saved by my sister, Nug. At my request she had driven with her family up to visit my parents, to see how Joy was getting on at the bleak and demoralising Tin Can Bay. They arrived to find a very miserable lady, covered in sandfly and mosquito bites, who hadn't had a proper shower for a week. Bathing in the saltwater estuary, with its questionable assortment of lurking creatures of the deep, had been the only option. Nug invited Joy to go back to Brisbane with them and stay until I returned to Sydney. Joy packed in record time. We never returned to my parents and had little contact with them until the death of my father, many years later. He was never to know or meet his grandchildren.

I had not, in fact, made it all the way back to Sydney from my urgent Qantas trip. I'd only reached as far as Guildford Aerodrome, later renamed Perth International Airport. I had then been co-opted into a vital search for Qantas Lancaster G-AGLX, piloted by my friend

Captain Frank Thomas. The crew of five, as well as five passengers, had gone missing after last radio contact 690 miles north-west of Cocos Island. It took me back to the war years and what it would be like to be stranded in the sea, but this time miles from any coastline. They had supposedly come down somewhere in the Indian Ocean between Karachi and Cocos Island.

Our search over the endless sea was monotonous. It was tinged with the ever-present anxiety of knowing, if we weren't vigilant, that we might miss a vital clue as to the whereabouts of these ten lost souls. The search began at first light and ended when the search aircraft were low on fuel or daylight faded. Our crew's day would start around 0400 and finish between 2300 hours and midnight, after the day's plots of area covered had been noted and new areas allocated for the next day. We flew at 50 feet above the water for twelve to thirteen hours, which was tiring and stressful work for the pilots. The search area for each aircraft was carefully planned and the sectors interlocked, with the total area to be searched expanded to cover all possible effects of position error by the lost aircraft, or wind and current drift if the crew was in a dinghy.

The next day there were reports of faint radio signals about 130 miles from where the Lancastrian was last reported, possibly from a rubber dinghy using the aircraft's emergency set. The signal was undecipherable. The weather was described as 'poor' on the evening they were lost. It was nothing we all hadn't been through. Frank wouldn't have had any problems, but there was lightning at play and they were within the inter-tropic area where the weather front was probably at its worst. The Lancasters were fitted with large petrol tanks in the bomb bay and the fumes could be overpowering.

We finished up with a total of fifteen aircraft, taking off each day as more and more became available. We found nothing except floating coconut palms, boxes, planks, tins, drums and a general assortment of sea debris. I had done a number of trips in G-AGLX and I imagined myself stranded on the open sea in a tiny life-raft. I gave every minute of search my total concentration, aware of how easily the positions could have been reversed. We endured six continuous days of fruitless searching before the search was finally called off.

I found it hard to accept that we couldn't find the crew or the missing plane. There were no distress calls from the aircraft and nothing in their position report that indicated any kind of trouble. Frank Thomas was a good man and a great pilot. I could somehow come to terms with an aircraft not returning in the war, but to lose an aircraft to the elements felt a bit below the belt. It must have been mechanical failure and it must have been sudden. I could only hope that the crew and passengers had a quick end and didn't languish for days in an open boat, trying to make the coast of Sumatra.

A report in the *West Australian* newspaper of Tuesday, 26 March 1946 was headlined:

MISSING PLANE
WEAK RADIO SIGNALS HEARD
PROBABLY IN SEA
EXTENSIVE AIR SEARCH

A haunting photo of Captain Frank Thomas looked out from a column containing full details of the incident and the possibilities. It had been described as one of the most extensive aerial and sea searches ever made. I'd duly recorded in my flying log book, now containing both wartime and civilian service, the coordinates of our futile search, between:

Longitude 1258 to 1400 South, and latitude 9520 to 9620 East.

In our efforts we had crisscrossed but one-thirtieth of 1 per cent of the total earth's surface area over six tortuous days; 70 hours of flying time ending in despair. Compared to wartime, the distances for the civil aviator were immense and mainly over water, the oceans covering more than 70 per cent of the globe's surface.

A year later, engineers found that the Lancastrian heating system, located in the wing of the aircraft, could generate sparks which could be fed down the air-conditioning ducts into the cabin of the aircraft. Possibly, when the crew changed from one fuel tank to another mid-flight, there had been a build-up of explosive fumes in the cockpit and the defective air-conditioning and heating system had provided the ignition. There would have been no warning and only the slimmest of chances for the crew and passengers to survive the explosion, let alone make it to the automatically dispatched life-raft. Nothing was ever found of Lancaster G-AGLX. I have never forgotten Frank Thomas or his ill-fated aircraft.

Joy and I had both been through a lot, but at last we were together. Finding a place to live in Sydney, where there were practically no houses or flats to rent, seemed inconsequential by comparison. We had, however, been lucky. After a couple of days at the Hotel Metropole, we found a room in a very run-down boarding house called Craignathan, which turned out to be a home for couples like us, desperately looking for somewhere to live. An imposing one-storey stone residence, built in the mid-1800s at Kurraba Point, Cremorne, it was in a glorious position overlooking the harbour, with small attic rooms tucked away in the roof. Our garret had only a view over the back yard but it included a healthy stand of emerald green, English spruce pines, which made Joy feel at home. We had an open fire and would happily buy and carry wood up the two flights of stairs, enjoying the warmth brought to our little haven.

For my part, I was often away working for periods of up to two weeks at a time but Joy showed a resolute determination to get on with things, to make good friends whenever she could. She had kept in touch with

Phyll, but she was far away, out of reach with Arthur in the west of New South Wales at their property in Coolamon. At the boarding house, we were fortunate to meet up with Olive and Dennis Adams, an unusual but artistic couple with whom we would forge a lifetime friendship. Dennis was to become godfather to our second son, Paul. He was a marine artist during the war and famous for his powerful paintings of the war at sea and in the air. His rendition of the rear gunner in action of a Halifax bomber brought to life for me the loneliness and vulnerability of warfare, the eyes of the gunner staring into the night. It now resides at the Australian War Memorial in Canberra.

Another good friend, Diana Baume, came through Joy's work at a local solicitor's office. She was to become Paul's godmother. She was the daughter of the well-known journalist Eric Baume. Di was younger than Joy, pretty with an educated and somewhat sardonic turn of phrase, reminiscent of her famed father. She'd realised how lonely Joy was and had invited her to her twenty-first birthday party to meet family and friends. It was Joy's first party in Australia.

Joy relished the ferry trips across the glory of Sydney Harbour, sparkling amid the luxuriant growth of the Botanic Gardens on the opposite shoreline. This scene had been set off by the aged stonework of Government House sitting atop the ridge above, like the crown on the head of our common distant monarch. Distant were her memories of the brown and grey waters of the Thames surging under Putney Bridge.

Our pleasures at the time were simple, as no one had any money worth mentioning but from these meagre beginnings would come a good life for us in Sydney.

I was now privileged to experience the 'Golden Age of the Flying Boat' and become a part of Australian aviation history. Flying boats lasted in service for little more than twelve years and became, at the time, the symbol of modernity.

My experience started in early 1946 with the luxurious Short S23 Empire Class flying boat, an all-metal cantilever monoplane termed 'the giant of the air', a 40,000-pound beauteous bird that could lift from the water in just 21 seconds. It measured 88 feet nose to tail and had a wingspan of 114 feet, surpassing the mighty Lanc's 102 feet. Designed by Short Brothers of Rochester, Kent, the Short Empire flying boat offered 'Shipboard Comfort at Airways Speed', with four nine-cylinder Bristol Pegasus–type engines, each developing 920 horsepower to give the boats a cruising speed of a sedate 200 miles per hour and, although unpressurised, the capacity to travel at 10,000 feet and above, to rise above the weather. The pitch or angle of the propellers had been specially designed to allow the boat to develop sufficient power to take off, then cruise at a higher speed without over-revving and wrecking the engines.

It was not that easy to get a flying boat to leave the water, as at full take-off power, the hull remained partly immersed creating a bow-wave. Once sufficient speed had taken it over the hump, it would begin skimming or aquaplaning across the surface. There was a 'step', or upward cut in the planing bottom, to allow the drawing in of a cushion of air and aid the release of the flying boat from the surface. This step was little more than halfway along the hull. On calm days the water had to be roughened up by a high-speed launch crossing in front of the flying boat, fracturing the physical surface tension and allowing the hull to break free from the suction.

These glorious flying boats reminded me of the stocky pelicans on the Burnett River at home, also needing a great effort and beating of wings to leave the river surface. Once free of their domain, they used the upward air pressure over the sea to ease their way forward in flight.

I also reflected on the considerable achievements of my distant mentor Donald Bennett in these machines before the war, and his famed 42-hour record flight in 1938 to South Africa's Orange River in a small flying boat, covering almost 6000 miles. It had been a long distance, straight-line record for seaplanes, that has never been beaten.

Qantas, in partnership with BOAC, became the first airline in the world to offer regular international passenger flights, providing all the comforts associated with luxury travel for sixteen lucky passengers who could summon the average annual wage to pay the single fare to England. The flying boats were pure romance, containing a promenade cabin, galley, wine cellar and plenty of space to stroll about and socialise. Now with large rectangular windows close to the water, passengers could enjoy the scenery in flight and on take-off and landing. The Short Brothers' catch-cry for these brilliant waterbirds was: 'We don't build aircraft that float, we build ships that fly.'

Australia's first international airport was established for Qantas at Rose Bay on Sydney Harbour. Passengers and crew travelled by launch to the boarding barge where the craft was tethered, reinforcing the perception of a marine experience. But this was where the similarities ceased. The thundering departure was in marked contrast to the slow travel of a luxury liner cruising out of Sydney Heads.

I have fond memories of our truly spectacular early morning take-offs, the sun glistening off the Sydney Harbour Bridge as our lumbering float plane lifted majestically from the mirrored tarmac of water, soaring effortlessly above the city to glimpse a reflection of this majestic iron structure, arching between the opposing shores of the harbour. The journey to England for the passengers would take nine days and 83 hours of flying time. There were up to 30 stops for fuel and provisions as we travelled through the exotic and colourful east, with nine of these stops being overnight stays at luxurious hotels. It all added to the excitement of the adventure.

Unlike my Bomber Command experiences, the crew quarters were no longer confined, and the pilot's cabin was now so big it could no longer be called a cockpit. I was located at the map table, behind the pilots on the upper deck of the Empire, with the rest of the flying crew of seven. We had ample space and a magnificent view of the surrounds as we came in to land. The sunset arrival into the tropics was truly inspiring. First a run over the landing area to ensure it was free of debris, then we returned to ease into the water, with a reassuring hiss on the silky smooth, rivet-recessed hull and the final gush as the two side-floats finally dipped in. This arrival into paradise preceded a refreshing overnight interlude, staying at such places as the famed Raffles Hotel in Singapore, or the Seaview out along the Malaysian east coast, with tennis nearby, swimming and excellent food. Warfare was now but a distant memory.

Navigation in an Empire Class flying boat on these long and lonely routes over water was a challenge, as radio navigational aids were often not available. Using dead reckoning and celestial navigation, I plotted the route on the map, called 'the track', to end up at the required port of call in time for the passengers to disembark for the night. The heading had to be adjusted to compensate for the wind and allow for the magnetic anomalies caused to the compass readings by splits in the earth's crust, deep below the ocean. The skylight behind the pilot could be opened so I could make observations with the sextant, this aperture having a windscreen to protect me from the rush of air. An aeronautical chart was always provided to identify expected ground detail along the route and thus aid visual navigation.

The Empire flying boats had not been pressurised and collisions in the air with unsighted obstructions were usually fatal. Towering peaks, like Mount Rinjani on Lombok in Indonesia, forced us to travel at an altitude of 12,000 feet to clear the summit, with consequent difficulty in breathing. We had viewed this impressive sight close up, with its glorious green-swathed apex piercing an iridescent quoit of white cloud, its impervious might set to threaten the unwary.

If you hadn't made landfall by the estimated time, flying in squares was the order of the day, searching for a shoreline or island lights at dusk to confirm the destination.

By August 1946, Qantas asked me to take charge of navigation for the newly arrived Hythe flying boat fleet. It had a longer 2000-mile range and a faster airspeed that had cut the previous nine-day journey to England to just a week. They were even more spacious than the Empire, carrying 24 passengers with 16 now having their own individual cabins with a bunk. Flying was now by day and by night, often over uncharted waters. Civil aviation authorities would lay flares on the water to make 'runways' for incoming pilots after nightfall, having 'swept' the area in a launch to clear any rubbish that might damage a flying boat's hull during landing. The sight of a floating Hythe seaplane at night was mesmerising, like a large luminous monster of the deep, with its array of windows from the top and bottom decks glowing an eerie light onto the rippling seascape.

Navigation after dark was by the stars and called celestial navigation. The engineer held the navigator firmly as he took his shots with a sextant through an opened hatch. Glimpsing between the gaps in the cloud cover, I was proficient in recognising the heavenly bodies by their colour, the blue tinted Vega and the yellow Capella; the planets of Mars and Saturn glowing a distinctive red and yellow; the bluish-white brilliance of Sirius, believed to have shone for 300 million years and which marked out the climatic events for the Egyptians and Greeks. It was also believed to have guided the islanders about the Pacific.

The amount of fuel able to be carried was still limited and required the navigator to allow for all contingencies, effectively calculating the Point of No Return back to the last departure aerodrome, taking into account the headwinds and tailwinds. It brought back memories of being in a Hudson over the Atlantic after my training in Canada, trying to reach Prestwick in Scotland and ferrying a much-needed aircraft to battle, with an engine playing up. It was always demanding work with a lot at stake. The navigator was still king.

I was advised that, on 9 August 1946, the then Governor-General of Australia, Prince Henry, first Duke of Gloucester, would be presenting me with a Distinguished Service Order (DSO) at Government House, for my services with Pathfinders. It had been recorded in the *London Gazette* on Tuesday, 24 October 1944 as follows:

> As navigation leader, Squadron Leader Goodwin has never hesitated to fly on operations with any crew likely to benefit from his advice. He has flown against the most heavily defended German targets including Berlin on 7 occasions. He has consistently displayed a high degree of gallantry and devotion to duty and his record is worthy of the highest praise.

As a matter of interest, I eventually made nine trips to Berlin and my indefatigable skipper, Philip Patrick, racked up ten. I found it incongruous that my tenacious skip, who had saved us on so many occasions and was rated as an 'exceptional bomber pilot', was never recognised with such an award. He was pleased that many of his faithful crew who had stayed with him for two tours had been so awarded. While receiving the Distinguished Flying Cross for his initial service in the Stirlings, Philip had received no recognition beyond his permanent Pathfinder badge and had joked that his DSO had possibly got lost in the post.

This capricious allocation of awards by the authorities at the end of the war was to be further compounded for all my compatriots in Bomber Command. All Allied armed services on land, sea or air received a group service medal recognising their work in the war in Europe. Bomber Command was the only notable exception, probably related to the controversy over the bombing of civilians. Politics not rectitude had become the order of the day. It would be another 66 years before this would be put right.

I was proud to receive this honour, the last reminder of my experiences of war.

25

CONNIES, SUPER CONNIES AND JETS

I was honoured to fly with Captain Robert (Bert) Ritchie on Qantas Empire Airways' first Lockheed Constellation 749 proving flight to England from Australia, arriving at London Airport on 21 November 1947. This was a simulated first commercial flight to demonstrate Qantas's ability to operate the aircraft. The 'Ross Smith' VH-EAA was a sleek aircraft with a neat triple-finned tail adorned with the 'flying kangaroo' on the outside and the Australian flag on the centre. The aircraft's registration, VH-EAA, would later take on significance for me at the end of my long Qantas service.

The name of our famed aviator, Ross Smith, rested on either side at the nose of our aircraft. He had piloted the first aircraft to fly from England to Australia in 1919, accompanied by his brother and two engineers. The journey took 28 days in a modified, twin-engined Vickers Vimy bomber from World War I. Smith had distinguished himself with many awards in the Australian Flying Corps and was even said to have been the pilot for Lawrence of Arabia. Our Constellation, powered by four big Wright Cyclone 3000-horsepower radial engines, was to follow in his footsteps and travel the official route length of 11,956 miles from Sydney to London, taking 93.5 hours elapsed flying time, and a wind-assisted 84 hours for the return journey. The cabin was pressurised allowing for comfortable travel at 18,000 feet, now with the ability for sustained flight above bad weather. Bert Ritchie was to become Chief Executive of Qantas twenty years later.

Qantas's decision to choose the Lockheed Constellations from the United States was its single most important post-war decision. It allowed for the strong growth and development of its operational and commercial expertise. There had been considerable pressure to maintain loyalty to the British Tudor II land-plane, derived from the Lancaster, but this was too slow at 205 miles per hour and its Merlin engines unproven over such distances. As it was unpressurised, the aircraft was also unsuitable for commercial use. The coming years would be highly competitive and Qantas could no longer afford to stick with the antiquated double service, express by Lancaster or slow luxury by flying boat, requiring added resources and excessive fares to cover costs.

Fergus McMaster had been the heart and soul of Qantas in its early developing years. His support for the bold purchase of the Lockheed Constellations and the nationalisation of the airline would make Qantas supreme on the Kangaroo Route until 1957. He'd been the first chairman, working with Paul McGinness and Hudson Fysh to build an air service for Western Queensland in 1920, now 100 years ago. He had lost his only son, Pilot Officer RF McMaster, during World War II at Aschaffenburg over Germany, flying a Lancaster with my old Bomber Command 460 Squadron. It was a terrible loss for him.

As a pastoralist, he was imbued with the red soil of the Queensland outback. His property was on the western Queensland plains, not far from Longreach where Qantas had its beginnings. Fergus was credited with the business acumen and undeniable skills in selling to his fellow graziers the need for better transport to the cities. He would remain the airline's chairman over its 27 formative years.

He reminded me of my own Queensland rural ancestors on my mother's side.

International airline travel and safe arrival in a Constellation relied heavily on the navigator. I truly felt the responsibility, with navigation now having the limited assistance of radio beacons, the last before Darwin being at Walgett, New South Wales, as I headed out over the vast emptiness of the Australian outback. The periscope sextant was mainly used to plot the aircraft's position, with the only connection to the air traffic system, en route to Europe, being through the dots and dashes of hand-transmitted morse code to our radio officer, or the occasional signal from a commercial radio station along the way. This allowed the use of the direction finder to plot the signal. The navigation skills and technologies I used over the long, often uninhabited track to England were not much more advanced than those used by Captain James Cook in his voyage to Australia on the *Endeavour* in 1768–71.

Constellation crews were virtually on their own. At night, as navigator, I would read the angles of the visible stars in relation to an artificial horizon, taking down the readings to check against the tables. During the day I'd use a sun sight, or a sighting of the visible moon or a planet such as Venus to check the aircraft's position against the planned course. As a good navigator, I used to pride myself on being accurate to within 5 nautical miles. During daylight and with clear visibility, landmarks or familiar islands could also provide an accurate fix. When neither skies nor ground were visible, I had to plot dead reckoning, by making allowance for the push of forecast winds on aircraft speed and heading.

Given the strong commitment to safety, a special bag was carried on all Qantas aircraft with landing charts for alternative airports. If engine failure occurred, I had to be ready to give the pilot a new course with distances to the diversionary airport. Constellations, known affectionately as 'Connies', didn't have radar and relied upon the eyes and skills of the pilot to penetrate weather fronts. With a maximum flying altitude of between 15,000 and 18,000 feet, our Connie often had to fly through the middle of towering cloud ramparts. This could, on occasions, create a rather unnerving phenomenon for both crew and passengers, called St Elmo's fire. Electrical potential would build up in the aircraft and be discharged in a blinding blue flash that speared along the wings or through the propellers. I'd heard reports that fireballs could appear in the cabin itself, yet no damage was done, except a cabin full of distraught passengers needing a stiff drink.

I was now flying Constellations all the way to England and would be absent for three weeks at a time. Joy and I had moved to a little flat in Bondi and started a family. Ian Derek had recently been born, his naming a gesture to our distant Scottish origins and the memory of Joy's brother lost in the skies over England. After Joy had adjusted to taking care of another little person, she decided to visit her best friend Phyll at Coolamon while I was away. The two friends hadn't seen each other in over two years and Phyll now also had a baby son, Tim. The memory of the twins lost in the war, although still with her, had been overtaken by new responsibility and the diversions of the hard life on the land. Joy was settled in her decision to go by herself. If Phyll could handle the isolation of Australian country conditions, after a life in London, then Joy felt she could certainly manage a visit with Ian for a week or so.

Coolamon is 25 miles from Wagga Wagga in country New South Wales. It was to be another eye-opening experience for Joy, exposing her to life in the outback—dry heat, dust, flies and the challenges of sheep and wheat. Although Phyll and Arthur had a large farmhouse, there were few amenities. There was no refrigerator, only a larder, and no proper running water, except for a tap on a stand-pipe in the kitchen. They had a large fuel stove but no sink for washing up. They left the cobwebs around the high ceilings to trap the flies, which were then eaten by the spiders. With no insect screens, their light at night came from Tilley lamps, filled with kerosene and pumped up with pressure to increase the light's intensity. Snakes were the order of the day coming out from the wheat to bake in the sun on the pathway. You had to step gingerly as you made your way down the back to the toilet outside. It was just a battered bucket that Arthur would take away from time to time to bury the contents.

At shearing time, Phyll had to take care of six shearers, as well as Tim, Arthur, the farm manager and two workers. Arthur killed a sheep every morning, butchered it then gave it to Phyll to cook on the fuel stove, chops on top and joints in the oven. After taking care of the meat, she baked several loaves of bread. All the men wanted for breakfast, lunch and dinner was meat with bread and butter. She even made the butter herself from the milk of their cows.

While Joy was at Coolamon, huge dust storms and gales hit thousands of square miles of eastern New South Wales. It was October 1948. They caused the closure of every airport between Sydney and Brisbane, even forcing a New Zealand flying boat to return to Auckland because of poor visibility at Rose Bay. You could see these deluges of dust coming across the flat, arid land from miles away. The tranquillity of the landscape was converted into a swirling turmoil that obliterated the blue of the sky. The blanket of red marched relentlessly forward, rising into the firmament, underscored by a thin line of train-engine green mulga, topping the horizon of brown parched earth. Howling winds and orange dust invaded, coating every nook and cranny. You couldn't even see inside the farmhouse.

Joy was pleased when I rang to say I was grounded in Sydney. She was lucky enough to catch a plane the next day and never returned to Coolamon. She kept in touch with Phyll by letter. Arthur was soon to take a senior aviation job in Brisbane after they decided they'd had enough of farming life. We were finally reunited when Arthur took on a major role in the National Civil Aviation Authority in Sydney. We had both admired how Phyll had given Coolamon her all, trying to adapt to this primitive life for the man she loved. She understood what it had meant to him to remain true to the land after all he had been through in the air.

In 1949, with the arrival of our second son, Paul, I took driving lessons and got my licence at the ripe old age of 32. I had gained proficiency in air navigation and all its technicalities but somehow, to this point, had not needed transportation skills on the ground. Now I just needed a car.

With the help of an aircrew counterpart in the Qantas radio operators' section, I secured a second-hand Austin 8 Tourer, with two doors and a statuesque dual-winged insignia on the bonnet. It was a marvel in antiquity in ebony, with canvas hood, canvas side curtains and plastic windows now opaque with age. When it rained, these little side windows had to be taken from the boot and fastened into position to the body of the vehicle, with imposing press studs. There was no such thing as air conditioning and the windows fogged up with rain or high humidity to the point where there was virtually no side vision at all, unless the occupants worked feverishly at clearing the windows while on the move. Our dear black mini-monster was all that was available, and all we could afford.

Surprisingly I met up again with my valued colleague and the undeniable hero of Pathfinders, Don Bennett, at Basra airport in Iran, just before the Christmas of 1950. I was now flying regularly in Constellations on the Kangaroo Route to London and he was flying, of all things, Christmas puddings to the British forces in the Middle East. I could sense he was not the man I had known in the Pathfinders, his demeanour was subdued, his professional confidence a little dented. He talked of how he had dabbled unsuccessfully in British politics after the war, initially gaining a seat in parliament, but losing it at the next election. He'd then stood as the Liberal parliamentary candidate for North Croydon, coming in a sorry third in the race. He had never been one for losing and found the wrangling of men in politics particularly unrewarding, soon leaving it behind.

Bennett had been brought back into aviation when the Russians had imposed a total land blockade on the city of Berlin, locked deep in the Russian-occupied zone of East Germany. He had formed a new company, Airflight Ltd, to join other civil operators supplying the city by airlift. Unlike Qantas, he had opted for the long-fuselaged Tudors, Avro's civilian successor to the Lancaster. He'd commenced commercial transport operations as owner, managing director and chief pilot. He had the help of one other pilot to take in 10 tons of potatoes to this desperate city, which he had so resolutely tried to bring to its knees a mere five years earlier.

In early 1950, Don had decided to become a civilian carrier, converting his Tudor aircraft accordingly. His reward was a disastrous accident, the worst in the air at that time and for many years to come. While flying 75 rugby supporters on charter from Dublin to Wales, the experienced pilot, who had worked for Bennett on the Berlin airlift, stalled the Avro on final approach to the airfield, which was perhaps too short for the aircraft. The airspeed had been allowed to decay to a dangerous point with the then resultant too rapid application of power ending in disaster. Bennett was clearly shaken as he talked of the death of all on board. While he'd been determined to maintain his commitment to the planes of British wartime manufacturing, his faith in the Tudor may have been misplaced, robbing him of satisfaction and purpose post-war.

He had proudly related to me how the Russian Defence Ministry had sent a special delegation to learn all they could about the operations of Bomber Command. They had wanted to know how we had developed such a high bombing success rate in the later years of the war. They sought every last detail of the workings of Pathfinders. He remained proud of our efforts and achievements.

Bennett was truly entitled to this vainglory. I include below an extract from the victory message he sent out to the Pathfinder Force, his men and women, on VE-Day 8 May 1945. It is recorded in a number of books including Gordon Musgrove's *Pathfinder Force: A History of 8 Group* and John Maynard's book *Bennett and the Pathfinders*, and appropriately in the chapter titled 'The Cruellest Betrayal'. I think it says it all:

> Bomber Command's share in this great effort has been a major one. You, each one of you, have made that possible. The Pathfinder Force has shouldered a grave responsibility. It has led Bomber Command, the greatest striking force ever known. That we have been successful can be seen in the far-reaching results which the Bomber offensive has achieved. That is the greatest reward the Pathfinder Force ever hopes to receive, for those results have benefited all law-abiding peoples.

Bennett had unfairly missed out in the wide sweep of victory honours and awards granted to other Bomber Command group commanders, and yet he had made the greatest contribution, later being recognised as the most notable of commanders. Perhaps it was the ruffling of conventional feathers higher up that had caused this oversight. Or perhaps politics prevented Churchill from granting recognition to Bomber Command, when service awards seemed to flow easily to the men and women of all other services. Bennett seemed unmoved by his own personal injustice but was angry for his gallant men of the Pathfinders. He felt that their sacrifice over Germany was all too easily forgotten. With an election looming after the war in Europe ended, British politicians at the time seemed quick to disassociate themselves from the necessary civilian sacrifice that was part of the destruction of German industry and duly ordered to win the war.

Bennett should never be forgotten as one of the great navigators of all time, both before and during the war, a demanding man devoted to the skills of finding the way, and forging ingenious methods for getting the bombs on target. His men would follow him anywhere.

By 1954, the L-1049 Super Constellation had progressively replaced the Lockheed 749. It was again a cigar-shaped aircraft, beautiful to behold, with the graceful sweep of the original design further accentuated by an added 17 feet in length. It could carry up to 80 passengers in comfort and travel at about 328 miles per hour. This marvellous flying machine was equipped with great advances in navigation, radio, landing aids and aircraft control systems. The Super Constellations would see Qantas through to the introduction of the jets in 1959.

Joy and I had found a more permanent flat in Maroubra, where we were to live for ten years, compiling funds to buy land and build a house. It was here that I met 'Old Cammack', the father of some good friends we made in the flats. He taught me everything I needed to know about rock fishing, being a blackfish man and an expert with a home-rigged, 15-foot Rangoon cane rod. He gave me a set of plates to bolt onto an old pair of shoes, and advice on rigging with line and float, and the purchase of rod and reel. He took me to his special haunts of 'Little Greenie' and 'Big Greenie' rocks at Maroubra Rifle Range. It was a rare day that we did not come home with a full bag of large blackfish.

I will never forget my necessary lesson in rock fishing. A moderate sea was running and every now and then Old Cammack would yell, 'Water!' as a large wave approached. I had to move quickly to higher rocks, but he could see my attention was on my float and not enough on the sea. Before I knew it, a large wave was breaking on the rocks at my feet, coming up waist high, washing me back, scraping skin from my knees and elbows. I had nearly lost my rod. He apologised, but said it was the only way for me to learn what happened if I took my eyes off the sea. If the waves had been bigger, I'd have been washed in with no choice but to swim for it all the way round to the beach. Lesson learned.

I had joined the patriotic fervour in 1954, carrying Queen Elizabeth II and the Duke of Edinburgh in Super Constellation VH-345 on their Australian tour, following her coronation. She was welcomed by over one million adoring Australians. Her husband was a bit of an eccentric, calling a spade a spade and not one really for regal protocol. He used to come up to the flying deck for a chat with the crew. Our paths crossed more than once, and I was forced to subtly discourage his regular invasion of my plotting table with his royal behind. The deft placement of the sharp end of my trusty dividers found their mark. He never did work out whether this was an unfortunate mishap or a considered assault.

I again travelled with Prince Philip in 1956 and '62, and with him and Queen Elizabeth in 1963, flying them from Christchurch. I enjoyed his company and welcomed these further visits, with sometimes humorous referral to the pointed dangers of navigation. Although a naval man, Philip loved to fly. He had achieved his 'wings' in record time in the middle of 1953 and I remember him extolling the virtues of Leonardo da Vinci and his prediction in the early sixteenth century of man soaring through the skies like birds. He quoted the great man: 'For once you have tasted flight you will walk the earth with your eyes turned skywards, for there you have been and there you will long to return.'

By 1956, Qantas had a fleet of 34 propeller-driven aircraft that carried a record number of passengers to the XVI Olympic Games in

Melbourne. In the same year Joy and I bought a one-acre block of land in Wahroonga, an Aboriginal name meaning 'our home', and started to build our house on a rustic rock shelf raised among the bracken. It looked out over a brush-filled valley. This suburb lies in the north of Sydney and our plot bordered on the bush, a place called Ku-ring-gai Chase. I hewed sandstone for drains, paths and walls from the landscape, and cleared the close-grown vegetation to make space for family living and reduce the significant risk from bushfires. I had seemingly returned to my days of unremitting toil on the land.

It was also a momentous year for the national carrier with the decision to enter the 'jet age'. Seven Qantas Boeing 707-138 jetliners were ordered, to be delivered between July and September 1959. Boldly inscribed on the red tail fin was the 'V-Jet' logo reversed out in white and derived from the Latin 'vannus' meaning fan. These Boeings were a shortened version of the 707, specially designed for Qantas, and were to be equipped with four brand-new Pratt and Whitney engines, called turbojets, and fitted with revolutionary turbofans that delivered lower fuel consumption, shorter take-offs, longer range and a faster cruising speed.

On 14 January 1958 I was again part of Qantas history, flying on one of two Super Constellations taking off from Melbourne on a pioneering 'round the world' service, circumnavigating the globe in opposite directions in just six days. One went via India along the Kangaroo Route; the other, for which I was the navigator, flew eastwards on the Southern Cross Route via the United States. The Qantas Flying Kangaroo, with its streaking red tail, had now become a familiar sight at airports in 23 countries.

On 29 June 1959, I joined the inaugural crew for the delivery of Qantas's first Boeing 707 'City of Canberra' from Burbank in the United States. Cruising at an exceptional 550 miles per hour, these 707s were to cut the Sydney to London flying time for the 80 passengers on board from 48 hours to 27. I was also there on 29 July 1959 on the day of the first Qantas jet service from Sydney to San Francisco. This was the first trans-Pacific jet passenger service. Qantas was the first airline outside of the United States to fly jet aircraft and was now firmly committed to the American aircraft industry. The company had a strong international future. I was excited to join the era of jet air travel, forsaking the robust four 15-feet grinding propellers of the Super Connie.

26

THE LAST NAVIGATOR

Aircraft had become my life. Even my earlier more primitive flights throughout the 1950s in a Douglas DC-4 Skymaster captured my imagination. Qantas was establishing much-needed shorter-haul services into Asia, including Djakarta (the original Dutch spelling), Singapore, Manila, Hong Kong and the south of Japan. Port Moresby, Norfolk Island and Auckland were also in need of civilian air transport. I remember so many contrasting episodes: one of my final trips in a DC-4 in 1957, where we transported 350 Rhesus monkeys in the hold between Singapore and Djakarta. Compare this to my first trip into South Africa on a Super Constellation 1049 at the end of 1955, to the 'Fiesta' Route proving flight on a Boeing 707 in 1964 from Sydney to London via Mexico City, and my involvement with the transportation of Australian troops to and from the Vietnam War by jet in 1966 and 1969–70.

The easy roar of the jet engine was to signify a permanent change to flying and air navigation. My relatively newfound profession was to become obsolete. A Super Constellation literally powered itself off the tarmac, just like the mighty Lanc—the thunderous four monster propellers grabbing the air as they churned and turned to pull the aircraft forward. This sleek aircraft would begin to move as the pounding pistons did their job, generating lift over the tapered wings and triple tail fins. The pitch of the engines would build into a thudding throb, reminiscent of the low-pitched sound of an Australian Aboriginal's bullroarer. This ancient instrument was used to send signals great distances through the bush. The wooden blade, shaped like a propeller blade, was rotated above the head on the end of a piece of twine, vibrating the air to produce the sound, as it in turn spun on its own axis.

A jet was an altogether different kettle of fish, reminding me of the evident power in the writhing body of a newly caught large blackfish, propulsion being effected by the thrust from the tail. A jet engine hummed, seemingly needing little effort as the might of the turbines built up, the whirring whistle of its fans delivering a new confidence in air travel, well above the clouds at 36,000 feet with minimal weather interference or complication, jet streams being the exception. Gone was the vibration and lack of mechanical certainty, just the purr of well-oiled machinery, the drone of the burly fans and internal combustion that would easily deliver the required ground speed for a smooth take-off as the craft easily lifted up towards the heavens.

Jet engines, also called gas turbines, worked by sucking air into the front of the engine using a fan. From there the engine compressed the air, mixed fuel with it, ignited the fuel and air mixture and shot it out the back of the engine, creating thrust. The turbofan at the front was made of titanium blades which drew tremendous quantities of air into the engine. The core of the engine was where compression and combustion occurred, with the remaining bypass air being moved through a duct on the outside, to create added thrust and cooling for the engine. This air also blanketed the exhaust air from the core for quieter running. The high-speed forcing of the air out the back of the engine pushed the early Boeing 707 aeroplane forward, allowing it to streak across the sky at an amazing 80 per cent of the speed of sound, with a maximum of 1010 kilometres per hour.

By the early sixties I had held the position of Chief Navigator for Qantas for over seven years, with training and technical responsibility for all Qantas navigation. Joy, the boys and I were now well settled on our acre block at Wahroonga, having built an architecturally designed, light-filled house with warm-coloured pine panelling in the bush.

From day one in 1920, Hudson Fysh had set the benchmark for air safety at Qantas and it had always been a high priority since. That culture of safety was key to the company's success and it was the first airline in the world to offer regular international passenger flights.

During the war, we had never quite believed in the strong tail-winds we encountered, helping us reach the target in record time, like surfing a wave to the beach. Now we had come to understand these jet streams' impact on aircraft. Jet streams were found mainly at higher altitudes, where our jet aircraft now chose to travel to get above the clouds and the weather. These winds in the upper atmosphere—between 30,000 and 40,000 feet—blew at 300 miles per hour and could have a dramatic effect on flying time. They were not visible to the naked eye and hard to detect, until you were well into them.

Once, coming back into Sydney, we were over Dubbo and our Boeing 707 just slipped through the air in freefall, as if the power in the engines and the lift of the wings had forsaken us. The captain countered the stall and got the aircraft under control once we reached 20,000 feet.

Jet streams are created where two air masses of different tempera-tures and densities meet, generating an immense wind along the boundary between these masses. The hydrostatic balance is upset vertically and the geostatic horizontally, causing great turbulence and

aviation wind shear. An aircraft can plunge from the sky. It seemed
the weather still controlled our destiny in the air, no matter how
sophisticated our machines were.

With the introduction of the L-1049 Super Constellation came
Doppler radar to revolutionise navigation. This device bounced a
microwave signal off a desired target and analysed how that object's
motion altered the frequency of the returned signal. Pulse-Doppler
radars were light enough for aircraft use and directly measured the
movement of the ground. This was compared to the airspeed from
the aircraft's instruments. Wind speed could then be determined,
allowing highly accurate dead reckoning by the navigator.

In the 1960s, with the advent of the Qantas Boeing 707 jetliners,
Doppler navigation was largely superseded by the inertial navigation
system (INS). This included a gyro-stabilised antenna platform with
four projected beams, allowing it to be aligned with the track of the
aircraft. The 'drift angle' could then be measured and the ground speed
determined. An additional 'Doppler Computer' drove the counting of
distance along track and across track, outputting the difference. With the
aircraft's compass integrated into this computer, a desired track could
be set between two identified waypoints. This was a great improvement
over dead reckoning and of great advantage over large tracts of water.

I had set high standards for my Qantas navigators with the
average error not to exceed 20 miles using celestial observations.
A quite small error in navigation could add 300 miles to the length of
the journey and cost in extra fuel consumed. Before Qantas decided
to fit Marconi Doppler in its aircraft on the Pacific run, we had established a 95 per cent probability of accuracy to within 1 per cent of
distance flown, with across-track errors of less than 0.38 per cent
of distance flown. Marconi Doppler, combined with the INS, now
delivered a high degree of automated navigation. Astrofixes were no

longer needed, removing any difficulties when the heavens were not easily seen. It was now 'navigation without the stars'.

Precise heading measurements had to be initially fed into the computer, as well as exact longitude and latitude of the place of departure. Having given the computer its location, the INS then aligned itself with true north by means of the gyro compass. Simply put, the INS now used computer, motion sensors, rotation and magnetic sensors, to continuously calculate by dead reckoning the position, orientation and velocity of the aircraft. Non-directional radio beacons at known locations along the track now transmitted a signal to the automatic direction finder of the aircraft to further assist with navigation.

It sounded the death knell for my profession.

In my time at Qantas I had watched over the many developments in aviation, including flying boats, Constellations, the introduction of Doppler navigation, the advent of the Boeing 707 and finally the jumbo jet, where navigators would no longer be needed.

When he became chief executive of Qantas in 1967, Bert Ritchie changed the airline's name to Qantas Airways Limited (cutting out any mention of empire) and championed the initial purchase of four 747s, catapulting Qantas into the age of the mass transit of travellers, with the first projected delivery date of August 1971.

I aided the airline in the computerisation of its navigation for these juggernauts of the skies, making my own profession obsolete. Boeing 747s now required only two crew to pilot the aircraft, more if it was a long haul. This seemed to me to be a somewhat full circle return to the pioneering days of flying—Ross Smith in his Vickers Vimy or Don Bennett in his Mayo Composite. One could not help but be impressed by the sheer presence of a 747, marvelling at its size and capacity for flight. You would have only been able to squeeze two jumbos into a standard soccer pitch with the wing tips and noses still floating over the lines. In comparison, twelve of my original warplanes, the Vickers Wellingtons, which had carried me into battle with Arthur in early 1940, would fit in the same soccer pitch.

On 4 November 1971, my flying log book, now up to Volume 3, recorded my swan song, from Honolulu to Sydney on a Boeing 707, VH-EAA. In the bottom right-hand corner sat, resplendent, my cumulative total:

13,700 hours, made up of 7710 hours daytime and 5990 hours flying at night.

The aircraft I took my last ride in as a navigator had the registration VH-EAA. This was the same registration as the Constellation I took my first flight on in 1947, with Captain Ritchie. This lettering was to be, significantly, again rebirthed in 1981 as a Boeing 747SP-38, the twenty-second of Qantas's fleet of jumbo jets, that would now carry up to 400 passengers and transform the airline industry for the mass market. The registration VH-EAA had been used three times, initially for Qantas's first Constellation, then as a Boeing 707 and lastly as a jumbo jet. This symbolised my own amazing journey in aviation— the transition from propeller to fan jet and lastly to jumbo, where my profession would come to an end. It had been quite a ride.

I retired from Qantas in November 1971, with the arrival of the Boeing 747s, bringing to conclusion my discovery and enjoyment of the meaningful profession of navigation. I had worked for Qantas for 26 years, thirteen as Chief Navigator, and spent over 30 years in the air in war and peacetime. I had witnessed the brutality of warfare and endured comrades lost, but it had delivered me from the tedium of a less than satisfying working life. The war had also brought me my partner, Joy.

AFTERWORD

Churchill had even failed to mention Bomber Command in his victory speech of 1945. Some suggest it was the evident politics of the time, the hope for re-election. For those who had not been to war, there was perhaps a shame and shock at the revealed level of destruction to Germany's cities and people, at the conclusion of the war in Europe. My father felt that Churchill had perhaps been a little too sensitive to this sentiment held by some of the voting public. This great wartime leader was perchance fallible, open to the vanity of remaining popular in peacetime.

Having lived through the experience, my father, though a temperate man, left me in no doubt that the bombing was justified. He had little time for the armchair analysts who argued as to the level of brutality needed for victory. He reminded me, before the bombers were effectively brought into action through Pathfinders, that Hitler was on the point of victory, a ferocious contest delicately poised that could go either way. Post-war analysis by so-called experts did not have the raw experience of all-out battle, the desperate effort needed for survival.

My father knew that nothing short of annihilation could stop the German war machine. The relentless despot would never give up, even though it meant the destruction of the German people and their cities. There are no delicate half measures in warfare and to suggest a reduction in the area-bombing formula of Bomber Command towards the end of the war, would be like leaving a last cancerous piece of a malignant tumour to fester and grow.

After losing government, Churchill did finally recommend Bomber Harris for a peerage in 1946. However, the then Labour Prime Minister, Clement Attlee, ignored his entreaties. Both sides of politics had been complicit, too easily forgetting Britain's darkest hour, when the motherland had teetered on destruction, an oppressive peace treaty with Hitler seeming the only option. Bomber Command and Pathfinders had stepped in to the fray to turn the tide of war.

Before his death in 1984, Sir Arthur Harris had given his permission and full backing for a commemorative medal. Although still not an official recognition of bravery, it allowed Bomber Command's stalwart commanders to pay tribute to their 125,000 brave aircrew and the untiring ground crews, airfield drivers, mechanics and armourers. In April 1985, under the tutelage of Lady Harris and Air Vice Marshall Bennett, this commemorative medal was struck, signifying the reward due to members of Bomber Command for their courage and skill. Lady Harris and Bennett were present at the mint to symbolically take off the production line the first and second medals created.

For my father, this medal's ribbon brought back lasting memories in blue grey, midnight blue and flame. The vertical stripes represented the North Sea, the night sky over enemy territory, the flame of the target and the return trip. Brevet letters designating each of the aircrew, 'O, AG, E, B, WAG and N' were contained on the face of this gleaming silver decoration. These were the letters originally included on the 'wings' awarded to aircrew on completion of their flying training, worn on the left breast above medal ribbons. Laurel-wreathed, they surrounded the pilot's designation on the medal, which was 'RAF' surmounted by a crown, symbolic of their support for their pilot and signifying the courage, team spirit and leadership of the time. The mighty Lanc glowed resplendent on the back.

Nearly half of those serving in Bomber Command had died during the war and too many of those who had survived had also passed on without due appreciation for all they had done. Bomber Command had made the difference. Not just those in the air but also those on the ground who had supported them valiantly in all weathers.

The memorial to Bomber Command was finally unveiled in Green Park, Central London by Her Majesty Queen Elizabeth II on 28 June 2012, in the year of her Diamond Jubilee. It is a 9-foot bronze sculpture of a seven-man crew in full flying kit, looking to the skies after a successful mission. It bears the inscription: 'We remember those of all countries who died in 39–45', a gesture of reconciliation towards all cities on both sides involved in the conflict. The plinth of the memorial is imprinted with the following text by Pericles, the influential Greek statesman, orator and general during the Golden Age of Athens: 'Freedom is the sure possession of those alone who have the courage to defend it'.

The opening ceremony was attended by 6000 veterans and family members of those killed. Avro Lancaster PA 474 dropped 800,000 red poppies over Green Park, reminiscent of the World War I poem 'In Flanders Fields', which refers to the red poppies that grew over the graves of the fallen soldiers. Those left had felt, somehow, once again united with those long gone.

Of particular note is the involvement in the campaign for recognition of Bee Gees singer Robin Gibb, part of an English-born pop group starting in Australia. This fine entertainer had fittingly given us such hits as 'Stayin' Alive' and was committed to keeping the memory alive of the 55,573 Bomber Command servicemen who lost their lives turning the tide of World War II against Germany.

There had been a growing groundswell, a call for a special campaign medal to recognise the 125,000 aircrew of Bomber Command and their supporting ground crews. The belated official service medal, the Bomber Command Clasp, was finally instituted on 26 February 2013, in due recognition of the brave men who took to the air with Bomber Command. It was awarded to aircrew members on aircraft who participated in at least one operational sortie in an RAF Bomber Command operational unit between 3 September 1939 and 8 May 1945 inclusive. This clasp is for attachment to the 1939–45 Star, already awarded. It is notable that the other clasp for sewing into the star's ribbon was instituted many years earlier in 1945. It was the Battle of Britain clasp.

Both clasps are struck in bronze and have a frame with an inside edge, perforated like a postage stamp. They are attached to a 32-millimetre ribbon, with equal vertical stripes, bands of navy blue, army red and air force blue, representing the equal contribution of all three service arms towards victory. It arrives in a simple blue box with the crown of Her Majesty Queen Elizabeth II embossed in gold on its face. Harris and Bennett did not live to see Bomber Command finally receive the recognition it deserved. It seems appropriate to include a small extract from the 'Special Order of the Day' sent out by Arthur Harris on 12 May 1945, at the conclusion of World War II in Europe. His words ring out the unpleasant, but necessary, achievements of Bomber Command, in helping to turn around the Allies' fortunes of war. I found this extract in my father's papers, an old yellowing circular from The Pathfinder Force Association in Australia published in October 1990:

With it all you never ceased to rot the very heart out of the enemy's war resources and resistance.

His Capital and near 100 of his cities and towns, including nearly all of leading war industrial importance, lie in utter ruin, together with the greater part of the war industry, which they supported.

Thus you brought to nought the enemy's original advantage of an industrial might intrinsically greater than ours and supported by the labour of captive millions, now set free.

For the first time in more than a century you have brought home to the habitual aggressor of Europe the full and acrid flavours of war, so long the prerequisite of his victims.

In their twilight years, Philip and my father often shared some whimsical words about the time it took for Bomber Command to receive this recognition. They were both well aware that, during the war, they had overcome the odds stacked against them. Some of their compatriots had not been so fortunate. Philip and Gordon had been part of the remaining few, holding the mandate for justice. This is what had made the long-coming recognition of the Bomber Command Memorial and the final official granting of the Bomber Command Service Medal so special.

My father, Gordon Goodwin, died peacefully on 21 July 2012 of pneumonia at 94 years of age. It was four weeks after his last conversation with Philip Patrick. They had talked after the unveiling of the Bomber Command Memorial in Green Park. The Bomber Command Clasp for Gordon Goodwin was applied for as a 'Claim by immediate family member' in September 2014 and finally received on 4 February 2015, nearly 70 years after the end of the war, and more than two years after his death.

My father remembered his five years with Bomber Command and Pathfinders as if it were yesterday. It was stamped indelibly into his psyche, just like his focus on the target and the task at hand. To the end, my father was filled with his recollections of warfare, and happily perused his extensive library of Bomber Command and Pathfinders books, fed regularly from England by his revered skip, Philip, with new war tomes just published, a meaningful annotation always in the flyleaf. When he died he was reading, yet again, *Pathfinder: A War*

Autobiography by Air Vice Marshal Bennett, written ten years after the war's end.

Gordon Goodwin was a man of strong commitment, dedicated and always trying to better himself. He grasped hold of any opportunity when it presented and was rewarded with a career in civil aviation with Qantas. He found his profession of navigation and helped to computerise this art form in the air in his own lifetime. As a decorated airman, he etched a place in the annals of aviation history, showing inspired leadership and technical achievement. He found many role models along the way but for me, my father Gordon Goodwin, would always be 'The Last Navigator'.

ACKNOWLEDGEMENTS

It has been a remarkable journey. One where I have met, been encouraged and guided by some amazing people along the way. Sitting among my piles of reworked and now-to-be-discarded papers, I reflect on this book, thirteen years in the making. My parents showed me the way, the joy of an early retirement with time to do the things you enjoy while the body is still able, but you need a project. Mine was *The Last Navigator*.

Talks with my father were always the stimulus, but I needed to hone the craft of writing. WEA writing courses were the key, allowing me to meet Yvonne Conoulty. A fellow writer, she got me going and gave me her time to perfect the early chapters and appreciate the need for the rewrite. She got me into the writing group, where I was fortunate to meet Peter Maxwell, Jan McCoy and Sylvia Levi. Peter, of UK origins, lived through and understood the war. He has been invaluable.

Then came the Mitchell Library and the welcoming Friends Room, under the able management of Helena Poropat. This was a haven for writing and research. Here I met Alex Gilly, a successful writer now publishing his second book, and Daniel Ryan completing his architecture PhD. They gave me all the support and friendship I needed. My first seven chapters were lucky to receive the able feedback of my bowling mate Ian Kimmorley and family friend Louise Cahill, who added her touch.

Family and friends have provided encouragement, like the *Flying Scotsman* receiving machine oil for its moving parts. They never thought I would finish. My hairdresser Sarah Ephraim never wavered in her belief, as she dutifully trimmed my sparse locks. Ian Patrick, himself with the RAF, provided able assistance with commentary on and photos from his dedicated father. My English second cousin Sue Akehurst, herself a writer, assisted my creative efforts and had a warm affection for my mother.

Qantas, through Nicole Kuttner at the Outback Founders Museum at Longreach and David Crotty, Curator of the Founders Museum in Sydney, made the link to Jim Eames. He is an eminent writer of books on Qantas' war years and it was he who was my champion, promoting my 'Bombing Berlin' chapter as proof for publication.

Now to publishing. Rebecca Kaiser from Allen & Unwin has been my editorial savior, recognising on my third attempt the value of my father's story and then reordering my work to fit and make sense. Deonie Fiford was next with the detailed edit to make it flow and be easily understandable. Tom Bailey-Smith has brought all the moving parts together for a fine book. Thanks to Samantha Mansell for her publishing ministrations.

My wife Tricia has always been there for me, with her love of history but not necessarily the machinations of aircraft. I couldn't have done it without her committed support. Early retirement has given us the freedom to travel, including such places as Montville, Temora, Duxford, Cambridge, Wimbledon Park and Montreal, researching the book and enjoying ourselves. Faithful dog Rosie has been by my side with sonorous snoring.

My father has also been there with me in spirit, providing the resilient spark to keep my focus and get the job done. He would have been proud that his story is now being told. This is just the beginning.

ENDNOTES

This book was based on my father's memoirs, the *Résumé of the Life and Times of One R. Gordon Goodwin*. Known as RGG Memoirs, it was completed in his eightieth year in 1997, somewhat tongue in cheek, always with a touch of whimsy. His last words of the memoir set the scene, even though the majority of the work was serious, matter of fact and without emotion: 'Anyone seeking to publish any of this must be out of their tiny minds. However my compassion for their state will not prevent me from suing for every dollar I can get under the copyright laws, because I need the money.'

As outlined in the Author's Note, this collaborative effort between father and son has used his extensive library of books on Bomber Command, interviews recorded with him and his 7 Squadron skip, Philip Patrick, his logs, his other documents and a lifetime of conversations with him. All entries contained in this book from my father's flying log books are exact extracts. Where my father's story was incomplete, I have drawn on other published sources and internet research to explain and expand on my father's work. My mother, Joy, also committed pen to paper to reflect her life and war years.

Where material has come from another source, it has been based on fact and events that actually occurred. Every effort has been made to maintain the authenticity of the original RGG Memoirs, to truly reflect my father's journey into the world of navigation with Bomber Command and Pathfinders.

Epigraph

This quote has been attributed to Leonardo da Vinci. An educational film in 1965, scripted by John H. Secondari, is said to possibly be the source. It was based on biographical information about Leonardo's life, depicting his dreams of constructing bat-like wings so humans could fly.

Chapter 1

RGG Memoirs form the basis of family origins and history. The carpet snake saga is a story of my father as a twelve-year-old boy. Tales of the Great Depression in Australia of the 1930s are sourced from Wikipedia, including the record-breaking batting of Don Bradman at just 21 years of age at the Sydney Cricket Ground in 1930 and the racehorse Phar Lap's domination of the Australian racing industry between 1929 and 1931. My father's Uncle Stan Moore was General Manager of the Millaquin Sugar complex and my father's saviour.

Chapter 2

After escaping to Bundaberg, my father started as a 'pan-boy', moving up to sugar-boiling and the study of sugar chemistry. Full accounts are contained in his writings. His grisly tale of chipping red-grey rust in the Babcock boilers is there. 'Blackbirding' from the Pacific Islands comes from Wikipedia and *Bundaberg: History and People* by Janette Nolan.

Chapter 3

'Linseed Lancers' comes from livinghistoryworldwide.com and Royal Australian Army Medical Corps from Wikipedia. The story of Bernard and Nell meeting is derived from a podcast transcript from La Trobe University of an interview with Ernest Raetz, by Dr Janet Butler on Australian Nurses in World War I, and also 'Casualty Clearance: The WW1 Nurses' by Roslyn Bell. Outline of the Empire Air Training Scheme comes from awm.gov.au and anzacportal.dva. gov.au, 'The Road to Bomber Command'. Reference to the opening of the Sydney Harbour Bridge in 1932 comes from Wikipedia as do details of engineer John Bradfield's birthplace, career and honours. The naming and history of Bradfield Park becoming an RAAF station where my father attended his Initial Training School (ITS) is sourced from Wikipedia. Both Bradfield and my father were born at Sandgate in Queensland with details of geography and history from Wikipedia. Thanks to Pam Verney at the Sandgate Museum for details on how country folk would come to stay in a pair of cottages with midwife present, awaiting the birth of their child. 'Scrubber Scott's' words of wisdom were given to my father. Matthew Flinders' historic material is sourced from Wikipedia, *Voyages of Discovery* by Tony Rice and *Matthew Flinders and His Scientific Gentlemen* edited by Juliet Wege, Alex George, Jan Gathe, Kris Lemson and Kath Napier. The rousing rendition of 'Rock of Ages' is sourced from *Journeys into Night* by Don Charlwood and the results of the Empire Air Training Scheme from *Chased by the Sun* by Hank Nelson. The database on clydeships.co.uk is the source for the information on the steamship MV *Aorangi*.

Chapter 4

The harbour scene from 1941 was sourced from illustrated vancouver.ca. *Journeys into Night* by Don Charlwood recounts the distant thundering of gigantic mile-long trains. Information on the Avro Anson Mark I, 'Faithful Annie', comes from Canadian www.wingsmagazine.com and also Wikipedia. The Avro Anson at Dunkirk and its vital role in the evacuation comes from Wikipedia. The story of Pilot Officer Phillip 'Pete' Peters of No. 500 Squadron is contained in the blog of Juhan Sotahistoriasivut (juhansotahistoriasivut.weebly.com) on the 'Deadly Avro Anson'. The story of Jeanne in Edmonton comes from my father. The practical training in the Fairey Battle aircraft is derived from Wikipedia, as well as information and exhibits at the South Australian Aviation Museum, allowing me to appreciate the claustrophobia of the bomb-aimer. The skill of making the astrofix using a sextant is sourced from *Shackleton's Voyage of Endurance* and Wikipedia.

Chapter 5

Max Hastings, in his book *Bomber Command*, gives the background on Donald CE Bennett. The history of 'Hustling Hinkler' is from Wikipedia. The description of the Avro Avian G-EBOV comes from the Australian Airways Museum. Bennett's story in Canada is based on my father's writings, those of Bennett in his book on Pathfinders and also the work of Max Hastings. The history and descriptions of the city of Montreal in 1941 come from a 1947 film documentary called *Montreal by Night*, livingin-canada.com and canadahistory. ca. The episode of fly fishing with the 'Silver Doctor' was from my father.

Chapter 6

Information on the basics of climate and weather come from weatherwizkids.com and Astronomy Online. The difficulty of gaining astrofixes over the Atlantic and the Point of No Return calculation come from my father. Information on icebergs comes from www. holloworbs.com. Background detail and history of John Cabot comes from Wikipedia and are also sourced from *The Voyage of the Matthew:*

John Cabot and the Discovery of North America by Peter Firstbrook. My father posed the question as to what happened to Hudson 9180, after its delivery to Coastal Command. My research indicated the possible involvement in forcing the surrender of German submarine *U-570*. Details of its capture are given in uboat.net. *Coastal Command: 1939–45* by Ian Carter and *Coastal Command at War* by Chaz Bowyer outline this incident involving Squadron Leader James Thompson and 269 Squadron.

Chapter 7

Details of the 'Wimpy' and its history, construction and engines come from 'Vickers Wellington' on Wikipedia and History Heritage Centre at www.raf.mod.uk. The story of Co-pilot Sergeant James Allen Ward is taken from *Strike and Return* by Peter Firkins. *Strike and Return* contains the history of 460 Squadron and is the source for life on the base including Bubwith, with its two pubs. Details of the first raid on Emden, with its U-boat construction yards, come from *Strike and Return*. The words of Wing Commander Hubbard come from my father. Descriptions of the chasing glow of the setting sun are from *Chased by the Sun* by Hank Nelson and *Journeys into Night* by Don Charlwood. The loss of Sergeant JFD Cooney and his crew as 460 Squadron's first battle casualties comes from *Strike and Return*.

Chapter 8

Pamphlet drops to the French are outlined in the 'Net Review' by Martin Moore in Tim Brook's book *British Propaganda to France, 1940–1944: Machinery, Method and Message*. The Cologne and Hamburg operations and the 'keg incident' come from *Strike and Return*. Heating details for a Wellington Bomber come from 'Vickers Wellington' on Wikipedia and www.raf.mod.uk. Details of the attacks on Lubeck and Rostock and small bomb containers are from *Strike and Return*. Poetic licence is taken with Arthur's old MG TA sports car in glorious British racing green. *Strike and Return* reports the demise of Pilot Officer Jimmy Falkiner and his brave crew in a Halifax.

Chapter 9

The last raid of the month of May 1942 on Cologne is well reported in *Strike and Return*, including Pilot Officer Arthur Doubleday and the role of 460 Squadron in this first 1000-bomber raid. This milestone is covered in Arthur Harris's *Bomber Offensive*. Hastings describes in his book *Bomber Command* the insight of Harris as he watched part of London ablaze from the roof of the Air Ministry in 1941 and his words 'They are sowing the wind.' Alan Clark's *Barbarossa* details the strategic significance of the Battle of Stalingrad and the role of Bomber Command in keeping the German fighters defending the homeland. Wikipedia outlines the key points in the Battle of Stalingrad. Pilot Officer Bert Walker's exploits as rear gunner are recorded in my father's flying log book with assistance from the excerpt 'Air Gunner Stories' taken by the Bomber Command Museum from *Sixty Years: The RCAF and CF Air Command 1924–1984* by Larry Milberry. Commentary on the lack of appreciation of super wind streams comes from my father. Descriptions of the Junkers Ju 88 are sourced from Wikipedia. Information on the Australian gannet comes from Richard Freeman's aloneatseaphotography.com.au. Statistics for the 20,000 air gunners who did not survive come from thewhpfamily.com. Details of the Emden concerted attacks come from my father's flying log book and the background on the Saint-Nazaire Raid is sourced from Wikipedia.

Chapter 10

The sea rescue experience is sourced from Firkins' *Strike and Return* about Sergeant R Lawton, a bomb-aimer. The Mae West life jacket comes from the RAF website. Operational details on Wilhelmshaven and Duisburg come from my father and also *Strike and Return*. Rob Davis's internet summary of the exploits of Bomber Command 1939– 1945 provides the meaning for 'Gone for a Burton' and 'Strike and Return', the motto for 460 Squadron. It also covers the dreadful losses of two crews under the exceptional leaders, Squadron Leader Leighton and Pilot Officer CH Burgess. *Strike and Return* documents the heavy losses of 460 Squadron in the June–August period of 1942. Breen's origins come from my father and *Strike and Return*. Background on Group Captain Blucke comes from www.raf.mod.uk. Firkins confirms 460's maintenance efficiency that was never surpassed by any other squadron in Bomber Command. Survival statistics for 100 airmen come from Rob Davis. History of 460 Squadron and Lancaster 'G for George's' move to the Australian War Memorial are from Wikipedia and the *Sydney Morning Herald* 'Spectrum' feature of 16 May 1998, 'Taking Care of George'.

Chapter 11

The anecdote of the barmaid is sourced from Rob Davis's summary of the exploits of Bomber Command, 1939–1945. My mother's memoirs of her wartime experiences document her own dices with death as a civilian in London. The friendship and radio banter on return of Doubleday and Brill comes from Hank Nelson's *Chased by the Sun*. Brill's bravery and resulting decorations are recorded by Firkins. Information on White Waltham Airfield comes from Wikipedia, as does the Distinguished Flying Medal and the explanation of Athena Nike. King George VI, shown in ww2db.com, with the wings of a flyer on his uniform and outlines his inspirational contribution, holding his people together throughout the war. It includes details of his 1927 visit to Australia. Background on Flying Superintendent Bennett's visit to the Air Ministry in December 1941 comes from *Bennett and the Pathfinders* by John Maynard. The summation of the three stages of progress of the bombing offensive by Bomber Command comes from an introductory speech made by my father when he was 'Commanding Officer of the Pathfinder Training Unit' at 93 Group Navigation Instructors' Course in mid-1943. Material outlining the new and effective radio and radar devices, including Gee and H2S or 'Y', was sourced from Pathfinders' display information on a visit to the Royal Air Force Museum, London, and from Air Vice-Marshal DCT Bennett's book, *Pathfinder: A War Autobiography*.

Chapter 12

Bennett's tale of escape is from his book *Pathfinder: A War Autobiography*. His impatience with some of the 'old guard' is sourced from John Maynard's *Bennett and the Pathfinders*. Background on the German occupation of Norway comes from the 'Norwegian history: World War II' internet site at cappalendamm.no. Bennett's initiative with radar navigational aids and the development of pyrotechnics to illuminate and effectively mark the target are well documented in Maynard's book. Also included is the explanation of the workings of 'Oboe', doubling the percentage of bombs reaching the target. His work with 'the boffins' is well documented in Bennett's autobiography. The book by Gordon Musgrove, titled *Pathfinder Force: A History of 8 Group*, outlines the Target Indicator types developed. The details of the raid on the Krupps Armament Works at Essen come from Maynard and the description of the attack on Dusseldorf is sourced from Musgrove. The history of the de Havilland Mosquito Bomber, the 'Timber Terror', comes from www.diggerhistory.info and details of the disruption of a German military parade in Berlin, to be addressed by both Goering and Goebels, is found on airforce.gov.au. The Mosquito's performance characteristics come from www.diggerhistory.info. The account of Bennett flying his Mosquito Bomber to assess the success of certain raids first-hand comes from my father. He understood Bennett's undeniable passion for flying, navigation and the Mosquito Bomber.

Chapter 13

The experiences at 27 OTU Lichfield come from RGG Memoirs. The history of the Regent Palace Hotel, London, is from regentpalacehotel.co.uk. Further insights into this magnificent building were provided by *The Guardian* article on the 'Battle to save London's Regent Palace Hotel'. Research on The Queens Head pub comes from queensheadpiccadilly.com. References to the Bundaberg Wintergarden theatre are from the qhatlas.com.au. Information on the V-1 'buzz-bombs' and V-2, the world's first rocket, comes from the historylearningsite.co.uk on the 'V Weapons'. There are differing reports on the length of the Battle of Hamburg. Both Hastings in Bomber Command and Middlebrook in his book *The Battle of Hamburg* confirm it lasting into August for eleven days. The significance of the Battle of Hamburg for Bomber Command and detailed descriptions, including the first use of 'Window', come from Max Hastings. He also describes searchlights wandering across the sky like drunken men. Details of 93 Group Navigation Instructors' Course at Tilstock and excursions out over the Irish Sea in an Avro Anson come from my father. The RAF Tilstock airfield history and descriptions are from controltowers.co.uk and derelictplaces.co.uk. A picture of Arthur's wedding party, including my mother, can be found in Hank Nelson's *Chased by the Sun*. My mother's memoirs include her father's wisdom in setting her free to marry, the Australian peaches and household cleaning episodes.

Chapter 14

The story about the Eagle Squadron crew comes from my father. Philip's own story about a Canadian crew comes from his chapter in Sean Feast's *Master Bombers*. The low cheer story when the briefing officer announced that Stirlings would be on that night came from my father. Philip Patrick's crew history comes from *Master Bombers*, including sergeants Lee, Sage and Brown as originals. All details on flight engineer Wally Lee come from RGG Memoirs, which includes a tribute speech made by Philip at Wally's funeral in April 2000. This is also where the reference by Philip to 'Foresakenheath' can be found, as well as www.lakenheath.af.mil. The wireless operator's 'left boot' syndrome and other 'Wop' material is sourced from an article on Douglas Radcliffe in the *Daily Telegraph* (UK) in 2008. Stories of the two gunners, Jimmy Brown and Jim Smith, come from my father and information from Ian Patrick from Philip's records. Philip's first mission to Berlin on the night of 2–3 December 1943 is covered in *Master Bombers* and in Martin Middlebrook's *The Berlin Raids*. The information on Leipzig mission, fighter attack near Zuiderzee and gunner defence plus heavy flak come from my father, his flying log and the *The Berlin Raids*. The location of Zuiderzee on the Dutch coast comes from Wikipedia, my father having a different spelling in his flying log book. Descriptions of Cambridge during the war come from my father and www.cam.ac.uk.

Chapter 15

Information on the layout and equipment of an Avro Lancaster comes from Wikipedia, including its development, design, crew accommodation, armament, bombs, radio and radar, operational history and general characteristics and performance. Peter C. Smith's book, *Avro Lancaster: Britain's Greatest Wartime Bomber* provides the blueprint and functioning of this aircraft including the Mark XIV bombsight. Gordon Musgrove's *Pathfinder Force: A History of 8 Group* gives information on the Mark XIV bombsight, target indicators and role of personnel and ground crew. Gee signalling comes from Peter Rees' *Lancaster Men* and the operation of the mighty 'Lanc' from Neville Franklin's book *Lancaster: Classic Aircraft No. 6*. Discussions with my father furnished the tricks to navigation, including dog-legging, in a Lanc. Warm descriptions of the WAAF personnel, ground crew and the resolute armourers is sourced from Gordon Musgrove. 'The Crew of a Lancaster Bomber' comes from ww2f.com and www.forces-war-records.co.uk. The 'Wop' responsibility for the pair of homing pigeons is from Wikipedia. The famed Elsan toilet information comes from www.rafmuseum. org.uk and the WAAF's bulbous-roofed motor transport bus from 75nzsquadron.files.wordpress.com. The WAAF ladies in the parachute section are from Keith Campbell's Bomber Command Reflections Speech at the Australian War Memorial in 2015. Descriptions of the *Flying Scotsman* are in www.railwaymuseum. org.uk and material on designer Roy Chadwick is from Wikipedia. Statistics on sorties, bombs dropped and Harris's quote 'shining sword' come from Wikipedia.

Chapter 16

The strategic importance of the Battle of Berlin originated from Sir Arthur Harris's book, *Bomber Offensive*, Martin Middlebrook's *The Berlin Raids: RAF Bomber Command Winter 1943–44* and Gordon Musgrove's *Pathfinder Force: A History of 8 Group*. The Berlin operations by 7 Squadron and 'Black Thursday' come from my father. Middlebrook provides detailed analysis of the Battle of Berlin and the effect on crew morale. The SN-2 Lichtenstein radar is sourced from Wikipedia. Musgrove imparts the terms for effectively marking a target. Input on D/F circuitry comes from chavfreezone.me.uk on restoring an R1155 receiver and the explanation of SBA (Standard Beam Approach) is sourced from Wikipedia, titled 'Lorenz Beam'. Marham's location is from Wikipedia and details of FIDO are found on www.rafmuseum.org.uk on Fog Dispersal. Middlebrook details each Berlin operation, including Query Field Elevation and is the source for the three quotes from Patrick, Canadian Pathfinder and the Lancaster bomb-aimer on run in to target.

Chapter 17

Craven A and Flying Dutchman tobacco come from you-smoke and www.tobaccoreviews.com. Middlebrook in the Berlin raids tells of the Luftwaffe resurgence with the airborne radar set SN-2. He outlines Zahme Sau or 'Tame Boar' strategy for the German fighters to overcome Window. The Junkers Ju 88s, Messerschmitt 109s and Focke-Wulf Fw 190s are well covered in Wikipedia. Zahme Sau is also explained there. The operations to Brunswick, Berlin and Magdeburg are outlined in detail by Middlebrook. My father was the source for the post of navigator II, known as the set operator, and the arrival and war history of Alan Coleman. Philip Patrick's chapter in *Master Bombers* by Sean Feast covers the Lanc going down in the sea and the Gee fix to assist. Bomber Command's conclusion to the Berlin raids comes from Middlebrook.

Chapter 18

Background on pyrotechnical skills, explosives, the Verey pistol and the 'standard bucket ascent' at Kelly's Brickyard come from my father. Levity was an important part of his war, leading to finally taking out all the windows of the control tower. The Oakington mess activities of drinking to the health of Cardinal Puff, ceiling footprints and 'kidney bean' are reported in detail by my father. He was amused. His rank of squadron leader did not deter him from the foam fire extinguisher revelry and the responsibility to lift spirits. The extreme winds on the Leipzig raid, dog-legging and the 9.6 per cent loss are well reported by Middlebrook. He covers the losses on the last raid to Berlin and the realisation by Bomber Harris that little more could be done against the targets of northern and central

Germany. The bombing of Leipzig in World War II is also analysed in Wikipedia.

Chapter 19

The brilliant corkscrew manoeuvre is best described by Peter Smith, in *Avro Lancaster: Britain's Greatest Wartime Bomber*. Details of the attempted escape from a burning Lanc come from my father and Philip Patrick's description in *Master Bombers*. Wally Lee's efforts in putting out the fire are recorded by my father. He then had to plot the course home to avoid any enemy contact. The reuniting of my mother and father after the trip to Augsburg is recorded in both my parents' writings. 'A Nightingale Sang in Berkeley Square' was my mother's favourite song at the time and was played at her funeral, two months after my father's death. Schrage Musik is well explained in Wikipedia and Martin Middlebrook's *The Berlin Raids*. This development by Oberleutnant Rudolf Schoenert, the champion of upward firing guns, is reported in Wikipedia.

Chapter 20

The death of KJ Rampling at the age of 31 is recorded by the Commonwealth War Graves Commission (cwgc.org). He is buried with his crew at Durnbach War Cemetery, Germany. My father recounted meeting with Bennett for the position of Group Navigation Officer. He also experienced first-hand Bennett's comments at a briefing that 'Limeys couldn't take it'. Philip Patrick's move to 582 Squadron Pathfinders is covered in Sean Feast's *Master Bombers*, including his loyal crew. My father outlines his new position as navigation leader at Downham Market and the first five trips risk. Christopher Coverdale's *Pathfinders 635 Squadron: Definitive History March 1944–September 1945* covers in detail each of my father's twelve operations with 635 Squadron. Joy's suitcase saga and wedding are happily recorded by my father and mother. The ban on the ringing of church bells during the war comes from www. ringbell.co.uk. Glorious detail of St Mary's Wimbledon is given on stmaryswimbledon.org. Research on the Dog and Fox Wimbledon comes from www.dogandfoxwimbledon.co.uk, the Queens Head pub, Keswick, Lake District from www.tripadvisor.com.au and the Sunbeam-Talbot luxury car from Wikipedia.

Chapter 21

The V-1 flying bomb strike on the Regent Palace Hotel, 30 June 1944, is reported in www.westendatwar.org.uk. The impact on Phyll and Arthur is from my mother's memoirs. Information on the V-1 comes from Wikipedia, militaryhistorynow.com, 'Buzz Kill–13 Remarkable Facts about the V-1 Flying Bomb' and express.co.uk, 'Terror of the Doodlebugs'. The information on the terrifying antlion and their pits comes from Wikipedia and www.antlionpit. com/popculture.html. Operations to Wizernes, Caen, Coquereaux, Tirlemont and Wesseling are well covered in Coverdale's *Pathfinders 635 Squadron*. The buzz-bomb strike on my mother's family home comes from my father. The role of Fort Kijkduin in Holland in World War II is found in www.tracesofwar.com. My father advised of this special action to retaliate against German naval artillery at the Fort. A picture and description of the bomb damage at the Stuart Road family home is provided on nortonbavant.co.uk, in an article titled 'A Boys War' by John Pincham. The trip to Ghent to settle the crew comes from my father and Wing Commander Clark's diary as recorded by Coverdale's book. Denis Richards in *The Hardest Victory* recounts the operations of 635 Squadron and the success of 'Crossbow' attacks against V-2 sites. The V-2 rocket's operational history is recorded in Wikipedia. Blue Bell Inn details come from whatpub.com and Arthur Doubleday's record with 467 Squadron and the command of 61 Squadron from Hank Nelson's *Chased by the Sun*.

Chapter 22

The rewarding of Daphne Pointer with chocolate rations comes from Coverdale's book on 635 Squadron as does Vines' difficult mission to Kiel. The message 'As ye sow . . . so shall ye reap' can be found on the inside cover of Denis Richards' *The Hardest Victory* and also covered is the importance of blanket bombardment and destruction of oil refineries. He recognises the need to clear the Germans from Calais and the Channel ports. The Second Battle of the Ruhr, including two separate 1000-bomber raids in 24 hours on Duisburg, is well reported by Coverdale. Descriptions of Duisburg, the city, come from Wikipedia. Ludwigshafen and Nuremberg, the duo of my father's wartime denouement, are well reported by Coverdale and Richards. Coverdale records Vinesy's last mission to Merseburg and Tubby Baker's 100th operation. The obituary of Wing Commander 'Tubby' Baker can also be found at www.telegraph.co.uk obituaries. The final demise of the *Tirpitz* is described by Wikipedia in its treatise on the German battleship and the last raid on Nazi Germany by a Mosquito bomber on 2 May 1945 is from www.bbc.com. The motto, badge and service of 635 Squadron come from its website. Statistics for the outcome of the war are from www.raf.mod.uk and www.bombercommandmuseum.ca and Wikipedia 'RAF Bomber Command'. The Old Ferry Boat Inn information is from www. oldenglishinns.co.uk and the River Great Ouse from Wikipedia. It was an idyllic conclusion to my parents' war. There is no doubt Churchill recognised the importance of Bomber Command and his quotation from September 1940 appears on the back cover of *The Hardest Victory* by Denis Richards.

Chapter 23

The history of Qantas's early days comes from John Gunn's *Challenging Horizons: Qantas 1939–1954*, including choice of aircraft and influence of Chairman Fergus McMaster. Background to

McMaster also comes from Wikipedia. The layout of a Lancastrian for civilian use comes from Gunn's *Challenging Horizons*. My father gives his detailed experiences on arriving back in Australia to be demobbed and join Qantas. The *RAAF Log* 1943 edition was published by the Australian War Memorial and included recognition of Flight Sergeant Rawdon Hume Middleton, the first member of the RAAF to win the Victoria Cross. Joy's departure from England comes from her memoirs and the rms-rangitiki.com.

Chapter 24

Joy's experiences on arrival of her new family and Australian life come from my father's and mother's writings. The loss of the Qantas Lancastrian G-AGLX and Captain Thomas is documented in aviation-safety.net and the report of the missing plane appeared in the *West Australian* of 26 March 1946. Details of the search come from my father and are recorded in his Flying Log. The North Sydney Heritage Centre describes Kurraba Point. Two Qantas publications *The Longest Hop* and *The Qantas Story 1920–1995* give a great appreciation of the early days in an Empire or Hythe flying boat. Leslie Dawson's *Fabulous Flying Boats* and sydneylivingmuseums. com.au 'Flying Boats' are also excellent, and the Wikipedia 'Short Sunderland' page gives details of operation. Flying boat design considerations including hump speed and transverse step come from globalsecurity.org. My father's receipt of the Distinguished Service Order was posted in the *London Gazette* of October 1944.

Chapter 25

Lockheed Constellation history comes from ashet.org.au and www. qantas.com history pages. Sir Ross Smith's details and Vickers Vimy are from Wikipedia, '1919 England to Australia flight' and aussieairliners.org. Wikipedia also informs about aircraft registration and prefixes. Qantas history, Fergus McMaster and choice of Lockheed from the United States is from Gunn's *Challenging Horizons*. Three Qantas story publications also give history, . . . *from the Dawn of Aviation The Qantas Story 1920–1995* by John Stackhouse, *I Still Call Australia Home: The Qantas Story 1920–2005* by Malcolm Knox and *The Longest Hop*. Super Connie, 707 delivery, navigation by astrocompass and periscope sextant and St Elmo's fire are well covered in *The Longest Hop: Celebrating 50 Years of the Qantas Kangaroo Route 1947–1997* by John Stackhouse. Dust storms and gales in New South Wales in October 1948 are reported in articles on trove.nla.gov.au. Coolamon memories come from my mother, Austin 8 Tourer details from my father. Meeting with Bennett at Basra is a lasting anecdote of my father's. Bennett's history is also captured adb.anu.edu.au. The Russian delegation story comes from Bennett's book. His Victory message is from John Maynard's book and includes commentary on the lack of recognition. Prince Philip's flying training is on www.rafmuseum.org.uk. The royal dividers story is from my father. The advent of the jets comes from www.qantas.com and Wikipedia 'Boeing 707'.

Chapter 26

Qantas service history is from my father. The bullroarer comes from www.instructables.com and Wikipedia. Turbofan engine operation is explained on www.grc.nasa.gov. Hudson Fysh's safety focus comes from Wikipedia and Jim Eames' *Courage in the Skies*. Jet streams over Dubbo is from my father, and also micklehamweather.com and Wikipedia. Air navigation 'without the stars', Doppler radar and INS are from Wikipedia. Introduction of Qantas Boeing 747 Longreach comes from hars.org.au.

Afterword

The BBC History website at www.bbc.co.uk addresses why Churchill lost the election in 1945. The uncertified commemorative medal and

Bomber Command Clasp are described from the objects themselves, sitting on my desk. The BBC News website at www.bbc.com reports on the championing work of Robin Gibb and rafbf.org gives all the descriptions of this commemorative icon, long awaited.

BIBLIOGRAPHY

Bennett, Air Vice-Marshal DCT, *Pathfinder: A War Autobiography*, Goodall Publications, London, 1988.

Bishop, Patrick, *Bomber Boys: Fighting Back 1940–1945*, HarperCollins, London, 2007.

Bowman, Martin, *Bomber Command: Reflections of War, Cover of Darkness 1939–May 1942, Volume 1*, Pen & Sword, Barnsley, 2011.

Bowman, Martin, *Bomber Command: Reflections of War, Battleground Berlin, July 1943–March 1944, Volume 3*, Pen & Sword, Barnsley, 2012.

Bowyer, Chaz, *Coastal Command at War*, Ian Allan Publishing, Hersham, 1979.

Carter, Ian, *Coastal Command: 1939–45*, Crecy Publishing, Addlestone, 1979.

Charlwood, Don, *Journeys into Night*, Burgewood Books, Melbourne, 2005.

Clark, Alan, *Barbarossa*, Orion, London, 1995.

Coverdale, Christopher, *Pathfinders: 635 Squadron Definitive History, March 1944–September 1945*, Pathfinder Publishing, Peterborough, 2009.

Dawson, Leslie, *Fabulous Flying Boats,* Pen & Sword, Barnsley, 2013.

Eames, Jim, *Courage in the Skies,* Allen & Unwin, Sydney, 2017.

Feast, Sean, *Master Bombers: The Experiences of a Pathfinder Squadron at War, 1944–1945,* Grub Street Publishing, London, 2008.

Firkins, Peter, *Strike and Return,* Westward Ho Publishing, Perth, 1985.

Firstbrook, Peter, *The Voyage of the Matthew: John Cabot and the Discovery of North America,* BBC Books, London, 1997.

Franklin, Neville and Scarborough, Gerald, *Lancaster, Classic Aircraft No.6,* Patrick Stephens, Cambridge, 1979.

Gunn, John, *The Defeat of Distance: Qantas 1919–1939,* University of Queensland Press, Brisbane, 1988.

Gunn, John, *Challenging Horizons: Qantas 1939–1954,* University of Queensland Press, Brisbane, 1990.

Gunn, John, *High Corridors: Qantas 1919–1939,* University of Queensland Press, Brisbane, 1990.

Harris, Arthur, *Bomber Offensive,* Collins, London, 1947.

Hastings, Max, *Bomber Command,* Pan, London, 1982.

Knox, Malcolm, *I Still Call Australia Home: The Qantas Story, 1920–2005,* Focus Publishing, Sydney, 2005.

Maynard, John, *Bennett and the Pathfinders,* Arms and Armour Press, London, 1996.

McKinstry, Leo, *Lancaster: The Second World War's Greatest Bomber,* John Murray, London, 2009.

Middlebrook, Martin, *The Battle of Hamburg: Allied Bomber Forces against a German City in 1943,* Allen Lane, London, 1980.

Middlebrook, Martin, *The Berlin Raids: RAF Bomber Command Winter 1943–44,* Viking, London, 1998.

Musgrove, Gordon, *Pathfinder Force: A History of 8 Group,* MacDonald and Jane's Publishers, London, 1976.

Nelson, Hank, *Chased by the Sun: The Australians in Bomber Command in World War II,* Allen & Unwin, Sydney, 2006.

Rees, Peter, *Lancaster Men: The Aussie Heroes of Bomber Command*, Allen & Unwin, Sydney, 2013.

Rice, Tony, *Voyages of Discovery: A Visual Celebration of Ten of the Greatest Natural History Expeditions*, Allen & Unwin, Sydney, 2010.

Richards, Denis, *The Hardest Victory: RAF Bomber Command in the Second World War*, Hodder and Stoughton, London, 1994.

Smith, Peter C, *Avro Lancaster: Britain's Greatest Wartime Bomber*, Midland Publishing, Hersham, 2008.

Stackhouse, John, *. . . from the dawn of aviation: The Qantas Story 1920–1995*, Focus Publishing, Sydney, 1995.

Stackhouse, John, *The Longest Hop: Celebrating 50 Years of the Qantas Kangaroo Route 1947–1997*, Focus Publishing, Sydney, 1997.

Wege, Juliet, et al (eds), *Matthew Flinders and His Scientific Gentlemen*, Western Australian Museum, Perth, 2005.